History, Memory, and Territorial Cults in the Highlands of Laos

This book captures the dynamics of history, memory, and territorial cults in Houay Yong, a Tai Vat village situated in the multiethnic highland frontier between Laos and Vietnam. By taking seriously the experiences of the villagers, it partakes in a broader movement to reintegrate highlanders and their agency into history at large.

Based on comprehensive fieldwork research and the examination of colonial archives, this book makes accessible, for an English-speaking audience, untapped French archives on Laos and early publications on territorial cults written by French ethnologists. In so doing, it provides a balanced perspective, drawing from the fields of memory studies and classical historical research. Following a chronological approach stretching from the nineteenth century to the present, it extends narrative analysis through a comparative ethnography of territorial cults, a key component of the performative and material presentification of the past.

Highly interdisciplinary in nature, *History, Memory and Territorial Cults in the Highlands of Laos* will be useful to students and scholars of anthropology, history, and religious studies, as well as Asian culture and society.

Pierre Petit is Senior Research Fellow at the Belgian Fund for Scientific Research and Professor at Université libre de Bruxelles, Belgium. His research interests include mobility, ethnicity, and interactions with the state among the Tai Vat of Houaphan.

Routledge Contemporary Asian Societies
Series Editors: Vanessa Frangville and Frederik Ponjaert
Research Centre on East Asia (EASt), Université libre de Bruxelles, Brussels, Belgium

Routledge Contemporary Asian Societies provides an original and distinctive contribution to current debates on evolutions shaping societies, cultures, politics and media across North and South East Asia. It is interdisciplinary in its approach and the editors welcome proposals across the social sciences and humanities; from political, social, cultural and economic studies to gender, media, literature, anthropology, philosophy and religion.

China's Youth Culture and Collective Spaces
Creativity, Sociality, Identity and Resistance
Edited by Vanessa Frangville and Gwennaël Gaffric

History, Memory, and Territorial Cults in the Highlands of Laos
The Past Inside the Present
Pierre Petit

History, Memory, and Territorial Cults in the Highlands of Laos
The Past Inside the Present

Pierre Petit

LONDON AND NEW YORK

First published 2020
by Routledge
2 Park Square, Milton Park, Abingdon, Oxon OX14 4RN

and by Routledge
52 Vanderbilt Avenue, New York, NY 10017

Routledge is an imprint of the Taylor & Francis Group, an informa business

© 2020 Pierre Petit

The right of Pierre Petit to be identified as author of this work has been asserted by him in accordance with sections 77 and 78 of the Copyright, Designs and Patents Act 1988.

All rights reserved. No part of this book may be reprinted or reproduced or utilized in any form or by any electronic, mechanical, or other means, now known or hereafter invented, including photocopying and recording, or in any information storage or retrieval system, without permission in writing from the publishers.

Trademark notice: Product or corporate names may be trademarks or registered trademarks, and are used only for identification and explanation without intent to infringe.

British Library Cataloguing-in-Publication Data
A catalogue record for this book is available from the British Library

Library of Congress Cataloging-in-Publication Data
Names: Petit, Pierre, 1966- author.
Title: History, memory, and territorial cults in the highlands of Laos : the past inside the present / Pierre Petit.
Identifiers: LCCN 2019027858 (print) | LCCN 2019027859 (ebook) | ISBN 9780367211257 (hardcover) | ISBN 9780429265501 (ebook) | ISBN 9780429556043 (adobe pdf) | ISBN 9780429564987 (mobi) | ISBN 9780429560514 (epub)
Subjects: LCSH: Black Tai (Southeast Asian people)–Laos–Houaphan (Province)–History. | Black Tai (Southeast Asian people)–Laos–Houaphan (Province)–Rites and ceremonies. | Ethnohistory–Laos–Houaphan (Province) | Collective memory–Laos–Houaphan (Province) | Cults–Laos–Houaphan (Province) | Group identity–Laos–Houaphan (Province) | Houaphan (Laos : Province)–History.
Classification: LCC DS555.45.T35 P48 2020 (print) | LCC DS555.45.T35 (ebook) | DDC 959.4–dc23
LC record available at https://lccn.loc.gov/2019027858
LC ebook record available at https://lccn.loc.gov/2019027859

ISBN: 978-0-367-21125-7 (hbk)
ISBN: 978-0-429-26550-1 (ebk)

Typeset in Times New Roman
by Wearset Ltd, Boldon, Tyne and Wear

Every effort has been made to contact copyright-holders. Please advise the publisher of any errors or omissions, and these will be corrected in subsequent editions.

With the collaboration of Sommay Singthong, Amphone Vongsouphanh, and Amphone Monephachan

Contents

List of figures viii
List of maps x
List of tables xi
Preface xii
Acknowledgments xviii
Dramatis personae xxi

1 Introduction   1

2 The setting   30

3 Traditions on origins   48

4 From the French colony to the present   85

5 The ethnography of territorial cults   116

6 Territorial cults in a regional perspective 145

7 Conclusion   173

References 188
Archives 195
Fieldnotes 198
Index 203

Figures

1.1	The maintenance of the lower canal	1
1.2	The valley seen from our resting place	2
1.3	The village post (*lak man*) of Houay Yong	8
1.4	People watching the film *Return Trip*	21
1.5	A meal during a *sén* ceremony	22
1.6	The author drinking with Thaao Chüaang	22
1.7	Dancing *lamvông*	23
1.8	Dancing *huup èèô*	23
1.9	Thaabun narrating the foundation of the village	26
1.10	Fieldnotes written on the spot	27
2.1	Houay Yong	31
2.2	Houay Yong (detailed view)	31
2.3	Thoongsôm and his family	35
2.4	The ceremony proclaiming Muang Èt as Cultural Village	40
2.5	Bunsoon receiving an agriculture promotion agent	42
2.6	Bunsoon speaking with Buasai	42
2.7	Thoongsôm as a young revolutionary staff	43
2.8	Thoongsôm in 2011	43
2.9	The communal hall: front scene	45
2.10	The communal hall: back scene	45
3.1	Thoongsôm with an almanac in Tai script	50
3.2	Thoongsôm's book of prayers in Tai script	50
3.3	The collective interview in Muang Van	51
3.4	The 1898 letter	55
3.5	Phèèngsoon during the historical recollection	58
3.6	Bunsoon during the historical recollection	58
3.7	Nguan performing a *khap* song	59
3.8	Koongvaa during his interview	62
3.9	The ruins of the temple of Xiang Kho	73
4.1	The 1902 census for gun owners	88
4.2	Spinning the silk in Nasan	89
4.3	Foropon's inspection itinerary of 1926	90
4.4	Mèèthao Leua interviewed	105

Figures ix

4.5	Somphan, a veteran	108
4.6	The boards of achievements of Houay Yong	111
4.7	The Tai Vat of Thongnamy watching performances from Yên Châu	114
5.1	Mèè Ua reciting *thaam* prayers for the New Year	121
5.2	Addressing the domestic shrine for the New Year	121
5.3	The *lak man* of Houay Yong in 2009	123
5.4	The *lak man* of Houay Yong in 2010	123
5.5	The *thiang seun* of Houay Yong in 2009	124
5.6	The *thiang seun* of Houay Yong in 2012	124
5.7	The *lak man* and *thiang seun* of *Naa Kuu*	126
5.8	Detailed view of the *lak man* of *Naa Kuu*	127
5.9	The *thiang seun* of *Naa Kuu*	128
5.10	The *lak man* of Houay Lom	129
5.11	The *thiang seun* for the spirits of Houay Lom and Houay Louang	130
5.12	The *lak man* of Ban Kang	131
5.13	The *lak man* of Ban Kang (detail)	131
5.14	Koongbun preparing for divination	136
5.15	Koongbun drinking with Thaao Chüaang	138
5.16	Koongbun leading the ceremony for the *lak man*	139
5.17	Koongbun in front of the *thiang seun* of *Naa Kuu*	140
5.18	Koongbun in front of the *lak man* of *Naa Kuu*	141
6.1	Screenshots of Bunsoon commenting on the *lak man*	150
6.2	Screenshots of Bunsoon on the *thiang seun* terrace	152
6.3	Screenshots of Buakham explaining the position of the spirits	153
6.4	The city pillar of Vientiane	159
6.5	*Taalèèo*	162
7.1	An old dome-shaped house in Houay Yong	179
7.2	The modern house of Buasai in Houay Yong	179
7.3	The *lak baan* of Nahit	180
7.4	The *lak baan* of Sop Hao	181
7.5	The *lak müang* monument in Sam Neua	181
7.6	Revolutionary scenes in the *lak müang* park	182
7.7	The *lak müang* painted on a long-distance bus	183
7.8	The *lak müang* pictured in the city's cultural hall	184
7.9	Laughter in Houay Lom	185
7.10	The *lak man* of Houay Yong in 2018	186
7.11	The *lak man* shrine of Houay Yong in 2018	187

Credit for Figures 3.4, 4.1 and 4.3: Archives Nationales d'Outre-Mer (France).
Credit for all other pictures: Pierre Petit.

Maps

P.1	Laos in its regional context	xiii
2.1	Houay Yong and the eastern edge of Muang Èt District	32
3.1	The eight principalities of Houaphan under the early French regime	53
3.2	The cross-border area between the Black River and the River Ma	69
3.3	Northern Vietnam	71

Credit for all maps: Pierre Petit and Isabelle Renneson

Tables

P.1	Romanization of Lao script	xvi
4.1	The 1896 population census in Houaphan	92
4.2	The 1899 population census in Muang Èt	92

Preface

This book captures the dynamics of history, memory, and territorial cults in Houay Yong, a Tai Vat village encapsulated in a multiethnic highland frontier between Laos and Vietnam. It questions the standard national narratives about the past by investigating, from a 'remote' valley unnoticed in the archives, the major developments that punctuated the last century-and-a-half in the region, from the scramble in Tonkin and Northern Laos on the eve of colonization, to the present dynamics of the Lao developmental regime. Decentering the focus of research from its usual lowland-based standpoint is an important step to refresh historical research in the region. There is more to do than detailing the royal chronicles from Luang Prabang and Huế, or glossing on the Vietnamese and American strategies during the war. Taking seriously history as it is experienced from a so-called back of beyond, the book partakes in a broader movement to reintegrate highlanders and their agency into history at large, a process catalyzed by the publication of James Scott's celebrated *The Art of Not Being Governed* (2009).

Based on fieldwork research carried out since 2003 and on French colonial archives, the book strives to find its way along the line between the booming memory studies and more classical history research. These two concerns are addressed here seriously. The volume discusses how the past is conceived, referred to, narrated, embodied, given material form, and purposefully performed by people and groups with their specific agendas. But it also engages with the usual concerns of history, and with the issue about what 'really' happened, following a more chronological approach that has faded away in many scholarly works fascinated with subjectivities.

The central issue of the first part of the book is the relationship between oral and written sources: how can they be used together to produce a better understanding of history, and of historical imagination? The case of the Tai Vat in Laos is very telling on the way these sources shed light on each other, because it is only through their entwinement that a plausible reconstruction of the past can be proposed. Under the pressure of the Chinese Flag armies who invaded the northwest of Vietnam in the 1860s to 1870s, some Tai Vat villagers, living in the region of Muang Vat (named Yên Châu nowadays, see Map P.1), fled southward into the region of Houaphan, nowadays a province of Laos. The population concerned by the present study eventually settled in Houay Yong, a village encased

Preface xiii

in the steep valley of a stream that holds the same name as the village. They cohabited in the place with an obscure group, the so-called Tai Soi, who eventually left the valley. Three generations later, in the early 1950s, many Tai Vat of Vietnam followed the itinerary of their forefathers, fleeing the violence of the First Indochina War to settle among their cousins in Laos. As a consequence, these 'animist' farmers presently straddle the Lao–Vietnamese frontier. If their society has evolved differently on both sides of the border, they keep a strong sense of their common origins, and visits to relatives living beyond the borderline uphold this feeling of belonging to a single group. Hence, if this book is clearly relevant for Lao studies, it can also be of interest for the anthropologists and historians of Vietnam.

Map P.1 Laos in its regional context (source: United Nations maps).

xiv *Preface*

The colonial history is analyzed based mostly on French archives, with focuses on demography, ethnicity, and economy. I then consider the installation of the revolutionary regime in the area (1953), the reunification of Laos in 1975 after more than 20 years of civil war, the local implementation of the policies of the People's Democratic Republic of Laos, all this until the present situation characterized by the rural flight of the youth to Vientiane. Mobility will appear as a thread running through Tai Vat history, which supports their self-perception as pioneers on the move.

History and memory cannot be limited to their narrative dimension. Landscapes, material culture, rituals, bodily practices, and other non-discursive elements have often been underestimated in the relationship people have with their past – and their present. The second part of the book redresses this unbalance by switching the focus to territorial cults. These cults are a central component of the presentification of the past: their main ritual concern is to engage in a relationship with the first occupants or settlers of the place, which leads us back to history. Based on observations and an extensive review of the literature, the book aims to adopt a relational perspective on territorial cults; it investigates their link with the local and regional hierarchies, analyzes their potential contribution to history, addresses their resilience in the post-revolutionary state, and questions their inscription into the monumental turn of the public space in present-day Laos. Such cults will be approached through extensive visual support, to highlight the importance of materiality, performativity, and embodiment.

Broaching, at the same time, history (based on oral and written sources), memory, and territorial cults is unprecedented in that region. I argue that there is much to gain from such a cross-perspective: cultual practices and the comments they elicit are a palimpsest from which historical hypotheses continually emerged during the inquiry. I therefore hope that this book can offer milestones for future research, and partake in general debates about the rekindling of historical anthropology in an area where oral and alternative sources to history are largely left untapped (see Michaud 2010).

Reference to fieldnotes

The field data used throughout the research have been indexed under 262 headings, of which 103 are used in the present volume, listed in the third section of the references (see page 198). Their reference number, in square brackets, is followed by: the date; the place in case it is not Houay Yong; the type of data (interview, observation, video, etc.); the people involved; and a summary of the topics. In the main text, they also appear in square brackets. So the reference "[4]" in the text means the information is based on heading 4 that appears in the field data section:

> [4]: 28/6/2009, interview of Bunsoon. The *lak man* and *thiang seun* of Houay Yong; the first settlers; the annual ceremonies; the *lak man* in *Naa Kuu*.

Preface xv

In other words, it is based on an interview conducted with Bunsoon (the village chief, or *naai baan*) in Houay Yong, on 28 June 2009, about the *lak man* (the shrine of the village post) and related topics.

Pseudonyms have not been used throughout, except when the information was deemed sensitive, or when the interview has been conducted under commitment of anonymity. This seemed to be the best way to balance the protection of our collaborators when coming to touchy information, and their legitimate right to acknowledgment and authorship in the locally valorized fields of history and rituals. I am aware that divulging the name of informants can be prejudicial in some contexts – see Salemink (2017: 3–5) for dreadful examples of abuse in the Central Highlands of Vietnam – but, after due consideration, anonymity has not been adopted as a norm in the book. The information presented cannot in my view be harmful to the reputation or the security of those who provided it; anonymity would hence be a poor reward for those who saw their interview as a contribution to a research that would precisely pull the group out of its present anonymity at the national level. This has been discussed with the collaborators of this book, and with the informants, of course.

Reference to archives

The archives mentioned here are all kept in the ANOM (*Archives Nationales d'Outre-Mer*), in Aix-en-Provence (France), and more specifically in two archival funds: Gouvernement général de l'Indochine and Résidence Supérieure au Laos. Documents are referred using the fund acronym (GGI and RSL, respectively), followed by the reference number, the date (which can be a precise day or a period), the title of the document (in brackets if it is my rendering of the contents), the name of the author (always in brackets), and the folder or sub-folder (or even sub-subfolder) in which the document is conserved. For example:

> RSL E4, 2/8/1909. *Au sujet de la demande de M. le Résident supérieur de l'Annam pour laisser partir les habitants à Than Hoa* (by Wartelle), sub-subfolder *Émigration et immigration. Province de Sam-Neua*, subfolder *1905–1935 Province de Sam Neua*, folder *Rapports de tournée 1925–1931*.

This is a document authored by Wartelle, dated 2 August 1909, conserved in a third-level folder in the file E4 of the archival fund Résidence Supérieure au Laos of the Archives Nationales d'Outre-Mer. In the main text, I refer to this document as "RSL E4, 2/8/1909," which is detailed in the archival sources (see pages 195–197). Archives are ordered by reference number and by date.

Notes on the transcription system

The use of Lao script has been limited to a few quotes of special interest. Lao has been Romanized elsewhere. The transcription of Lao for an English text is challenging. The systems usually adopted show neither the syllable tones (Lao is

xvi *Preface*

Table P.1 Romanization of Lao script

Lao consonants	Phonetic	Transcription	Lao consonants	Phonetic	Transcription
ກ	[k]	k	ນ	[n]	n
ຂ, ຄ	[kʰ]	kh	ບ	[b]	b; p (ending)
ງ	[ŋ]	ng	ປ	[p]	p
ຈ	[tj]	ch	ຜ, ພ	[pʰ]	ph
ສ, ຊ	[s]	s	ຝ, ຟ	[f]	f
ຍ	[ɲ]	ny	ມ	[m]	m
-ຍ	[j]	i	ຢ	[j]	y
ດ	[d]	d; t (ending)	ລ	[l]	l
ຕ	[t]	t	ວ	[v]	v
ຖ, ທ	[tʰ]	th	ຫ, ຮ	[h]	h

Vowels		Phonetic		Transcription	
Short	Long	Short	Long	Short	Long
-ະ, -ັ-	-າ	[a]	[a:]	a	aa
◌ິ	◌ີ	[i]	[i:]	i	ii
◌ຶ	◌ື	[ɯ]	[ɯ:]	ü	üü
◌ຸ	◌ູ	[u]	[u:]	u	uu
ເ-ະ, ເ◌ັ	ເ-	[e]	[e:]	é	éé
ແ-ະ, ແ◌ັ-	ແ-	[ɛ]	[ɛ:]	è	èè
ໂ-ະ, ◌ົ-	ໂ-	[o]	[o:]	ô	ôô
ເ-າະ, ◌ັອ-	◌ໍ, -ອ-	[ɔ]	[ɔ:]	o	oo
	-າວ		[a:ɔ]		aao
	ແ-ວ		[ɛ:ɔ]		èèo
ເ◌ິ	ເ◌ີ	[ə?]	[ə:]	eu	euu
ເ◌ັຍ, ເ◌ັຍ, ◌ັຍ-	ເ-ຍ, ເ-ຍ, -ຍ-	[ja?]	[ja:]	ia	iaa
ເ◌ຶອ	ເ◌ືອ	[ɯa?]	[ɯa:]	üa	üaa
◌ົວະ, ◌ັວ-	◌ົວ, -ວ-	[wa?]	[wa:]	ua	uaa

Lao special vowels	Phonetic	Transcription
ໄ-, ໃ-	[aj]	ai
ເ◌ົາ	[ao]	ao
-ໍາ	[am]	am

a five-tone language) nor the vowel lengths. The system I used here displays the latter but omits the former. It is based on Lissoir (2016: 9–10) but adapted following Becker and Mingbuapha (2003: 20–33), whose system fits more with English spelling.

Toponyms regularly transcribed in the Roman alphabet (typically, names appearing on boards or maps or in the literature) will be reproduced as such. This is why I write Houay Yong (it should be spelled "*Huai Yoong*" according to my Romanization system), Muang Van (*Müang Van*), Nasan (*Naa Saan*), Houay Lom (*Huai Lôm*), Houay Louang (*Huai Luang*), Ban Kang (*Baan Kaang*), Nong Thop (*Noong Tôp*), Muang Èt (*Müang Èèt*), Muang Vat (*Müang Vaat*), Ban Sot (*Baan Sôôt*), Xiang Kho (*Siang Khoo*), and Muang Soi (*Müang Sôôi*). Although all village names should be preceded by the word "Ban" (*baan*, "village" in Lao and Tai), the latter word will be used only for names of one syllable, as for Ban Kang or Ban Sot. All toponyms that are not regularly transcribed for official usage will be Romanized and italicized. This applies mostly to mountains or streams, such as *Phuu Kup* Mountain or *Huai Yoong* stream. Toponyms in Vietnam will be written in the Vietnamese script, with its diacritics.

Personal names (and their indissociable titles if any) will be Romanized but without italics. As for the ethnonyms, I write Tai Vat (*Thai Vaat*), Tai Soi (*Thai Sôôi*), Tai Dèng (*Thai Dèèng*), and so forth, because most references about the region omit the "h" marking the "t" as an aspirated consonant.

Single and double quotation marks are used respectively for scare quotes and direct quotes. Square brackets inside quotes refer to my own remarks.

Acknowledgments

This book is published 16 years after my first contact, in June 2003, with people from Houay Yong, more precisely members of the pioneer families who had settled in Thongnamy three years earlier. They were facing hard conditions at the time. Our relationships were not only friendly since the beginning, but also loaded with emotional links. Part of this is due to my insertion in the group as the *luuk hak* of Mèè Chét, an elderly woman. *Luuk hak* (literally "beloved child") and its symmetrical *mèè hak* ("beloved mother") are elective kinship terms, which denote a relationship of affection as between mother and child. Mèè Chét has been an extraordinary mother; I miss her. Other people were central in this insertion, among whom are Phuu Vông (Mèè Chét's son), Banliu (Chaak), Mèè Ông, Imphaan, Phonsiikéo, and Mèè Ua. Without them and their friendship, I would never have thought of going to Houaphan, in search of their home place, which fascinated me when they talked about their distant origins.

My relationship with the population in Houay Yong was very similar to the one I had with the Tai Vat in Thongnamy. Here again, I can hardly consider people as mere "informants", because coming over and over during nine years, sharing everyday life, and enjoying parties led to pleasant relationships and sometimes friendship. A long list of those people who collaborated with the research could not be comprehensive – I will keep it short. *Naai baan* Bunsoon has been and remains the key person in this success. Always positive, friendly, and responsive despite his many responsibilities, he was a great host for the demanding guests that we were. He is mentioned more than 130 times in this book, a token of his central role in the research. Thoongsôm was our second host, and our tutelary 'traditional elder' for all obscure issues related to the Tai Vat society of the past. Free discussions with him in his cottage in the fields, evoking the underground dragons, the lost king, and the sacred mountain of his home place in Vietnam, were golden moments. Thaabun (deceased in March 2018) and his half-brother Koongbun, from the family of the first settlers of the village, were respectively great specialists in history and rituals. Through the four of them, I would like to warmly thank all the villagers who took part in our research or who simply welcomed us, not only in Houay Yong, but also in Houay Lom and the neighboring settlements of the valley mentioned in this study.

Many colleagues at the National University of Laos (NUoL) worked with me during the five years of research in Thongnamy, and have already been mentioned and thanked in former publications. Sommay Singthong, Amphone Vongsouphanh, Amphone Monephachan, and Vannaseun Chaiyavad have been excellent research assistants during the seven stays in Houay Yong. The publication of this book owes much to the repeated involvement of the first three in the field research, hence their full acknowledgment as direct collaborators. The first two played a central role in the continuous institutional support of our program, which was a further challenge deserving warm thanks. Somxay Khampavong, retired professor of the NUoL, has been my teacher of Lao language and helped me with transcriptions and translations. Gioa Chanthaly Tong Van, a Tai Dam friend in my home city (Namur, Belgium), and Mimy Keomanichanh, PhD student at the Université libre de Bruxelles (ULB), have been very helpful in this time-consuming work. Ms Phouvan Sommixai, from Houay Yong, should also be thanked for her help with transcriptions during our last stay. Isabelle Renneson, from ULB, deserves warm regards for drawing the five maps of this book with her full dedication to this detailed work.

Diverse authorities at NUoL should be mentioned for their constant support, at department, faculty and central administration levels. I always felt lucky to have positive answers to my repeated requests. Thank you, *achaan* Saleumsack Phabouddy, Phout Simmalavong, Dexanourath Seneduangdeth, and Phouvong Phimmakong.

The research has been funded by my employer, the Belgian Fund for Scientific Research (F.R.S.-FNRS) and by my university, ULB. The fieldwork in Thongnamy (2003–2008) was conducted under the aegis of CIUF–CUD (Conseil Interuniversitaire de la Communauté Française de Belgique–Commission Universitaire pour le Développement). The same institution, renamed ARES–CCD (Académie de Recherche et d'Enseignement Supérieur–Commission de la Coopération au Développement), funded the field seminars in Yên Châu, in collaboration with the Vietnam National University of Agriculture of Hà Nội (VNUA) (2010–2014).

The present book benefited directly from discussions with many colleagues, among whom (in alphabetical order) are: Vanina Bouté, Olivier Évrard, Holly High, John Holt, Peter Jackson, Marie-Pierre Lissoir (who accompanied me in Thongnamy and Houay Yong as a PhD student), Michel Lorrillard, Jean Michaud, and Oliver Tappe. Rosalie Stolz, as well as the two anonymous readers of the manuscript, did an extraordinary job commenting on the full document and providing insightful remarks on the structure and contents. Oliver Tappe, whom I met in a Stanley-and-Livingstone manner in Sam Neua in 2011, generously shared hard-to-find documents on the early history of the province, and Sèng Aloune Keovanthin helped me to find elusive Lao archives transcribed in the Thai language. May they all receive the expression of my gratitude for sharing ideas and information on the different topics discussed in this book.

An ethnographer's family always deserves a special mention for due reasons. A book can hardly compensate for the repeated absences of a husband, a father, a son, or a brother. But at least, it gives them some sense: they eventually had a purpose. May this volume be a token of deep gratitude to my wife Violaine, my daugthers Louise and Alice, and all my family – to the living and, even more, to the dead – for these last 16 years.

Dramatis Personae

This section briefly presents the main characters of this 'anthropological drama,' both as a preview and as a short reminder in case the reader is lost. Our team's main impressions of the personalities have not been concealed. Where they appear the figures are mentioned in brackets.

Buakham: a lively and expressive elder of Houay Lom, in charge of the resolution of conflicts in the village (Figures 6.3 and 7.9).

Buasai: a former chief of the village (from 1998 to 2004), Buasai is the present head of the *kum baan* (subdistrict) including Houay Yong and nine other settlements. His father married the mother of Bunsoon after their coincidental widowing. With his large stature, loud voice, and political pedigree, Buasai is an imposing figure in the village arena. His daughter married Vôngkham, creating an alliance between the old settlers' lineage and the present representatives of the Party (Figure 2.6).

Bunmaa: the *chao süa* ("master of the shirt", that is, the ritual master of the first settlers' lineage) of *Naa Kuu*, the northern hamlet of Houay Yong. He sustains a sense of distinction in 'his' hamlet (Figures 5.17 and 5.18).

Bunsoon: born in the mid-1950s, Bunsoon is the *naai baan* (village chief) of Houay Yong since 2008. A short-sized, dynamic, and friendly figure appreciated by his fellows, he was our host during our seven stays and a central informant for all the topics covered in this book. He clearly played an active role in the research design as well. He is the brother of Mèè Ua and the stepbrother of Buasai (Figures 1.7, 1.10, 2.5, 2.6, 2.10, 3.6, 5.3, 6.1, and 6.2).

Koongbun: the very talkative *chao cham* (ritual leader) of the village shrines of Houay Yong and *Naa Kuu*. He was in charge of the annual rituals we observed in January 2012. Half-brother of Thaabun by his father (Figures 5.14–5.18).

Koongthéé: the *chao süa* of Houay Lom. Bound to his place due to his ritual status, he is well known across the valley for the afflictions that befell him each

xxii *Dramatis Personae*

time he attempted to settle away from Houay Lom. He is a younger relative of Koongvaa (Figure 7.9).

Koongvaa: a direct descendant of the first settlers of Houay Lom, renowned for his knowledge of historical traditions. We interviewed him in June 2011. He died a few months later from a lung disease (Figure 3.8).

Laankham: both a spirit and a generic name for all the dead ancestors of the Tai Vat, especially the first settlers and their descendants.

Lak man: the "strong-" or "stable post" designates both the wooden post a bit above the village on the mountain slope, and the spirit inhabiting it and protecting the villagers of Houay Yong – very efficiently, according to most of them (Figures 1.3, 5.3, 5.4, 5.16, 6.1, 7.10, and 7.11).

Mèè Chét: a humorous elderly woman from Houay Yong who settled in Thongnamy in 2000. Mèè Chét is the elective mother (*mèè hak*) of the author.

Mèè Ua: the elder sister of Bunsoon, the *naai baan*. She settled in Houay Yong as a refugee with her family in 1953, when she was a child. Mèè Ua was an impressive *moo môt* (medium), with a penetrating gaze; she commuted between Houay Yong and Thongnamy, where some of her married daughters had settled. She died in 2012 or 2013, apparently from a cancer (Figure 5.1).

Mèèthao Leua: a famous performer of *khap* songs, Mèèthao Leua is an elderly woman who settled with her family in Houay Yong around 1953, when she was a child. She is the widow of Phongsai, a celebrated composer of *khap* who was the last *chao cham* (ritual leader) of the *dông khuaang* ritual in the valley. She is a humorous character and a great orator (Figures 1.4 and 4.4).

Phèèngsoon: former chief (2004–2008) and present deputy-chief of the village, Phèèngsoon was in charge of research on history and territorial issues at the sub-district level, in the late 1980s (Figure 3.5).

Phii: generic term for the spirits, who people every place from the sky to the river, as well as the village, the house, and the body.

Thaabun: holding the honorary title of *chao kôk chao lao*, "master of the foundation and of slashing the forest," Thaabun was a direct descendant of the first Tai Vat settlers in Houay Yong. He was repeatedly presented to our team as the most knowledgeable historian in the village. He died in March 2018 from a heart attack, aged about 80 (Figures 1.9, 5.14, 5.15, 6.1, and 6.2).

Thoongsôm: born in Vietnam, Thoongsôm settled with his mother in Houay Yong in the late 1940s, when he was a child. A former policeman, Thoongsôm had important responsibilities as a leader of the Party at the subdistrict level. He was village chief for over two decades (circa 1971 to circa 1993). He is extremely knowledgeable about various aspects of the past society, and is presently the only person in Houay Yong who is able to read Tai Dam scripture. He housed the team in 2017 (Figures 2.3, 2.7, 2.8, and 3.1).

Vôngkham is an adult man holding the charge of *chao süa* (ritual representative of the first settlers) in Houay Yong. He is the son-in-law of Buasai (Figures 5.14 and 5.15).

1 Introduction

The stakes of history in a highland village

June 9 2010. A busy day in Houay Yong: the canals of the rice fields have to be maintained. Teams of workers are constituted in the morning, each house providing one laborer. Bunnyèng, head of the Youth Union and son of the *naai baan* (chief of the village) Bunsoon, supervises the activity; he explains to us precisely how it is organized based on *chu*, the smallest administrative units of the settlement. We follow up the workers who proceed upstream along the canal close to the village, removing the dirt and other elements that congest the water flow.

We chat with some workers and are eventually invited by Bunsoon, the *naai baan*, to take a rest with his stepbrother Buasai and some of their friends, mostly male adults and elders (*phuu nyai*), who speak proudly – and loudly – about their

Figure 1.1 The maintenance of the lower canal (9 June 2010).

2 Introduction

coconut trees in the place. After that pause and some coconut tasting, we walk upstream with the *naai baan* alone to complete the visit of the village's irrigation system. We cross the small river *Huai Yoong* and climb eastward up the terraced rice fields on the mountain slope. Bunsoon and the two Lao members of the team (Sommay and Amphone V.) can easily find their way on the narrow embankments between the paddies, but I feel much less at ease, and end up after the climb quite muddy, which is great fun for my younger colleagues. The height we reach, just above a little canal, offers a splendid view of the valley (Figure 1.2). We pause and gaze – we often joked saying we had chosen the fieldwork site for the beauty of the landscape. We launch the discussion about the former inhabitants of Houay Yong village, the mysterious (to us, at least) Tai Soi, switching on our small voice recorder.

I provide here two excerpts of this discussion to immerse the reader into the complexities of oral narratives [51]. The first one explains how the Tai Vat, the present inhabitants of the village, eventually replaced the Tai Soi, who were settled in the valley when the former came. The Tai Soi could reportedly not compete with the industrious Tai Vat, and went back to their place of origin, Muang Soi.

Figure 1.2 The valley seen from our resting place, above the higher canal, on the day of our visit. Note the terraced rice fields (front) and the swiddens on the mountain slopes on the other side of the valley (9 June 2010).

ນາຍບ້ານ ບຸນສອນ: ເຮີ! ໄທໂສຍ ລະ ເຂົາ...
ເຂົາບໍ່ຕີນາ. ເຂົາບໍ່ເຮັດ ເຂົາເຮັດແຕ່ໜ້ອຍໜຶ່ງ
ກ້ອງບ້ານພຸ້ນນັ້ນເນ. ລະໄທເຮົານີ້ມາປຸ່ວມ ລະ
ໄທເຮົາຈຶ່ງເຮັດ. ໄທເຮົາເຮັດ ໄທເຮົາໝັ່ນ ລະ
ເຮັດມານໍາໄທໂສຍ.[1]

ໄທໂສຍບໍ່ເຮັດ ແຕ່ໄທເຮົາເຮັດ. ໄທໂສຍ ລະ: "ໂອະ!
ຜູ້ໄທນີ້ໝັ່ນເຮັ້ງ" ລະເຂົາຢູ່ບໍ່ໄດ້.

ສົມໝາຍ: ຕອນນັ້ນເຂົາລະບໍ່ເຫນີໄປເບາະ?

ບຸນສອນ: ເຍາະ. ໄດ້ຫນີ ເຂົາລະເຮັດຝັ່ງເຂົາ. ເຂົາເຮັດລະ
ເຮົາໄດ້ບາເສົາ. ເຍັກ ໄທເຮົາເຮັດ ລະງ ເຮົາລະໄດ້ບາ
ເຄິ່ງງເຂົານັ້ນ ຂອງເຂົາລະຍັງໃຫ້ເຂົາ. ຈົນຮອດປີ
1945-1946 ນີ້ເຂົາ: "ໂອ! ຢູ່ບໍ່ໄດ້ແລ້ວ
ໄທເຮົານີ້ມາຫຼາຍແລ້ວ" ລະ ແຜ່ຂະຫຍາຍອອກແຕ່.

ສົມໝາຍ: ເຂົາຄ່ອຍງໆຍ້າຍອອກໄປເບາະ ຫຼື
ຍ້າຍອອກໄປໝົດບໍ?

ບຸນສອນ: ເຮີ! ໜີໄປພາດກຸ່ມເດຍວເນາະເຂົາບະ. ເຂົາວ່າ:
"ບໍ່ຢູ່ແລ້ວນີ້ບະ" ລະກັບຄືນເມືອງໂສຍເລີຍ.

ສົມໝາຍ: ຄືນໄປເມືອງໂສຍ...

ບຸນສອນ: ຈົນວ່າຕົ້ນໄມ້ ກິກ ໂອຍ! ຈົນ
ໂກະເໝັດແລ້ວ. ເຂົາຍັງວ່າມີຊຸມເງິນໃໝ່ແຕ່.
ມີກິກຂາມ ເຂົາສາບຫີນເຊັຕົງຍັງນ້ອຍ ແຕ່ຍັງນ້ອຍ
ສ່ຳແຂນ ສ່ຳແຂ່ງນີ້.
ກຸ່ງນີ້ມັນເຖົ້າມັນແກ່ເປັນໂກງໂກະໝົດລະ.

ສົມໝາຍ: ເໝືອງໃຕ້ນີ້
ກະແມ່ນທາງໃຕ້ບ້ານເຮົາເຮັດ?

ບຸນສອນ: ເໝືອງມານີດ ກະໄທບ້ານເຮົາເຮັດ.
ແຕ່ໄທໂສຍລະເສິ່ເຮັດກະ ບ່ອນງບ້ານເຮົາພັກກິນ
ໝາກພ້າວນັ້ນເນ. ຢູ່ເທິງນັ້ນໜ້ອຍໜຶ່ງເນາະ ຝາຍເສົ້ານັ້ນ
ແລ້ວລະເຮັດໄປເໝືອງເຂົາລອງກ້ອງບ້ານ ນັ້ນເນ.

ລະໄທເຮົານີ້ມາຫຼາຍຄືນ ລະ: "ໂອຍ ບ້ຶໄທໂສຍ
ເອົາເສຍລະ". ເຂົາຈຶ່ງແຫກ ມາງຕໍ່ເອົາກະ ນັ້ນນ່າ.

ແຕ່ກີ້ ເປັນ ເໝືອງນ້ອຍ ເປັນເໝືອງນາກີເຂົາ

Introduction 3

Naaí baan Bunsoon: Oh, the Tai Soi (*Thai Sôôi*)! They built no paddy field. Or rather, they built some, but on a limited scale, over there, just below the village. Our group eventually came and the situation changed, for we started building. We made new paddy fields; we are active. We worked with the Tai Soi.

The latter did not work, but we did. They used to say: "Oh, those people are hardworking!" Then, they could not stay.

Sommay: So at the time, they had not yet moved away?

Bunsoon: Not yet. They had not yet moved. They worked on their side, in their paddy fields. We made our fields close to theirs. The latter still belonged to them, until 1945–1946. Then, oh!, they could not stay anymore. Our group had settled by great numbers and had extended.

Sommay: Did they move away gradually or suddenly altogether?

Bunsoon: They moved away at a single time. They said they would not stay here. They went back to Muang Soi.

Sommay: So they moved to Muang Soi…

Bunsoon: As for the trees, oh! They have grown old and died. People say that the Tai Soi hid treasures under the trees. There is a tamarind tree they marked with a stone in the bark [to find it again, later]; [at the time] it was not broader than an arm or a leg. By now, it's already old, and hollow.

Later on, showing the canal just below the place where we discussed:

Sommay: Has this irrigation canal been built by the people of our village [in the sense of the people of Houay Yong]?

Bunsoon: This canal of *Naaiit*[2] was built by our group. The Tai Soi had built the canal close to the place where we have eaten coconuts when we took a break, a bit above the paddy fields. That was their part. They have also built the canal below the village.

Our group came by large numbers. The Tai Soi had already occupied the area, so we extended the constructions next to the places they had already put up.

In the past, it was a small canal. Anyway, it was their fields and their canal.

4   Introduction

ສົມໝາຍ: ວັດຖືກເຜົາປີໃດເກາະ?	**Sommay**: In which year was the Buddhist temple [of the Tai Soi] destroyed?
ບຸນສອນ: ໂອ! ບໍ່ຈື່ແລ້ວ ເຂົາໄປລະ ເຂົາລະມ້າງສະຄອກ ແຕ່ປີ 1940 ປາຍພຸ້ນແຫຼະ	**Bunsoon**: Oh! I do not remember. When they moved away, they dismantled it, in the 1940s.
ປີແອດ: 40 ປາຍ?	**Pierre**: In the 1940s?
ບຸນສອນ: ມີ 46, 47 ນີ້ລະ. ພວກເຮົາ ຂຸດເຫີບໂຮງຮຽນ ພວກເຮົາຂຸດລະຍັງໄດ້ທອງຕິດໂອບບາດ, ໂອບສັງຂອງວັດນີ້ລະ.	**Bunsoon**: Yes, around 1946–1947. When we excavated the soil for the schoolyard, we found the base of a bronze *baat* [monks' begging bowl], and things like this. They had not built a stupa (*thaat*), there was just a monks' dormitory (*kadii* or *kutti*).
ບໍ່ແມ່ນຕັ້ງທາດກະໃດຕັ້ງກຸງກະທີ	
	After a long exchange to spot out the precise location of Muang Soi:
ອຳພອນ ວ.: ແລ້ວ ໄທໂສຍ ຍ້າຍໄປນີ້ເຂົາທີ່ຍ້າຍ ດ້ວຍຄວາມເຕັມໃຈ ເອາະ?	**Amphone V.**: When they moved away, were the Tai Soi willing to move, or not?
ບຸນສອນ: ເຮີ! ຄວາມເຕັມໃຈແລະ ເພາະວ່າ ຢູ່ນີ້ລະ ຜູ້ໄທເຮົາມີຫຼາຍລະ ຜູ້ໄທເຮົາອ່າວຫຼັບກວ່າເຂົາ. ເຂົາລະຂີ້ຄ້ານ.	**Bunsoon**: Yes, they were willing, because we were numerous, hardworking, more than them. While they were lazy.
ປີແອດ: ຂີ້ຄ້ານ?	**Pierre**: Lazy?
ບຸນສອນ: ເຮີ! ຂີ້ຄ້ານ! ເຮັດນາກະເຮັດໜ້ອຍ.	**Bunsoon**: Yes, lazy! They cultivated in their paddy fields, but not so much.
ອາໄສ ຢູ່ເຮັດ ລຸງລຸ່ມ ນັ້ນດອກ. ໄທເຮົາມານີ້ ໂອ ຂຸດເໝືອງຕື່ມ ຕີນາຕື່ມ ລະໄທເຮົາຫຼາຍຄົນລະ ບໍ່ຢຸດເຊົາເບີ່ ມີສວນແຕ່ ຂຸດໜອງແຕ່ ຕີນາແຕ່ ຕັ້ນບ່າ ໂອ!	They just lived in that area below, no more. Then we came. Oh! We dug more irrigation canals; we enlarged the paddy fields; many of us did not stop working. We made gardens, dug fishponds, enlarged the paddy fields. And so on. Oh!
ໄທໂສຍລະ ບໍ່ຢູ່ແລະ ບໍ່ຢູ່ນຳໄທເຮົານີ້ ກັບຄືນໄປບ້ານເກົ່າ ເມືອງເກົ່າໂທຍ ເຂົາລະຄືນເມືອ.	This is why the Tai Soi could not stay with us. So they settled back to their home region. They just moved away.
ແຕ່ເຂົາພ່າຍກະ ບໍ່ໄດ້ຂາຍ ລະບໍ່ໄດ້ຂາຍ. ເຂົາທາກຈົງໃຈນີ້ພ່າຍ. ລະໄທເຮົາ ປະເລີຍ ປະເລີຍ ລະເປັນຂອງໄທເຮົາບ້ານ.	When they left, they did not sell their land. They moved away on their own will. We …. The Tai Soi left definitively. Since that time, that land is the property of our village.

After explaining how the Tai Soi left the place to the benefit of the Tai Vat, the *naai baan* explains the origins of other villages in the valley. From where we stay, we can see Houay Yong on the right (the North, downstream), and the vicinity of the village of Ban Kang on the left (the south, upstream) (see Map 2.1). As appears in the following excerpt, Ban Kang is a new village compared with Houay Yong. It has been displaced three times, moving upstream on the *Huai Yoong* stream, pushing out some Khmu (a Mon-Khmer people widely distributed in northern and central Laos) to their reported place of origin, the village of Nong Thop, in the mountains on the west (see Map 3.1).

ບຸນສອມ: ບ້ານເຮົານີ້ເກີດກ່ອນ ຫຼັງນີ້ຈຶ່ງເກີດ
ບ້ານກາງນີ້ນ່າ. ໄຕເຮົານີ້ຜູ້ເລິຊັນນະ ບ່າເມື່ອເຮັດ
ນຳທ້ອຍນີ້. ເມືອບ່ອນເລີພຽງເຮົາລະກໍເລີຍ.

ບະແລ້ວແມ່ນລາວເທິງ, ຂະມຸ ມາຢູ່ນີ້ນະ. ກໍມມຢູ່
ກໍມມ ເທິງລົງມາຢູ່ ເຂົາກໍລະ ເຂົາວ່າ ໄທເຮົານີ້ເມືອ
ເຂົາລະ ຄືນເມືອໃໝ່.

ປີແອຣ: ບ້ານ ເຂົາ ຂະມຸ?
ບຸນສອມ: ຄືນເມືອຢູ່ບ້ານເຂົາ ຂະມຸ ບ້ານໜອງຕົບ
ນັ້ນເນ.
ປີແອຣ: ບ້ານ ເຂົາ ຂະມຸ?
ບຸນສອມ: ເອິງ!

ບຸນສອມ: ເຜິ່ນນັ້ນ ທາງໄຕນົກຮອກ ທ້ອຍນີ້ ໂອ!
ປ່າກິງຕິບເປັນຕາຢ້ານ.

ລະບ້ານກາງນີ້ ລະ ມາຢູ່ນີ້ກ່ອນ ໂອ! ປ່າມ່ວງເຮົານີ້
ປ່າມ່ວງໄທບ້ານກາງເໜີດ.

ສົມໝາຍ: ແຕ່ກ່ອນບຢູ່ບ້ານນີ້ຂະມຸ?

ບຸນສອມ: ບໍ່ ໄທດຳນີ້ແຫຼະ. ຂະມຸ
ລະແມ່ນຢູ່ກາງເທິງຜູ້້ນ. ໄທບ້ານກາງນີ້ ລະ
ເຂົາລູກມາແຕ່ທາງຸກວນາມ.
ປີແອຣ: ບ້ານກາງ?
ບຸນສອມ: ເອີ! ບໍ່ຢາກຢູລວມນຳໄທຫວາດນີ້ລະ
ເຂົາມາຕັ້ງຢູ່ນີ້.

ບຸນສອມ: ບ້ານກາງເຮົານີ້ ເປັນບ້ານທີ3. ແລ້ວນັ້ນບ່າ
ທຳຮິດລະຢູ່ແລ້ວ ເຂົາພັດຍ້າຍເມືອຢູ່ທ້ອຍທາງ
ນັ້ນໃໝ່. ເຂົາຕົບນັ້ນເນ. ເຂິດຮອບນີ້ ເຂົາຈຶ່ງຍ້າຍໃໝ່
ປີ... ໂອ! ປີ 60 ປາຍ ນີ້ແລ້ວ ເຂົາຍ້າຍເມືອ 68-69
ນີ້ລະວາ. ເສົາຍ້າຍເມືອບ້ານເສົາ ປະຈຸບັນນີ້.

Bunsoon: Our village Houay Yong was built before the village of Ban Kang. We are really hardworking. We moved upstream of this river. Wherever we stay, we make paddy fields.

Some Lao Theung, or Khmu, had settled here. They had come from the upland to stay and cultivate. They saw that our people had come, so they moved back to their place.
Sommay: Where did they settle back?
Bunsoon: In their old village, Nong Thop.

Pierre: Was it the former village of the Khmu?
Bunsoon: Yes, it was.

Later on, showing the path below us:
Bunsoon: In the past, these people, this river, oh! It was a dense forest: that was chilling!

The village of Ban Kang was settled on that area before. You see our grove of mango trees right there? All this belonged to Ban Kang before.
Sommay: So in the past, the village of the Khmu was there?
Bunsoon: No, I was speaking about the Tai Dam [of Ban Kang]. The Khmu were upstream. The people of Ban Kang, as for them, originated from Vietnam.
Pierre: The people of Ban Kang?
Bunsoon: Yes. They did not want to live among the Tai Vat [of Houay Yong], so they settled apart, here [where the mango trees grown].
Bunsoon: Ban Kang is presently on its third location. At first they settled here [he shows the grove of mango trees below us]; then they moved up to the brooklet *Huai Vaang* and built paddy fields there; eventually, they moved again in, oh!, in the 1960s, around 1968–1969. They settled their village on the site where they live up to the present day.

These transcriptions provide a glimpse of how history is narrated by villagers – a village chief, in this instance – to visiting scholars interested in their past and their society. In this rural highland context, orality is the main source of history, because no manuscript in the village keeps a written record of past events. It has always been a challenge, first of all, to make history from such statements because of the confusion linked with the oral style: actors are ill defined, information is thick, sometimes contradictory, consisting of shortcuts, and laden with elements that have been taken for granted. In addition to these trivial elements, which are rarely addressed in the literature, scholars ascribe the difficulty of making history from oral statements to the scarcity of written sources for crosschecking the data, and to the complete intertwinement of the past and the present. As the historian Jan Vansina wrote, long ago, in his seminal book on oral traditions:

> One cannot deny either the past or the present in them. To attribute their whole content to the evanescent present as some sociologists do, is to mutilate tradition; it is reductionistic. To ignore the impact of the present as some historians have done, is equally reductionistic. Traditions must always be understood as reflecting both past and present in a single breath.
> (Vansina 1985: xii)

The interview excerpt brings out the fluidity and complexity of the human settlement in the valley: it refers to no fewer than six resettlements, four ethnic groups, and five ethnonyms – and this is just the tree hiding the forest. Dates, the cornerstone of history, are often absent in such oral accounts. The narrative above, with two reliable dates, is an exception. As a state officer, Bunsoon is eager to refer to specific years, in line with what is expected in official documents. But if plausible dates are sometimes provided about recent events, this hardly applies to ancient times. At some point, Bunsoon mentioned 1769 for the settlement of the Tai Vat in the valley, a date he got from another villager presented as the local historian, Thaabun [42, 250]. This last date is, however, not plausible from a chronological point of view, as is demonstrated later.

Despite all this, historical research in this regime of orality is very rewarding for historians as well as for anthropologists. It is the central topic of the first half of this book. History, in the common sense of event-driven history, is a never-ending issue many villagers indulge in discussing at length with passing researchers, because it deals with questions of origins and identity, of morality and legitimacy. This last point appears strikingly in the excerpt, when Bunsoon compares the industriousness and diligence of the different populations to explain and justify how the Tai Vat took over the leadership from the Tai Soi, and how the Tai Dam of Ban Kang eventually displaced the Khmu. Rather than a statement on chronology, the whole excerpt can be deciphered as an assertion of the group's virtues and its legitimate rights to land. The local interest in history is also motivated by the fact that narrating the past is an important enactment of one's status, especially for adult and elder men.

The reference to history and memory in this book's title reflects that, in line with the inspirational quote of Vansina above, my interest is limited neither to the objective aspects of history nor to its subjective dimension. The historical accounts reported throughout the volume are in no way 'neutral' oral archives, but situated assertions. In this sense, the present book is a contribution to ethnohistory, if we characterize the latter as research on "folk history," or "the view a society has of its past," as Carmack defined it in his seminal article (1972: 239).[3] How do the people narrate their own past in specific contexts? Who is entitled to do so? How is this narration supported, or enacted, by non-verbal supports? How do the current stakes of a society inform the whole process? Whatever the interest of such issues, they can hardly be addressed if one ignores the alleged referent of these discourses and performances, that is, the past, in the sense of events that happened some time ago. This deserves a chronological approach as well, which is underdeveloped in the current research in Laos.[4] The twin concerns I have raised here are in line with the commitment of ethnohistory, in opposition to memory studies, which often lack an interest in the objective aspects of the past, and to classical history, which usually lacks an interest in the present stakes for the past. The late Grant Evans told me a few years ago he regretted how few historians were involved in research in Laos, compared with the huge contingent of anthropologists. I hope the present monograph, a study of history through the lens of anthropology, will contribute to a better balance between the two disciplines.

Another relevant point of our ethnographic vignette is the role played by materiality and visuality in the discussion with *Naai baan* Bunsoon. Our dialogue was geared by the landscape in front of us. He referred to the canals we had just crossed to emphasize that his ancestors built them; he mentioned the place where the temple of the Tai Soi formerly stood, where bronze artifacts were discovered when the school was built later on; he pointed to the mango trees down on the road as a reminder of the time when the population of Ban Kang had not yet resettled upstream.

On a subsequent visit in 2017, strolling down the mountain slope after a washed-down lunch on the opposite side of the valley, a fellow guest pointed to the eastern side of the valley to tell me that this area used to be reserved for the village chiefs before the communist revolution, which happened in 1953 in this province [218]. Indeed, as recently argued by Pholsena and Tappe (2013: 6–7) about post-conflict landscapes in former Indochina, landscapes are much more than a "setting": they are meaningful. But their meanings change with time and with the vantage point of the speaker.

The landscape is only one of the material supports of memory in the valley. The second part of the book is devoted to village shrines and territorial cults. Most settlements in the valley have a shrine for village spirits, typically a wooden post imbued with a power of protection for the village, and miniature houses for the local spirits. It is placed under the responsibility of a descendant of the first settlers. This is very much in line with other founders' cults that have been described across the whole subcontinent of southeast Asia (Mus 1933, 1975; Tannenbaum and Kammerer 2003; Schlemmer 2012). The shrine is not a commemorative monument: it is activated through ritual performances taking place every year, or when a special event requires a ceremony. The distribution of roles in the ritual is still related to pre-revolutionary lineage hierarchies, despite the 65 years that have elapsed since the communist revolution in

Figure 1.3 The village post (*lak man*) of Houay Yong. The date of its enhancement (2 February 2010) has been molded on the cement when it was fresh (June 2010).

Houaphan (1953), and despite the policy restricting or prohibiting reportedly 'superstitious' rituals at the turn of the 1970s/1980s. Such resilience is much more than the conservative perpetuation of a frozen past. Some rituals have disappeared – this is the case of a territorial cult involving about ten villages in the vicinity of Houay Yong – whereas some others have transformed. New political incumbents have been coopted in the narratives about the village shrine in Houay Yong, and are materialized through a specific spirit house. In 2010, the wooden post has been encased with cement and inscribed with dates, similar to new memorials erected throughout Houaphan, under the influence of a neo-traditional monument built by the authorities at the province capital. The subtitle of this book – The Past Inside the Present – originates from my own surprise: I was impressed that a village pillar so intimately attached to the historical memory of the group had been enclosed in cement, a material associated with modernity by the Tai Vat. It was for me a strong metaphor about the way the past survives inside the present, encapsulated, framed, and veiled by it.

This transformation of the shrine, through cement and writing, has been the first occurrence of modern monumentality in Houay Yong. It opens the question about "places of memory" (*lieux de mémoire*) in this local and rural context. The concept was coined by the French historian Pierre Nora to describe material, but also immaterial institutions created with the intent to support memory, such as monuments, museums, popular books on history, commemoration ceremonies, and so on (Nora 1997 [1984–1992]). Intentionality is a very important component of the concept, compared with non-intentional traces of the past that are to be found everywhere (ibid. 37–38). According to Nora, the *lieux de mémoire* are typical of (post)industrial societies, like France, that underwent an acceleration of history, a rupture from their past, due partly to rural flight to the cities. If a society has to sustain a specific memory through such institutions, it is because it is not anymore a "memory-society" (ibid. 23), that is, a society where the transmission of values, worldviews, and practices is spontaneous. As Nora observed, "the less memory is lived from inside, the more it needs external supports and tangible benchmarks of an existence that goes on only through them" (ibid. 30).

Nora's book has been a turning point in historical studies, and triggered a wave of research on memory, with a focus on spatiality, emotions, identity making, and political use of the past. As Berliner (2005) rightly notes, memory has since become a buzzword in anthropology, due to its capacity to reformulate old debates on culture and identity. This present book tries to avoid the traps of this "memory boom" by focusing on *historical memory*, defined as the situated narration of past events of collective importance, through discursive and performative statements. The larger issues of cultural transmission and continuity covered by the flow of memory studies are not the central theme of this book, although the latter does contribute to this larger debate.

To come back to Nora's seminal work, it has been criticized for being unquestionably based on the French nation-state, which limits its comparative use. The "peripheral" societies Nora refers to in his introduction were brought to historicity after they were "awakened from their ethnological sleep by the colonial rape" (Nora 1997: 23). Many authors have disapproved of such a conception of a great divide in the regimes of historicity (Moniot 1999: 18). Despite this obvious flaw, the question remains: can the concept of *lieux de mémoire* be used in contexts wholly different from France? Can we use Nora under the tropics, as Moniot (1999) asked provocatively?

The challenge has been partly taken up in Laos. In 1998, Grant Evans published *The Politics of Ritual and Remembrance. Laos since 1975*, which investigates the rhetoric of political legitimacy at the turn of the last millennium. The book can be read as a study about the continuity of symbols despite political changes in Laos. The transitions from a monarchy to a republic, from a Buddhist state to a Marxist–Leninist state, from revolutionary socialism to market socialism, all failed in Evans's view to produce a new symbolic order. Hence the regime progressively relied on older references to sustain its legitimacy through ceremonies, statues, iconography, and the like. However, this process does not amount to a simple restoration of former symbols: no overt reference is made to the pre-revolutionary monarchic regime or to touchy aspects of the early post-revolutionary past. This triggers a paradoxical memory, half-performed, half-unspeakable, and hardly acknowledged as such by the authorities who rely on it. This present/absent memory is quite different from the memory effervescence in France, characterized by proactivity and intentionality according to Nora and the other contributors to *Les lieux de mémoire*.

Nora is not mentioned by Evans, but he is referred to in the recent volume edited by Pholsena and Tappe (2013) I have already cited. The authors analyze how landscapes linked to the Indochina Wars are imbued with memories. The tragic background of the war creates for sure the kind of rupture that Nora presents as a prerequisite for the production of *lieux de mémoire*. Some places directly affected by fighting (such as Viengxai in Laos [Tappe 2013b]) have been turned into sites of memory and received an aura they did not have before. These sites play an important role in the present national narratives. The contributors to that volume show, however, that memory can never be monopolized: such state narratives coexist with more particularistic memories about this violent past. Their book can be read as an invitation always to go beyond the national chronicle.

The present research about Houay Yong will certainly follow this invitation, even if the Indochina Wars have not affected the inhabitants of the valley as dramatically as the people who faced massive bombing, or the *Khmer Rouges* camps. As we shall see, wars are vividly remembered in Houay Yong, but the local memory embraces many other fields and is not really focused on that aspect. Memory studies have a predilection for traumatic pasts: the present volume can be seen as a contribution to compensate this usual leaning, although anxieties and violence will remain part of the whole story.

To come back to the use of cement to encase and strengthen the village post referred to above, it raises a question in line with Nora's reflection on historicity. Does it mark a turning point in the relationship people have with their past? Do people think that a rupture is occurring in their society, and that historical memory must be upheld by new devices? Are we turning from a natural "environment of memory" (*milieu de mémoire*) to "sites of memory" (*lieux de mémoire*) created self-consciously (Pholsena and Tappe 2013: 9, based on Nora 1997: 23)? Even if most elements of our research do not clearly head in this direction, I take this possibility into account. The very notion of cultural heritage, which is closely linked to the new memory processes described by Nora, has been popularized these last years by state officers and mass organizations, even in remote areas of Laos. For example, *Naai baan* Bunsoon declared that, if the village had to build a new office house, it should be a traditional Tai Vat dome-shaped house, precisely the type that has disappeared during the last decade [196] (see Figure 7.1). Bunsoon considers that the younger generation tends to forget the "traditions", *sing thii banpabuulut phaa hét* – literally, the things ancestors did and taught us to practice. He also used the word *muunsüa* (literally, heritage from the ancestral line) to describe such practices inherited from the past. This heritage should henceforth be encouraged actively through their performance, to show the new generations how to celebrate the *kinchiang* New Year,[5] how to sing and dress along the traditions, how to perform the ceremonies for marriage or for lifting misfortune (*sén*), and how to behave in relation to the domestic ancestors' altar or with the village shrines [260]. Even if the *naai baan* is more sensitive than most villagers about such issues, the concern of "losing one's culture" (Berliner 2018) is shared today by highlanders, or at least by some of their elites.

In sum, this book explores the intricate relationship between the past and the present in Houay Yong and its neighboring area. As a preliminary step to a more general attempt to capture the social changes triggered in that village by the intensified mobility of the population turning to a rural flight, in this volume I provide a glimpse on the 'present past' of the place, not for the sake of history alone, but to understand how historical trajectories and memories constitute the present, and how narratives of the past are used as a resource by the villagers today. Oral traditions of origins, intimate accounts of past events, shrines devoted to village founders, and rituals conducted to renew the communal pact with the spirits all articulate the past with the present in a constructive tension.

The usefulness of this endeavor can be questioned. Why should scholars devote time to investigate such marginal areas? Does it make sense to broach large historical issues from Houay Yong, a remote village that never played a central role even in Houaphan's provincial history? The answer probably lies in the shift of historical perspective such research creates. For 15 years now, scholars have argued that the historical trajectories of highland populations in mainland southeast Asia must be addressed in their complexities, and not as footnotes or annexes to mainstream history. These societies' reported marginality reflects the political standpoint of standard national historiography, but is not a decent posture for research. On the contrary, to adopt, following Salemink's (2011: 44) felicitous formula, "a view from the mountains" is an intellectual commitment to contribute originally to the history of southeast Asia, and to induce relevant effects of knowledge for understanding its interconnected societies.

To situate the present research in a broader movement, I very briefly list books that have participated in the reassessment of history in the region. Salemink (2017 [2003]) wrote a critical re-evaluation of the way knowledge of highland societies has been produced in the course of history – a violent history – in the Central Highlands of Vietnam. Michaud (2007) analyzed the early Catholic missionaries in Upper Tonkin and Yunnan, in their relationship with colonial expansion and the production of anthropology. Scott (2009) has written a very ambitious book defending a paradigm where lowland state societies and highland anti-state societies are to be understood through their relationships, because they are mutually constitutive. Scott's *Art of Not Being Governed* was met with international success. One of the uncontested benefits of the volume was to trigger discussion, and heated debates, across the boundaries of national traditions of research. Following a French monographic tradition, Bouté (2011, 2018) analyzed the ethnohistory of the Phounoy of northern Laos whereas Le Failler (2014) authored a detailed historiography of the integration of the Black River societies into the Vietnamese national space. Jonsson (2014) wrote a multisite history of the Mien in different countries of southeast Asia and in the USA, challenging assumptions of Scott on 'escapism.' In *Imperial Bandits*, Bradley Davis (2017) has investigated the turmoil triggered by the Black and Yellow Flags armies that invaded the north of Vietnam during the second half of the nineteenth century, showing notably how oral traditions challenge the official Vietnamese and Chinese narratives, and unveiling the trauma experienced by highlanders during that violent period. Eventually, Lentz (2019) has questioned the history of Điện Biên Phủ and the Black River region between 1945 and 1960, with a concern for the various ways actors imagined and constructed a 'territory' centered on that area; far from the usual focus on the famous battle, the book attempts to capture the successive subjectivities of the actors involved in the conflict (mostly the Tai and the Kinh), through a fine-grained analysis of archive sources in Vietnamese and in French.

I limited this evocative inventory to single-authored books – many more contributions can be found in the references quoted at the end of this volume. My intent was to show that a growing body of literature is now available to question the grand narratives positing the lowland states as the mandatory departure point of any research. There are alternative views to the canonical versions of history that have been adopted successively by the precolonial, colonial, and postcolonial states of the region, which reproduce the relations of power between the lowland centers and their margins.

My specific contribution to this collective reassessment is first to anchor the research in a small valley, along the *Huai Yoong* stream, which remains the locus of the research throughout the book. As already mentioned, it might seem challenging to investigate, from an area unnoticed in the archives, the major developments that punctuated the last century and a half in the region. It is at least worth trying. Of course, I recontextualize the local history on a larger frame, but the valley of the *Huai Yoong* stream will remain the axis around which the book revolves. Another specific aspect is the preeminence of orality and observation in my empirical data: this makes the local setting and its actors more tangible to the reader – a trademark of anthropology I absolutely endorse. This also reveals the basic concerns people have about the past: beyond wars, major historical figures, ideology, and political revolutions that figure prominently in the historical literature, this book voices other views and concerns of the local populations, which embrace mobility, kinship, spirits, rituals, village divisions, village fusions, resettlement, ethnicity, self-protection, coping strategies, political pragmatism, and collective self-praise. I also try to connect oral and written sources more than this has been done hitherto in the literature, which often calls for this integration but rarely puts it into practice. Finally, broaching history and territorial cults to make their connections more apparent is another research challenge I take up here. I hope that all these specificities will produce original insights.

Origins, scope, and contents of the research

If the villagers of the valley have their own history, so do this book and the research from which it emanates. Between 2003 and 2008, I was involved in a cooperation project ran by the French-speaking universities of Belgium (Conseil Interuniversitaire de la Communauté Française de Belgique–Commission Universitaire pour le Développement or CIUF–CUD) and the National University of Laos (NUoL). One focus site of the program was the multiethnic village of Thongnamy, in the lowlands of Bolikhamxay province, in the center of the country (see Map P.1). Thongnamy had been peopled since the mid-1990s by waves of migrants from the northern half of Laos, who settled there in the wake of the government's measures against shifting cultivation in the highlands. Hmong formed the bulk of the population, but there were also ethnic Khmu, Phuan, and about 50 Tai Vat families originating from Houay Yong village, in the district of Muang Èt, Houaphan province.

This research resulted in articles on the strategies of these migrants and on the way they adapted to land policies, the national culture, the Lao standards, or new religious practices (Petit 2006, 2008a, 2008b, 2012, 2013a, 2017). These orientations were in line with the many studies devoted, during the first decade of the century, to village resettlement in Laos.[6] However, it turned out that, apart from Rigg's (2007) early contribution on those "left behind," little attention had been dedicated to: the people who remained in the villages from which the migrants came; the reasons why they have not moved; their living conditions after the departures of their relatives; the relationships they kept with the latter; the transformations of the local culture and society prompted by the migrants; and similar questions centered on the home villages of the migrants rather than on the migrants themselves.

Due to the very good relations developed with the Tai Vat of Thongnamy during those five years, and due to the extensive data already gathered about them in their new settlement, I proposed, with colleagues from the Faculty of

Social Sciences of the NUoL to plan a new research program about the migration process grasped from their place of origin. To this end, a Memorandum of Understanding was signed by the University of Brussels (Université libre de Bruxelles, ULB) and the NUoL, and eventually endorsed by the Lao Ministries of Foreign Affairs and of Education. From 2009 to 2018, I stayed over seven short periods (from three days to fourteen days each) in Houay Yong, together with one or two collaborators from the NUoL: Sommay Singthong, Amphone Vongsouphanh, Amphone Monephachan, and Vannaseun Chaiyavad.[7] The first three came several times and were in charge of the administrative tasks related to research authorizations. They played a central role during interview sessions, and in the detailed translations we completed afterwards based on their recordings. We frequently discussed the ethnographic data based on our respective backgrounds, which in their case involved details on culture, society, and religion in different parts of Laos. Hence, this book is the result of a collective work, as acknowledged in the credits: they fully fulfilled their role of research assistants in the strongest sense of the term.

The total of 66 days spent in the village of Houay Yong is a limited timespan based on ethnographic standards. However, this brevity was compensated for by: the extensive research carried out previously or simultaneously in Thongnamy and Vientiane with migrants from the village;[8] the collective dimension of the research that broadened the possibilities for inquiries and the range of attention; and the added value of successive field stays that allowed a comprehensive and extended analysis of previous data before beginning a new research stay. Doing research through repeated visits, compared with one or a few extended stay(s), has the great advantage of deepening one's experience and understanding of a social setting, because anthropology does not progress through a simple, continual accumulation of 'data,' but through a process where presence and absence, gaps and memory also play a role. As Fabian nicely says:

> there is a kind of quantum leap our efforts can take after a period of absence. Our interlocutors are more willing and eager to help us, they are more talkative and tell us things they held back earlier, meetings become more productive and enjoyable when they are reunions, even short visits make us feel more at home now than an extended stay did when we started out. Copresence, to be experienced consciously, needs a shared past, and it is during absence from each other that we find the time to make pasts that can be remembered.
>
> (Fabian 2007: 133)

Indeed, beyond the benefits in terms of trust and emotional ties, repeated field stays produce specific effects of knowledge, where interpretations deepen and metamorphose, rather than accumulate.

I also conducted a series of yearly field seminars from 2010 to 2014 in Chiềng Pằn, Chiềng Sàng, and Chiềng Đông (see Map 3.2), in the district of Yên Châu, the home region of the Tai Vat in Vietnam. I was in charge of a seminar of rural sociology with students and colleagues from the Vietnamese National University of Agriculture in Hà Nội. Although I was much involved in the guidance of the students, I was able to carry out observations and interviews, on a much more superficial mode than I did in Laos, and to get a sense of the difference between the Tai Vat societies in the two countries.

The original focus of research was mobility and the way in which it affected the local society through economic, social, and cultural changes. This entailed a deep interest in the impact of remittances, the changing relationships between parents and their migrant children, the way access to land has been transformed due to massive departures, etc. However, if such issues have been central since the beginning of the research, other topics progressively surfaced. I did not intend to investigate religion in detail at first, but I eventually had to, because domestic rituals were observed almost every day in the village, proving the vitality of the religious system, and its central role in maintaining kinship and other social ties between villagers, including youths who moved to the city. As for history, I intended to have no more than a short historical background to the migration issue. But this topic of conversation was vividly appreciated by our hosts, besides which, information on the past unceasingly surfaced during interviews on other themes, or when strolls along the valley elicited casual comments on the landscape's history. The village shrines did not rank either among the initial themes of research, but we have been invited to these places since our very first days in the village. Being a central institution for constituting the village as a corporate unit, in the sense of a group feeling united and distinct from its neighbors, under the aegis of a spiritual presence, it became more and more central in the research, especially in 2012, when we were invited to attend the annual ceremony for the village spirits. Eventually, so many different issues had been investigated that it turned out to be impossible to discuss them properly in a single monograph. Hence the present volume has a limited scope compared with the research at large.

This book is made up of seven chapters. This present introductory chapter has already discussed the overall aim of the volume, and situated the genesis of the research. The following sections of this chapter describe in detail the conditions of fieldwork, to give a clear account of the practicalities of our team's insertion into the village and the methodology we used over our seven stays. The archival research conducted in France is also presented.

Chapter 2 provides the basic elements of context needed for understanding the following chapters. It briefly develops the local geography to cast Houay Yong amidst the neighboring villages, because their history and territorial cults are intimately interconnected. Ethnicity is evoked second, to highlight the importance of ethnic ascription in the local area and to remind the reader of the need to approach such categories in a relational, non-substantive way. The subtleties of the two self-ascribed ethnonyms used by people of Houay Yong to refer to themselves, Tai Vat and Tai Dam, are discussed accordingly. The official discourse on ethnicity, and the unofficial centrality of the Lao in this system, deserve attention as well. Ethnicity is also approached as a diachronic process, as I analyze the shift of ethnic labels in the district center of Muang Èt. Finally, I present the local administrative and political system, which provides the opportunity to introduce some informants and discuss their political pedigree, but also to describe the state as an everyday reality for the villagers. Each of these three sections ideally deserves a full chapter, but they are developed here as elements of context for the volume.

Chapters 3 and 4 address the first main topic of the book: history and memory. Chapter 3 reconnects first with the issue of orality and written culture evoked in the introduction. The local context can be described as literate, or semi-literate, which questions why history remains mostly based on oral accounts. I contrast this with the culture of writing that appears in more important political centers of the area. A Lao archive of the first half of the sixteenth century is described first to give an idea of the early charts that linked the principalities of Houaphan with the Kingdom of Lane Xang. I analyze with more details a colonial archive dated 1898, in the light of the larger regional history of the province. The latter shows the involvement of the local elites in the struggles opposing factions of the colonial bureaucracy, as evidenced by many documents conserved in the French colonial archives in Aix-en-Provence. I also describe the performative dimension of oral history, which is a prerogative of the male elites.

I then report five oral narratives about the coming of the first settlers from Yên Châu, in Vietnam, transcribing one of them with more detail. Their comparison shows the centrality of the kinship idiom to frame the current relationships between the villages. I then confront these oral traditions with other sources on the regional history (accounts by travelers and missionaries, military and administrative archives), especially those related to the invasion of Northern Vietnam and Laos by the Chinese Flags, often referred to as the Hô, in the late 1860s/early 1870s. I also address the enigma of the former inhabitants of the valley, the Tai Soi, already mentioned in the introductory vignette, as well as the Lao and the Khmu, who have presently disappeared from the valley but are still vividly remembered. A tentative chronology is proposed, while the ideological dimension of these episodes is also stressed throughout the chapter. The last section elaborates on the present moral appraisal of the former political order.

Chapter 4 carries on with colonial and postcolonial history. A section is devoted to Muang Van, the seat of the subdistrict authority since the 1880s, and to the larger system of nested polities in the province. I turn thereafter to the colonial regime, for which I elaborate on archives related to politics, demography, ethnicity, taxation, trade, religion, and infrastructure. The blind spots of the colonial documents are discussed as well, because they are key indicators for the French governance in the highlands of Laos. The French colonial period came to an end with the Japanese invasion (1945) and the First Indochina War (1946–1954). I mostly base the reconstruction of this last episode on Vietnamese sources, because they help to understand why, from 1951 to 1953, many Tai Vat fled the war in Vietnam to take refuge in Houay Yong. The next periods analyzed are the Second Indochina War, the early revolutionary regime, the economic overtures in the 1980s, the resettlements of the 1990s, and the massive out-migration and the development of local infrastructure in the twenty-first century. The chapter concludes by a reflection on the use of archives when doing ethnography, the system of indirect rule during the colonial period, and the relationship the villagers keep with their place of origin in Vietnam.

Up to the present day, most villages of the valley have a "solid post" (*lak man*) erected on a nearby mountain slope. Close to it, one usually finds small huts for the communal ancestors and spirits. Chapters 5 and 6 address this ancient ritual institution of the Tai people, which has remained central in the present identity of the villages: it constitutes the second main topic of the book. Chapter 5 begins with a state-of-the-art look at the literature devoted to territorial cults in southeast Asia, which have been described and analyzed for a century, notably by French ethnographers such as Mus, Maspero, and Archaimbault, whose ideas remain inspiring. I thereafter provide an ethnographic description of these shrines in the valley. The material structures and the local comments on the spiritual presences attached to these shrines are presented first. Following this, I investigate the identity and function of the different incumbents involved in the cult, the most important being the "master of the shirt," a patrilineal descendant of the first settlers of the place, who is responsible for carrying out the yearly rituals for the village community. I describe at length the annual and non-annual ceremonies celebrated in the village to ensure the continuous protection of the spirits, based notably on observations carried out in 2012. I eventually delineate the *dông khuaang*, a territorial cult centered in Houay Yong that involved other settlements taking their water from the *Huai Yoong* stream, which has disappeared two decades ago.

Chapter 6 analyzes, along different axes, the ethnographic material presented in Chapter 5. It uses comparative data from other regions of Laos or from nearby areas to elaborate hypotheses of a general nature, addressing first the annual ritual on the village shrine and second the disappeared regional cult, *dông khuaang*. To start with, I discuss Mus's (1933) very relevant thesis that territorial cults can be approached as a "cadastral religion" at a supralocal level. Indeed, both the rituals and the historiography of the village shrines demonstrate the central role of territorial cults in identifying each community and its boundaries. Village fissions and fusions are key indicators to test this relational argument. Next, I disentangle how the commitment to stability inherent to territorial cults can paradoxically coexist with an ethos of mobility in a group with a history intimately linked with migration. I then demonstrate how the cults are part and parcel of a larger system of hierarchy and exchange linking the living and the spirits through the symbolism of verticality and offering. Not surprisingly, the modern state interferes with such representations of authority, as appears in the current commentaries on the village shrine. Thereafter I question the pervasiveness of dual structures in territorial cults throughout southeast Asia, which provides incentives to rethink the link between the local sphere and the encompassing political–religious order.

The later sections of Chapter 6 resume with the analysis of the *dông khuaang* ritual that involved nine villages depending on the *Huai Yoong* River. I first question the apparent absence of reference to autochthony in the territorial cults of the present day. This contrasts with the observations made in their time by French ethnologists, who envisioned territorial cults as mediating the authority of the current occupants with the former powers of the place. Then I formulate the hypothesis that Houay Yong formed a second-level polity nested in a larger system of *müang* polities, and survived as such only through its ritual centrality for a century. Thereafter I discuss the interaction of Buddhism with those territorial cults, exploring the ambiguous relationship these two spheres maintain. After a glimpse on the local memories about the revolutionary period, when prohibitions against "beliefs" put at stake the old religious and social systems linked to territorial cults, I conclude with a reflection on the disappearance of the *dông khuaang* ritual.

The conclusion (Chapter 7) recaps the main topics discussed in the whole volume, highlighting the core arguments and perspectives for prolonging the research. Its final pages connect even more directly the issue of territorial cults with the present national society. As appears in Figure 1.3, the village post has recently been strengthened with cement, a material intimately linked to modernity and to the future in Lao imaginaries. This change is partly related to the construction, in 2008, of a huge city pillar in Sam Neua, the provincial capital, adorned with political slogans and pictures of the "liberation war." This Sam Neua post has triggered a new model of monumentality diffusing now throughout the villages of the region, as if yesteryear's hierarchical system of territorial cults was given a new impetus by the Lao State. The ambiguous reactions of the Tai Vat to the modernization of their territorial shrines – between fear and laughter – are illustrated in the last two vignettes closing the book with a touch of local humor.

As a selection of only two topics among the many that were broached during this long-term research, this book provides the historical and territorial bases to explore other themes in the future. I am unable to address, in the limits of this volume, the changing economy of the village: its burgeoning economic differentiation, land issues, and the process of migration seen from the village's perspective. Another absence is precisely migration as it is conceived from the migrants' point of view: in particular, how do the Tai Vat youths in Vientiane see their relationship to the city and the village through their practices, their imagery, the New Year's celebration, or their attitudes to marriage? Also left in a blind spot is the domestic religion: ancestors' shrines, rituals of birth and death, and mediums' ceremonies against affliction – all institutions of prime importance to understand the resilience of kinship and hierarchies in the social fabric of the village, despite the disruptions provoked by two decades of migrations. I plan to unpack those topics in future publications.

The fieldwork

This section describes how our team was immersed in the local society and how we proceeded to produce data for the research. Reflexivity is mandatory to introduce any ethnography: no one speaks from nowhere. But it often takes an individual, ego-centered, abstract, or confessional mode that overlooks practicalities, interactions, and methods. The following paragraphs aim rather to clarify how we developed relationships with our hosts, and how we conducted the research practically. This is an important key to contextualize the contents of this book and to engage in dialogue on disciplinary practices with fellow anthropologists, whether or not they are Lao.

The contact trip in 2009 aimed at establishing relationships and getting basic information on the place. We were the first team of university researchers to work in Houay Yong and were welcomed as such. Some villagers had already heard about us from their relatives in Thongnamy. I was surprised to find, on the wall of one house, pictures of myself and my wife (who visited Thongnamy in 2008, with our two children), and other pictures I had taken in that village: they had been sent by Mèè Chét, my 'adoptive' mother in Thongnamy, to her younger sister in Houay Yong. I had also brought pictures from Thongnamy, and I offered them to different people on the first day that I was present. At the time, smartphones and social networks were still unknown in the place, and pictures were much appreciated, leading to discussions about faraway relatives.

Conducting field research in upland socialist Asia is usually not a long, quiet river for scholars, especially for westerners. At the margins of the lowland centers, peopled by ethnic minorities, close to international borders, sometimes touched by social unrest, rebellions, or messianic movements, these places rouse state anxieties in the whole region. In an edited volume, Turner (2013) and other scholars discussed at length the peculiarities of this context: the difficulties for obtaining a research permit; the role of local officers as gatekeepers, who can provide or not their "red stamp" for validating such permits; and the uncertainties relating to the information flow, which can stop anytime due to decisions of bureaucrats, security agents, or anyone who considers the researcher addresses sensitive issues. As for our team, we were confronted by that kind of problem only once, in 2010 (Petit 2013b). When our team presented the mission order validated by the university to the provincial authorities in Sam Neua, it turned out that the document could not be approved (or rejected, in fact). The main problem was the mention of research on "migrations" (*kaannyaaithin*), which, phrased as such, seemed to interfere with national policies, as if we aimed at their assessment. Thanks to contacts, we were eventually able to meet a senior officer to plead our cause, that is, to explain our proper scholarly intents. This officer was convinced and became quite jovial, suggesting that we change some phrases of our document and that we label it "The living conditions of the Tai Dam ethnic group." We endorsed his proposal. We soon received the new mission order from the university; it was stamped by the provincial administration and we began our research the same day. The whole process took us less than 48 hours.

We faced no problem during the following years: the research permit was renewed by the university every year; we had it stamped by the provincial authorities when we arrived in Sam Neua, then by the district authorities in

Muang Èt, and we handed it eventually to the chief of the village, Bunsoon. At the district level, during one of our first stays, an officer insisted that we would sleep in the district center and proceed every day to the village of Houay Yong to conduct research, but we were able to convince him that it was not feasible for practical reasons. Once or twice, a security agent came into the village to check our documents – the matter was settled quickly. To cut a long story short, our work was not hampered by the administration, and our repeated comings and goings made things easier and easier over time, because trust had been progressively achieved.

By comparison, the research trips to Yên Châu District, in Vietnam, were uneasy. Despite the active support of the National University of Agriculture in Hà Nội, which sponsored this seminar lecture, it was always difficult to receive the approval of the provincial authorities of Sơn La; spending a night in any village was forbidden "for security reasons," and, during our December 2014 seminar, the groups of (mostly Vietnamese) students were each accompanied by a security agent every day. The reason for this difference is difficult to explain. At the time, tensions were high between Vietnam and China which both claimed rights on the sea between the two countries; it was explained to me that "external enemies" could try to ally with ethnic minorities. More globally, state control seems much more enforced in Vietnam than in Laos, and tensions between the (mostly Tai) population and the authorities was palpable in the region at the time, due notably to the enforcement of development projects not approved by the population.

The relationships with state officers in Laos were much easier and more casual. As for our relationships with the villagers, they were very good. How they perceived us remains partly unknown, but our daily interactions with the inhabitants were smooth, kind, and friendly. Some people, especially authorities (but not only), might have seen our successive visits as a sign of esteem for their community – a good opportunity for status advancement in the micro-politics of precedence among the neighboring villages of the valley. For most, our whereabouts seemed in line with the friendly visits that villagers used to pay to their acquaintances or with routine bureaucratic surveys. We explained the aim of our research whenever possible, and always before interview sessions. In 2014, our film *Return Trip*, shot in 2012 in Houay Yong, was screened on six occasions in different houses (Figure 1.4), and twice in the central place of the village, in front of an audience of several hundred villagers: it was a turning point for some people still unsure about our goal.

It is likely that some villagers developed apprehensions about our intentions. Coming from the National University and working in close contact with the village authorities related our presence to an investigation by the state (see page 178 for an instance of our perception as state agents), and most foreigners coming to the valley are involved in development projects, or in a business. However, we had no hearsay about any hidden motives to our presence, despite our alertness to that issue. This climate was quite different from the situation described, for example, by Bouté (2011: 23–27), where the ethnographer was

Figure 1.4 People watching the film *Return Trip*, here during a screening in the house of *Naai baan* Bunsoon. That movie turned out to be a transactional object in our relationship with the villagers. Besides generating fun from self-recognition, it was a good way to clarify the aim of our research, and people felt rather proud to have a film about their community (June 2014).

received with mistrust, despite her strong commitment and good will. The difference can be explained partly by the local context: during the civil war, the region of Houay Yong was a faithful ally of the Pathet Lao; being on the communist side preserved the area from some hardships more common in regions that did not have such a good reputation. A second point is that we assumed our position of 'official' researchers – any other explanation about our presence would have been a matter of surprise, or rather of concern, for our hosts. However, we never acted like authoritative state officers pressed with time – quite the contrary. The National University has a good reputation in the countryside, with higher education being valued in Lao society at large. A third point was the composition of the team, which included two research assistants (Amphone Monephachan and Amphone Vongsouphanh) born respectively in the district and a neighboring district: both of them could easily find, after a short exchange, personal links with the villagers. Fourth, and last, the fact that we came repeatedly, year after year, was certainly a landmark for establishing trust: villagers appreciated our constancy and reliability. We hope that the publication of this book will fulfill their hopes for a better acknowledgment of their society in Laos.

Besides our formal activities of research, we did our best to share the everyday lives and the usual forms of sociability of the villagers, as anthropologists usually do. This includes showing consideration to everyone, respecting the village hierarchies, asking the village chief first before taking initiatives, accepting invitations, sharing meals, and making short visits as much as we could. We

Figure 1.5 A meal during a *sén* ceremony for lifting a household's misfortune. Amphone Vongsouphanh and Sommay Singthong are in the center left, wearing sport T-shirts (June 2010).

Figure 1.6 The author drinking *lao hai* (rice beer) with Thaao Chüaang, the commissioner of the *sén* ceremony illustrated above, and his wife. The man on the right adds water from a buffalo horn while the drinkers swallow the beer using a straw (June 2010).

Figures 1.7 and 1.8 Members of the team dancing *lamvông* (Figure 1.7, left) and *huup èèô* (Figure 1.8, right) with villagers of Houay Yong in the communal hall during the feast following the inauguration of the new school (June 2011).

bathed in the public fountains of the village, as most villagers did. Food and drink turned out to be of central importance for acceptance, because it is a key vector of sociability in this farmer society. To be honest, we enjoyed local food. We showed no reluctance for any meal that was offered to us, including dog, cat, mice, or curdled blood of various animals. This was always highlighted by our hosts when they presented us to external visitors.

The Tai Vat serve alcohol generously to their guests during the various parties that gave the rhythm to the everyday life in the village.[9] This often led to "participant intoxication" (Fiskesjö 2010), especially when there was a special event to celebrate. Indeed, we were sometimes quite drunk due to our attendance, but it was a token of trust and proximity with our hosts. Accepting vulnerability – someone intoxicated is deprived of one's usual protections and emotional barriers – can be an important step for involvement in a community, and for sure that was crucial in Houay Yong.

Dancing was another important bodily involvement with the village's community. It is a mandatory aspect of sociality in Laos, where events of importance and all parties are supported by dances, either Lao *lamvông* or local dances (Figures 1.7 and 1.8). Beyond drinking, fieldwork requires dancing.

We certainly held a high status in the village society. This appeared, for example, in the fact that, when there was a collective meal, we were usually invited to share the table of the authorities and male elders, as appears in Figure 1.5, due to our position as guests and official researchers. Similarly, drinking alcohol, contrary to its apparent casualness, is usually outlined by the social hierarchy. The first rounds of people invited to share the *lao hai* beer prepared for a ceremony with the commissioner are high-ranking participants (see Figure 1.6). Likewise, dancing *lamvông* follows a protocol, during the first rounds at least: the invitations to take a place in the dancing procession are made along a decreasing order of precedence. Downplaying this high status conferred by our hosts would have been very vexing to them, because they themselves participated in this system.

However, to mitigate this assigned male seniority, we mixed with all the segments of the local society, joining youths for a party, circles of women eating and drinking during ceremonial events, farmers in their field cottages, local students and teachers celebrating the end of the year, and meeting people of all economic statuses during our interviews (all the more during the socioeconomic survey). This was met with some success, because Tai Vat society is rather casual for social interactions across genders and age, and my research assistants were about 15 years younger than me, which made our team able to straddle generations. The most difficult part was interviewing teenagers (especially the girls), who could feel stressed on the first contact and were not used to taking the floor in the presence of adults; but, here again, our repeated visits made things easier over time. In short, if we had been appointed into the circle of male elites, and if this certainly constrained our viewpoint, we were neither passive nor naive in the process of our social insertion.

It is certain that this insertion cannot be reduced to a professional practice, even if it is informed by it. It left traces in our lives, and over these years all the team developed an emotive attachment to the village and its inhabitants. The technical (and a bit strained) word "informant" used to describe our working relationship with interviewees in the next chapters should in no way obscure that we had close relationships, and developed friendship, with many of them. But despite the fact that this word is used less and less in the anthropological literature, to the benefit of the euphemizing "interlocutor" or the developmental-milieu-driven "research participant," I will keep it here and there as a reminder of the asymmetrical relationship on which anthropological research rests in effect, despite pretenses.

During our stays, we lived in the house of Bunsoon, the *naai baan* who has been quoted in the introductory vignette. The only exception took place in 2017, when his house was being repaired: we moved to the home of Thoongsôm, who used to be *naai baan* long ago. Hosting official guests in the house of village authorities is the usual practice throughout Laos. We had our meals with these families, providing our own contribution for expenses when possible, and, of course, slept in the house. We brought no special modern convenience into the house, except laptops (which we never used during interviews). With the exception of the fourth research period when we made the film, we had no car and relied on our feet for visits, or on villagers for driving us to the district center, Muang Èt, by motorbike or van when needed. Such precautions helped to avoid exacerbating differences in living standards with our hosts.

Bunsoon has been our main contact in the village. He has always been eager to introduce us to people who could help us for the research, or to accompany us to places of interest inside or outside the village. He is extremely collaborative and has never made any restriction on our investigations. He is a very talkative, friendly, convivial, and casual person, absolutely in line with the village standards of sociability; staying in his house never seemed to threaten our relationships with anyone in the village because he is very popular. The outcome of this research owes much to him. Among our other close collaborators is Thoongsôm, a key informant since 2010. Born in Vietnam around 1940 and still very active, he has a deep knowledge of Tai Vat history and society. These two figures often appear in the following chapters, and their biographies are shortly developed (see pages 41–43). We had, of course, many other informants, collaborators, or simply friends, among common people, the youths, elderly women, the poor and the rich. The Dramatis Personae section gives a good summary of our main contacts during the research. Our knowledge is based on information obtained from men as well as women, from elders as well as adults and youths. However, the present volume is an exception to this general rule: oral lore about ancient history and rituals conducted in the village shrines are a privilege of elder men, who are the gatekeepers of such traditions. This androcentric standpoint is a reflection of the way information, institutional positions, and practices related to these two issues are organized in the village. Authority on narrating historical events in the region (I do not speak about biographies or family history) and on performing community ritual is definitely a prerogative of the male elite. The informants about other topics of our research at large are much more balanced between genders and generations. I elaborate more on that issue on pages 56–59, 133.

As has already been said, our original program aimed at understanding the social, economic, and cultural transformations of Houay Yong triggered by migrations. We gathered data on these topics using, not a questionnaire, but, sometimes, a protocol of inquiry, that is, a list of topics to be developed more freely, adapting to the specific case of each and every interviewee. On that basis, we got formal information for a socioeconomic survey from a sample of 25 families (about a quarter of the village), interviewed mostly in 2010 or 2011.

Besides this, the bulk of the information came from interviews carried out with specific topics in mind. The questions during interviews were phrased based on what the interviewee had said before, not on queries listed in advance. We interviewed key informants on specialized matters, such as elders reputed for their knowledge of history or village rituals, or female mediums about their dealings with the spirits. We made long and often repeated interviews with informants who had a story about migration, like returnees, with elders who were often an inexhaustible source on rituals, or with educated teenagers who had decided not to go to Vientiane, but who eventually did, etc. Contact has been kept up to the present with about 15 youths and young adults through Facebook, which has become very common for those who have traveled to the city.

We also learned a lot during everyday observations and conversations. Casual discussions could often be more rewarding than formal ones: for example, an unplanned breakfast with elders during the New Year proved to be thought-provoking about the difference between youth and elderly people on the issue of mobility, and a lunch turned out to be an extraordinary occasion to learn how villagers discuss history among themselves (see pages 57–58). Our knowledge on some touchy topics, such as prostitution, was also often triggered by casual remarks from villagers.

26 *Introduction*

The interviews were conducted in Lao and in Tai Vat/Tai Dam languages, which are mutually understandable with some effort, but still different. I have an intermediate-level understanding of Lao, with a decent understanding of vocabulary but a poor proficiency in tones (Lao and Tai are tonal languages). I read it but write it with difficulties, due to the tones. The NUoL colleagues are, of course, absolutely fluent in this language and were in charge of the interviews. Amphone Monephachan and Amphone Vongsouphanh are, respectively, Tai Dam and Tai Dèng from Muang Èt and Xiang Kho districts (see Map 3.1), which means that they have a very good understanding of the Tai Vat dialect. This was most useful during the research, because the use of specific locutions, especially by elders, made translation a real challenge.

Farmers' lives are busy, and this is why we made short visits (often in the early night-time) to make appointments with our potential informants. Interviews took place in their home, or quite often in a cottage in their field. We brought small presents, like tea, coffee, glutamate, or candies, to share with our hosts and their children. After casual discussion, we explained the aim of our research to start the interview. The permission to use a voice recorder was always explicitly requested after that presentation – no one bothered about it, or about our use of a (video) camera. I launched the interview with a first set of questions, which were trans-

Figure 1.9 Thaabun (on the front right) was acknowledged as the authority on history in Houay Yong until his death in March 2018. He narrated the foundation of the village to our team in 2010 (Amphone Vongsouphanh at the front left; Sommay Singthong behind him) [8]. Another elder listens, and sometimes intervenes at his back. Offering herbal tea and fruits are usual tokens of politeness with guests among Tai Vat. The voice recorder close to Thaabun allowed a full transcription of his version of the story (Narrative a, see page 60–61) (June 2010).

lated by one of the colleagues. He prolonged the conversation with sub-questions for one or two minutes, and then summarized the contents in English. Based on that, and on my own understanding of the informant's answer, new questions were devised, the process repeating during the whole interview (which lasted from half an hour to up to one and a half hours). We were always attentive to the use of specific vocabulary and tried to use it whenever possible. Fieldnotes were written down on the spot during the interview. After thanking our informant, we always took the time to have a lighter discussion before leaving. We translated and transcribed the interview in a handbook on the very day of the interview if possible, or soon afterwards. We often repeated interviews with the same informant, after having assimilated the content of the previous session to engage more deeply in concerns that had only surfaced during the first session.

Although we stayed in the village of Houay Yong most of the time, we visited other villages in the surrounding area, and conducted interviews on their history. Ban Kang was visited three times; we spent two full days in Houay Lom, and we visited Nasan, Muang Van, Nangiu, Pakfèn, and Ban Sot for short periods to conduct interviews.

Figure 1.10 Fieldnotes written on the spot. This interview was part of the socioeconomic survey, the interviewee sitting on the left. *Naai baan* Bunsoon (center) provides here elements of contextualization, notably for the uneasy calculation of cultivated surfaces in hectares – he usually did not take part in our interviews, however (June 2011).

Besides interviews and informal discussions (the relevant elements of which were also written down in a handbook when we had spare time), we devoted a lot of time to observation. We have been invited to many rituals, and documented various activities, such as handicraft, agriculture in the paddy fields, and in the swiddens, the collective maintenance of the canals, the inauguration of the new secondary school and its annual closure ceremony, or the different phases of the *kinchiang* New Year. Here again, I wrote down syntheses of such observations and of the comments heard on the spot.

We took a lot of pictures and videos, which have been useful in many ways. First, they were used as gifts or for entertainment. Despite the accessibility of smartphones throughout the country for four or five years, printed pictures remain uncommon, and are much-appreciated personalized presents. The film *Return Trip* was screened eight times in the village, in 2014, and DVD copies were widely distributed. Second, visual data have been a very useful research instrument, completing fieldnotes and sound recordings of interviews. They can be watched long after their capture, providing new information previously unnoticed, and sometimes even challenging the first interpretation of an interview or sequence of facts. Third, they allow decentering from the usual 'logocentric' perspective of anthropology: they switch the attention from discourses to gestures, atmospheres, audiences, and, of course, materiality. And fourth, images are a very convenient way to bring the field to the fore in an anthropological publication – unlike sounds, they can be printed in a volume. I use photographs and screenshots extensively in this book, because in my view they are part and parcel of any ethno*graphy*. The Greek etymology of the word (γράφω, gráphō) refers both to writing and to drawing, and it has always seemed obvious to me that anthropology is also visual by nature. I do not use pictures as 'illustrations,' but in dialogue with analysis, or with longer captions than usual. I hope that the use of pictures provides a better idea of the context in which interactions took place and knowledge was produced. The anthropologists at work are not concealed. If the photographs taken with a Nikon camera are usually of good quality, the screenshots from Sony Handycams are, of course, coarser, but they help to capture specific movements during interview sequences, and are helpful to discuss the gestural dimension (see Figures 3.5, 3.6, and 6.1–6.3).

Apart from ethnographic research, this book also draws first-hand material from colonial archives. I spent six working days consulting the French colonial archives in Aix-en-Provence (at ANOM – Archives Nationales d'Outre-Mer), unpacking tens of cardboard boxes filled with reports, telegrams, maps, and letters selected from the main archival funds on the region.[10] The library of the ANOM also contains published colonial sources that are difficult to find elsewhere. Despite my expectations, I found almost no information pertaining specifically to Houay Yong: out of around 5000 pages that I consulted, focusing on the documents related to the districts of Muang Èt or Xiang Kho that successively included the territory of Houay Yong, I could find only one casual mention of the village. In a document dated 1902, three villagers of "Hua Yong," in the district of Muang Èt, are listed as paying taxes for their guns (RSL E3, 4/5/1902). This silence of the archives is addressed on pages 87–91, 112.

Notes

1 Lao is normally written with no space between the words. I use some to highlight syntagms for non-native readers.
2 The toponym *Naaiit* refers to the paddy fields (*naa*) that were constructed after slashing down a forest of trees of the species locally called *iit*.
3 Carmack (1972: 236, 238) acknowledges other possible meanings of ethnohistory.
4 To have a better idea on the pressing need to reconsider critically the accepted chronology of Laos, see Lorrillard (2006).
5 *Kinchiang* is a three-day celebration held in January to February, at the same time as the Vietnamese New Year (*Têt*). Many young migrants living in Vientiane come back to visit their relatives in the village, and to enjoy parties, visits, and celebrations. This is also a time for displaying the group's identity through clothes, music, songs, dances, games, and rituals.
6 The articles by High (2008), Petit (2008a), and Baird *et al.* (2009) provide a state-of-the-art view of the literature on resettlements at the time.
7 A short trip (with Amphone Monephachan, 27–29 June 2009) aimed at establishing a first contact and at getting basic information on the village. The second stay took place from 2 June 2010 to 7 June 2010 (with Amphone Vongsouphanh and Sommay Singthong); the third one took place from 24 May 2011 to 6 June 2011 (with Amphone M. and Sommay S.). The fourth included the members of the preceding stay as well as Marie-Pierre Lissoir, an ethnomusicologist from the Université libre de Bruxelles who wrote a PhD (Lissoir 2016) under my direction; it took place from 18 January 2017 to 27 January 2012 at the time of the *kinchiang* New Year festival, and was aimed at making a film on youth migration. The film, titled *Return Trip. Portraits of Tai Dam migrants* (2014), has been podcasted on YouTube and can be watched as a visual support to the present book. The fifth stay took place from 30 May 2014 to 9 June 2014 (with Amphone M.), the sixth, from 8 June 2017 to 18 June 2017 (with Amphone V.), and the seventh and last, from 27 November 2018 to 7 December 2018 (with Sommay S. and Vannaseun Chaiyavad). Ms Phouvan Sommixay, a villager of Houay Yong, was also included in the team to help with transcriptions during our seventh stay.
8 My research in Thongnamy spans from 2003 to 2012, and was carried out there as well in collaboration with scholars from NUoL; two teams of colleagues from NUoL filmed and interviewed migrants established in Vientiane and Thongnamy during the *kinchiang* New Year of January 2012; I conducted research in Vientiane with young migrants, but also with adults and elders (in 2012, 2014, 2017, and 2018).
9 See Lissoir (2017) on the role of alcohol during her fieldwork among the Tai Vat. The importance of alcohol in the contact with foreigners and during festive events at large is reported by archives on the region (RSL E2, 1/12/1896a; RSL E4, 3/3/1926), and by Foropon (1927: 45). An interesting and lively description on drinking *lao hai* and its protocol is provided by Raquez (1905: 1233, 1323–1324). According to him, failing to respect the customs of hospitality related to sharing food and *lao hai* would (partly) explain the assassination of the scholar Odend'hal by the Jarai in the highlands of Vietnam, in 1904. His explanation is not fanciful in my view.
10 Tappe (2015, 2018) has also recently consulted these archives about Houaphan. His work has been more focused on the relationships between the administrators and the local elites, especially during the early period when the eastern districts of Houaphan were incorporated into Annam (1893–1903). Our researches are complementary.

2 The setting

This chapter aims to provide the reader with a basic background to the research. Located in the mountainous northern half of Laos – often described as a glimmering ethnic mosaic – and more precisely in Houaphan Province – the cradle of the Lao socialist revolution – Houay Yong could be associated with exotic and anachronistic images that must be unraveled from the start. Taken together, the three entries that follow – geography, ethnicity, and the state – aim to highlight the inclusion of this village society into the wider context of the Lao nation-state.

Elements of geography are needed to describe the constraints of the mountainous environment but also the insertion of the village into networks connecting people along roads, rivers, and shared infrastructure. In the second section, I question the issue of ethnicity, in a country that proclaims its multiethnic character in the national constitution, but addresses this diversity in a catalog-like fashion and considers the Lao Buddhist mainstream culture as a *telos*. For social anthropology, ethnicity has nothing to do with such discrete categories, although the production of such categories is part of the issue. It should rather be approached in terms of processes of identification and categorization resulting from intergroup relationships, in a context marked by local tensions, and by policies and politics in the nation-state. The third section unravels the insertion of Houay Yong into the multi-layered structure of the Lao State. The latter is presented as a constitutive dimension of everyday life, not as something alien, or by nature alienating, to the villagers' existence. Its pervasiveness is linked to the presence of representatives, artifacts, and institutions linked in *dispositifs*, the banality of which contributes to efficacy. Through them, all villagers, whether or not elite, are engaged in "state relations," that is, social relations indexed to state practices and imagery.

Geography

The village of Houay Yong shelters 530 inhabitants based on the statistics of 2017 [233]. It is located 396 meters above sea level, in the deeply embanked valley of the *Huai Yoong* stream that flows from south to north (Map 2.1). The name of the village obviously derives from the river: *huai* means "stream, small river" in Lao and Tai. About 1 or 2 km east and west from the river, the mountains on both sides

The setting 31

Figures 2.1 and 2.2 The village of Houay Yong seen from *Phuu Kup* Mountain, looking southeast. Streams, fishponds, paths, villages, terraced paddy fields, patches of forests, swidden fields, and mountains form the landscape of the valley (May 2011).

32   The setting

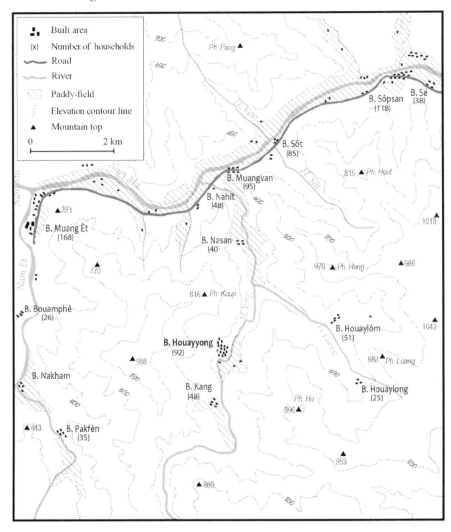

Map 2.1 Houay Yong and the eastern edge of Muang Èt District in 1983. Spellings have been conserved as on the source map (*Service Géographique d'État*, F48–113, 1983). Numbers under the villages' names refer to the number of houses at the time. Unreported on this map are the villages of Nalèng (between Muang Van and Ban Sot), Nangeun (between Nahit and Muang Èt), and Navan (facing Ban Sot on the opposite side of the River Ma).

of the valley reach an altitude between 800 m and close to 1000 m.[1] A direct consequence of this geographical setting is that irrigated rice fields are limited for topographic reasons, even if the population has built terraced hillsides.

The *Huai Yoong* stream flows into the River Ma (*Nam Maa*) in the vicinity of Muang Van village. Leaving Muang Van and climbing up the *Huai Yoong* stream for 2 km, following a dust road, one comes first to Nasan, on the west side of the stream. Then, 1 km further upstream, the *Huai Yoong* receives a tributary on its right bank: the *Huai Lôm* ("H. Luang" on the map), on which one finds the village of Houay Lom, 2 km upstream; 1 km upstream of Houay Lom is the former location of the village of Houay Louang, the inhabitants of which have been resettled as explained on pages 147–148. The village of Houay Yong is 2 km upstream from this confluence with the *Huai Lôm*, on the west side of the *Huai Yoong* stream. And 2 km further upstream is Ban Kang (already evoked in the introductory vignette), still on the west side of the stream.

Muang Van lies on Road 6A, which leads westward to the district headquarters of Muang Èt (named after the River Èt [*Nam Èèt*] which enters the River Ma on that location), and eastward to the district headquarters of Xiang Kho.[2] Road 6A runs alongside the River Ma, which flows eastward parallel to the border with Vietnam (only 20 km north of Muang Van, see Map 3.2); in fact, the River Ma flows on its first 100 km in Vietnam and on its second 100 km in Laos, and re-enters Vietnam to spill eventually into the Gulf of Tonkin. The River Ma and the River Èt used to be important axes for trade and communication until the end of the colonial period (see pages 95–96).

As for infrastructure, Houay Yong and all the villages of the valley were connected to the national network of electricity in late 2012. There is no domestic water supply in Houay Yong, but eight public fountains were built in 2003. In June 2011, the old primary school on the north end of the village was pulled down and replaced by a bigger building, including a lower secondary school. Next to the school is the health center, run by three employees. Both the school and the health center are intended for the populations of Houay Yong, Houay Lom, and Ban Kang [6, 41, 215, 230].

Ethnicity

According to their respective inhabitants, the villages of the *Huai Yoong* valley have different ethnic compositions. Muang Van has a mixed population of Lao, Tai Dam ("Black Tai," including Tai Vat), Tai Dèng ("Red Tai"), and Tai Soi (included among the Tai Dèng or the Lao) [113], Nasan has a balanced population of Tai Dèng and Tai Vat,[3] Houay Lom and Houay Yong are Tai Vat villages, and Ban Kang is a Tai Dam village [71, 76]. This variability carries on along the River Ma: going west from Muang Van, the first villages are Nahit (Tai Dèng) and Nangeun (Yao/Iu Mien); going east, one crosses the villages of Nalèng (Tai Vat, with a few Tai Dam and Tai Dèng) and Ban Sot (Tai Dam); facing Ban Sot on the opposite side of the River Ma is Navan, which hosts a population of Singmun, a Mon-Khmer subgroup [222, 237].[4]

The area is for sure an "ethnic mosaic," but this overused metaphor does not capture the fact that the same people can acknowledge themselves under different ethnic labels. For example, the inhabitants of Houay Yong identify themselves alternately as Tai Vat (*Thai Vaat*) or Tai Dam (*Thai Dam*). Tai Vat is not a common ethnonym in Laos: there are only four villages exclusively or predominantly populated by Tai Vat, all of them in Houaphan Province.[5] Tai Vat is listed neither among the 49 ethnic labels officially endorsed by the Lao State, nor among the 54 endorsed in Vietnam (Lao National Front for Construction 2005; Nguyen Van Huy *et al.* 2009). This lack of administrative acknowledgment explains why they are classified as Black Tai (Tai Dam in Laos, Thái Đen in Vietnam), a more generic category. However, among themselves and on the micro-local scene, they use the more precise denomination of Tai Vat. This is a clear example of the way nation-states impact ethnic ascription.

Through their lines of descent, all the Tai Vat presently in Laos originate from Yên Châu District, in Sơn La Province, Vietnam. They also call this region Muang Vat (*Müang Vaat*), which refers to a pre-colonial *müang* (polity) centered along the River *Nam Vaat* (see Map 3.2), a secondary tributary of the Black River.[6] Despite this obvious etymology, which relates their ethnic name to the river of their home region, some elders from Houay Yong have an alternate folk etymology of their ethnonym: when their ancestors in Vietnam were asked by other inhabitants of their valley of origin about their intention to stay or not, they answered "*taam vaat*," meaning "in an uncertain, non-definitive way." They did not know how long they would settle there before possibly continuing on their way. This narrative underscores the mobility of the Tai Vat people, their 'unsettledness' [87, 90, 107] (Petit 2015: 412).

The unusual nature of this ethnonym in Laos partly explains why the Tai Vat often present themselves (or are referred to) as Tai Dam, a much better-known ethnonym in Laos and in Vietnam. Depending on the context, Tai Dam can refer to a generic category including Tai Vat and some other Tai peoples, or refer to a specific subgroup of this category, the Tai Dam in the narrow sense of the term.[7] The Tai Vat of Houay Yong feel very close to the Tai Dam (in the narrow sense), but they are prone, in specific contexts, to underscore their differences: pronunciation (even if their language is basically the same), singing (their *khap* songs are different), traditional clothes, and place of origin, Muang Vat. Cầm Trọng, a specialist of the Tai populations in Vietnam, acknowledges the specificity of this group among all the other Tai Dam, notably from a linguistic point of view (Cầm Trọng 2004: 21).

The use of alternate ethnonyms by the same people illustrates the contextual and relational nature of ethnicity. Ethnic groups are not cultural units. They have more to do with social processes of categorization and identification that permanently reshape the ethnic landscape in a given context.[8] The cultural elements mentioned above as differences been Tai Vat and Tai Dam (pronunciation, clothes, etc.) are diacritical emblems related to traditional culture, rather than sound cultural differences between the two groups in the present. They would fall into the category of "overt signals or signs – the diacritical features that people look for or exhibit to show identity" mentioned by Fredrik Barth in his pioneering work on ethnic relations (Barth 1998 [1969]: 14). Barth mentions a second category of diacritical features for ethnicity: the "basic value orientations: the standards of morality and excellence by which performance is judged" (ibid.). We have already come across one of these in the ethnographic vignette in

Figure 2.3 Thoongsôm, his wife Mèè Soong, and some of their grandchildren. The old couple wanted to have their picture taken wearing traditional Tai Vat suits. The *piau* headdress of the woman and her shirt with a vertical row of metallic clips in the form of butterflies are the most conspicuous emblems of Tai ethnicity up to the present. On the contrary, only a few elders wear the male suit during ceremonies. Children wear the regular uniform for pupils, with the typical Lao *siin* (tubular skirt) for girls (June 2009).

the introduction (see pages 3–5), when *Naai baan* Bunsoon highlighted the industriousness of the Tai Vat and Tai Dam (compared with the Tai Soi and the Khmu), and their never-ending endeavor to move up the rivers making new fields. This ethos was opposed to the reported cultural leanings of the Tai Soi and the Khmu, the former inhabitants of the valley who eventually had to give way to the new, overactive settlers. Another component of these "standards of morality and excellence" is the group's self-perception as a migrating people, which appeared in the folk etymology mentioned above, or their self-ascription as *saatsanaa phii*, that is, people whose rituals devoted to spirits fall outside the Buddhist (or any other world religion) frame.

Interestingly, during the interview mentioned in the introductory vignette, Bunsoon used different expressions to refer to his group in distinction to others. Most often, he simply said "*Thai hao*," which means "our Tai" or "our people," in the sense of "us." The word *thai* is both a classifier for any group (the inhabitants of Muang Èt, for example, are the *Thai Èèt*; the members of the Sing Loo clan are *Thai Loo* [242]), and an ethnic classifier distinguishing Tai subgroups from other ethnic groups, such as the Lao, the Khmu, or the Hmong. When he came to the episode relating how the people of Ban Kang progressively settled up the river, built new rice fields, and eventually displaced the Khmu, Bunsoon phrased Tai identity in inclusive terms: he introduced Ban Kang as "the village of our people/ our Tai" (*baan Kang khoong Thai hao nii*); he later used the same expression of "our people/our Tai" when he stressed how the ethos of hardworking pioneers made the Khmu move away. In that part of the discussion, the villagers of Houay Yong (including himself) and of Ban Kang were presented as forming a single group, by opposition to the Khmu. However, a minute later, Bunsoon used the word "Tai Dam" to refer specifically to the inhabitants of Ban Kang, explaining that they settled separately because they did not want to live among the Tai Vat of Houay Yong. In this second context, ethnic categories are used to mark the difference between the two Tai groups, rather than to stress their unity.

This exemplifies that, depending on the situation, the boundaries of identity change. The inhabitants of Houay Yong identify themselves as Tai Dam (in the broad sense of the term) when they want to state their similarity with the other Tai Dam subgroups, or to stress their difference with other groups like Khmu (as in the former example), Tai Dèng, Hmong, or Lao. In Thongnamy, far away from their home province, they form a tiny minority and tend to identify as Tai Dam because this category is more easily acknowledged by other people. Identifying as Tai Dam is, in this context, a strategic resource to connect to other groups sharing this label, and to trigger solidarity with them. This was visible, for example, during the *kinchiang* New Year ceremony in 2005, when they invited a delegation of Tai Dam (in the narrow sense of the term) from a nearby village [55]. In contrast, they present themselves as Tai Vat when they want to highlight their specificity, for example, when explaining the distinctive settlement of Ban Kang, as in the above excerpt, or when they want to stress the corporate nature of their village and their respect of traditions compared with the people of Ban Kang, who in their opinion do not share these concerns as much as themselves (see page 150).

I have already mentioned that the villages in the neighborhood of Houay Yong are mostly populated by other ethnic 'minorities,' such as Tai Dèng, Tai Dam, Iu Mien, or Khmu. What about the presence of the Lao, who make up most of the population at the national level and have given their name to the country? Here again, there is no simple answer, because 'Lao' does not constitute a category with a clear-cut boundary: who does or does not identify as Lao, and who is acknowledged or not acknowledged as such, may change along with the circumstances and the interlocutors. Muang Èt, the urban seat of the district in which Houay Yong is located, provides a good example to discuss this issue.

Paul Le Boulanger is the author of the first history of the Lao kingdoms published in French (Le Boulanger 1930). He was serving as a colonial state officer in Houaphan when his book was issued. In his report after an inspection tour throughout the province, he wrote that "Muong Het is a large Tai Dam village"

(RSL E4, 22/3/1930). Eighty years later, when I asked *Naai baan* Bunsoon which is the main ethnic group settled in the district center, "the Lao" came as a natural answer, with the emphasis that the Tai Dam probably predominate when considering the whole district [237]. As the hypothesis of a large-scale migration of Lao people into the area is not sustained by the facts, we should consider that this is another instance of "Laoization," that is, the process through which ethnic minorities tend to identify with the Lao mainstream culture, and discard their specificities by the same token (Evans 2000: 285). This is more visible in the urban setting than in the hinterland villages, if we follow the difference reported by Bunsoon about the population of the district center and its hinterland.

During the first decades of the twentieth century, the ethnonym "Lao" was, however, not in common usage in Houaphan. The Catholic missionary Mironneau, very active in the area of Muang Soi that is evoked later on, does not use it when he comments on the provincial census of 1930: among the 41,741 inhabitants of Houaphan at the time, about 16,850 were "Tay Nura inaccurately called Laotians" (Mironneau 1935–1936: 715). Tai Nüa (*Thai Nüüa*, that is, Northern Tai) is an interesting ethnic category to explore. Historically, it was the specific ethnonym used to refer to the Tai populations of Houaphan who had adopted the Lao culture and its religion, Buddhism. In the long term, it turned out to be an intermediate step before the generalization of the ethnonym "Lao." The process was already engaged in the 1930s, as appeared in the remark made by Mironneau, who denounced the inaccuracy of the label "Laotians" to describe "Tay Nura": his remark makes sense only if the two ethnonyms were used concurrently at the time.

The process can be assessed in Muang Èt. An early observer of the region was Alfred Raquez, a colorful character who conducted an ethnographic survey in French Indochina in 1905, with the view to contributing to the colonial exhibition of Marseille in 1906 (Gibson 2018). Raquez reached Muang Èt in January 1905:

> The population is made up of Black Tai, but they have adopted everything from the Tai Nüa: their clothes, their houses, and their festivals; they present themselves as Laotians. Only one village in the *huaphan* of Muang Èt, Ban Na-Hoi, claims to be Black Tai.
>
> (Raquez 1905: 1328)[9]

I have reported above that Le Boulanger noted, in the 1930s, that the inhabitants of Muang Èt were of Tai Dam stock. Much later, in 1991, Tanabe reported that the dominant population of Muang Èt was Tai Nüa (Tanabe 2000: 303). And I mentioned that, presently, they are called Lao, as appeared in the conversation with Bunsoon.

To cut a long story short, the category of Tai Nüa has evaporated with time. I never heard it during my research in Houaphan. In 2005, only 2354 people were classified as Tai Nüa throughout Laos (Lao National Front for Construction 2005: 21), and the category was not concentrated in Houaphan Province. The progressive disappearance of this category, already in progress when Raquez (see next paragraph) and Mironneau made their observations, has to do with the superiority attached to the identity of Lao, a superiority probably vivified since the nineteenth century by the elites related to the kingdom of Luang Prabang, by the Siamese occupants, by the French colonizers, and by the present authorities who acknowledge Lao culture as the *telos* of the nation (Petit 2008b). This explains why the inhabitants of Muang Èt have been successively described as Tai Dam, Tai Nüa, and eventually Lao.

This switch has not been a smooth one, and tensions between the Laoized Tai Nüa and the other Tai groups remained very tangible in the early twentieth century, possibly fed by the resentment due to violence of late nineteenth-century wars (see pages 69–75). Raquez observed this tension during a colonial festival gathering representatives of different groups from the province[10] celebrated one month before his coming to Muang Èt:

> The Lao, who are in fact Tai Nüa, consider themselves as superior to their Phu Tai [Tai Dam and Tai Dèng] neighbors and make it feel clearly to the latter in many circumstances. Today, during the celebration, they [the Lao] keep them apart.... Offended by this separation, the Phu Tai women consider leaving the festival ... the [Lao] female singers involve themselves in the issue. Taking an innocent, honeyed attitude, with a silk cloth covering their mouth, they exchange sweet-and-sour compliments.
> (Raquez 1905: 1322)

This excerpt demonstrates that, if ethnic categories were relevant for the administration, they were even more so for the local people. We are not here in the situation of an ethnic grid imposed by a colonial administration: ethnicity seems to be all the more anchored in the regional history and everyday experiences of categorization. Laoization is one dimension of the process, but it has nothing to do with a soft, 'natural' transition. It is related to local hierarchies, precedence, power, and conflict.

This detour by the distant past provides the background for reframing our original question about the presence of 'Lao' in Muang Èt: the question must be cast on that background of cultural processes and social tensions, and cannot be answered in a substantive way. To document further the current expressions of ethnicity in the area, we need to introduce a new actor: the state, which has been largely ignored by Barth in his seminal work. Laos is officially defined as a multiethnic nation, and state institutions have promoted the imagery of harmonious ethnic diversity (Petit 2008b, 2013a). A pervading iconic element of the latter is the trio of women in traditional garments typifying the three cultural meta-ensembles peopling the country: Lao Lum, Lao Theung, Lao Sung, that is, the Lao of the plains, of the slopes, and of the upper lands. This trio can be seen everywhere across the country, on boards welcoming the visitor at the national airport, on banknotes, on advertisements for tourism or mobile phones, and during various occurrences of state pageantry. Despite the abusive simplification of this triple icon, which has been discarded by the state authorities themselves, it is still much used today, even in official contexts as appears in the next ethnographic vignette. Beyond this imagery, the state has also promoted more or less explicit national standards about what the "fine customs" of ethnic groups should be, that is, consensual elements related to clothes, handicrafts, dance, music, architecture, ceremonies, and other traditions, as long as they do not "impede the development, unity and mutual assistance among the ethnic groups" (Lao National Front for Construction 2005, p. b).

The politics and policies of ethnicity are not a distant reality in the highlands of Houaphan. There are many opportunities where they are given a concrete form. I take here as an example the ceremony for awarding the official status of "cultural village", *baan vatthanatham*, to Muang Èt (see also pages 110–111 on this issue). The ceremony, organized in June 2011, staged the iconic group of three women in ethnic clothes, backed by banners, and surrounded by people grouped by villages (wearing their specific ethnic costumes), or by mass organizations or schools (Figure 2.4). Such pageantry informs the local representations of ethnicity and the state in the whole area. Despite the very modern character of such representations – or, rather, because of it – people adopt them when they come to discuss their culture and their identity. It is tempting to stress the authoritative top-down aspects of such policies and discourses, but one should not forget that they are also resources for action and for self-acknowledgment.

In Figure 2.4, a picture taken during the ceremony of awards, the woman occupying the central position and holding the board with the name "Muang Èt" wears a Tai Dam suit; usually, this central position is devoted to the Lao representative, who is in this occurrence sitting on the right side of the picture (Petit 2008b: 484–490). This shift is not mere chance. It shows that, despite the reported Laoization of the district center, despite the fact that its inhabitants identify – and are categorized – as Lao in some contexts, the sense of being 'somehow' Tai Dam is given a tangible expression, especially when local cultures are valued, as in the ceremony under discussion. Such a symbolic highlight is prone to boost the sense of being Tai Dam, and to raise self-esteem in this identification. This situation demonstrates that Laoization does not amount to a unilinear acculturation to the national standard. The process is more complicated, because ethnic identity is made up of different layers that actors use through their agency. Furthermore, the times have changed, and the "liberation struggle" of the socialist government has for sure modified many hierarchical orders of the past. The present state-sponsored appraisal of ethnicity partly explains why the Tai Vat and Tai Dam are proud of their ethnic identity nowadays.

Before closing this section, it should be stressed that ethnicity is obviously not always the relevant dimension people use to demonstrate their collective identity. Being a villager, and not a city dweller, is certainly a very strong social classifier throughout Laos, especially for the migrants in Vientiane. Identifying as 'animists' is common to differentiate from Buddhists.[11] The provincial identity of Houaphan is also often put to the fore, as appears in songs or on social

Figure 2.4 The ceremony for awarding the title of Cultural Village to Muang Èt. Sitting from left to right are three women representative of the Yao/Iu Mien, the Tai Dam, and the Lao. This iconic embodiment of the multiethnic population of the country is facing the authorities, mostly senior men and monks, who deliver speeches about the urban center's achievement (May 2011).

networks; this has a political connotation in some circumstances, for Houaphan used to be the cradle of the revolution, and its inhabitants are still suspected of holding political privileges in the country. And, of course, the national identity is of prime importance in many contexts, notably in Muang Èt, due to the proximity of the border with Vietnam.

Political and administrative status

Houaphan was one of the two 'liberated' areas governed by the Pathet Lao during the civil war, from April 1953 to December 1975. Presently, Houay Yong is located in the district (*müang*) of Muang Èt, which was autonomized from the district of Xiang Kho on 20 October 1997 [252] – we see on page 86 that Muang Èt had already been a separate district at the turn of the nineteenth and twentieth centuries. One administrative rank below is the *kum baan*, "group of villages." The district of Muang Èt is made up of 10 of them, representing 78 villages altogether [237]. The *kum baan* including Houay Yong is Muang Van. It includes ten villages: Muang Van, where the office of authority is located; the four villages in the valley of *Huai Yoong* (Nasan, Houay Yong, Houay Lom, Ban Kang); and five other close villages on the road along the River Ma (see Map 2.1).[12] In the past, the *kum baan* used to be called *taasèèng*, and this administrative level had important prerogatives (and often a larger geographical extension), but it disappeared in an administrative reform in 1993 (Bouté 2011: 34). However, *kum baan* remains a significant institutional level for the Party and for mass organizations. I sometimes call it 'subdistrict' for convenience.

Below the village unit, the lowest level of the political–administrative structure is the *chu*, a group of 9–13 neighboring households in Houay Yong. The *chu* plays a role for mostly practical concerns, such as the recruitment of workers for collective works, evoked in the vignette on the maintenance of the canals (see pages 1–2) [50, 215]. There are currently ten *chu* in Houay Yong; there were twelve in the past, but the population has receded due to migrations.

As for every village in Laos, Houay Yong is under the authority of a *khana baan*, a village council made up of the chief of the village (*naai baan*) and deputy chiefs (*hoong naai baan*). Applications are ratified by the Party, and go through elections at the village. Since 2008, the *naai baan* is Bunsoon.[13] Until 2017, he had two deputy-chiefs: Phèèngsoon [73] and Khamphian [103]. The elections of early 2017 have confirmed them all in their positions for five more years. The *khana baan* has been extended to five people, the two new members being Nang Hom, a woman formerly in charge of the Women Union (see Figure 1.8), and Khamphét, who is in charge of the finances and statistics of the village.

Becoming a member of the village authority requires one to have a good political pedigree, and a good position in the micro-politics of the village. Let us take the example of the three main members of the *khana baan* [13, 27, 43, 154, 215].

The *naai baan*, Bunsoon, is the son of Koongvaakhuu, or Khuu, a refugee from Yên Châu who fled the war in Vietnam in 1953. Koongvaakhuu's father, Thoom, had been village chief in Bản Ngùa, in the present Vietnamese commune of Chiềng Pằn (see Map 3.2). After his arrival in Laos, Koongvaakhuu became a teacher in Muang Èt and was noticed by the authorities for his cleverness in mathematics and accounting; furthermore, he could speak Lao as well as Vietnamese. This is why he was incorporated into the committee of the *tambun*, the subdistrict administrative unit that would be called *taasèèng* and *kum baan* later on. He remained in the position for about a decade, and was head of the committee for two years [42, 43, 154, 215].

Bunsoon, born in Laos after 1953, was a child when his father Koongvaakhuu died suddenly (around 1960); he was seven when his mother, O, married again. In the 1970s, he became a soldier for two years, then village guardian in Houay Yong, and eventually head of the Youth Union. In 1985–1986, he was appointed deputy chief of the village and he maintained this position for 22 years until he attained the status of *naai baan* in 2008. His own son, Bunnyèng, is presently the head of the Youth Union. Coming back to Bunsoon's mother, O, she married a widower in the early 1960s: the latter had children from his first marriage, among whom Buasai (born in 1950), who had been *naai baan* before his stepbrother Bunsoon, from 1998 to 2004. Buasai has a remarkable political track, because he had been head of *taasèèng* in the past and is now head of the

Figures 2.5 and 2.6 Bunsoon, in his everyday activities as *naai baan* of Houay Yong. Figure 2.5 shows him receiving an agriculture promotion agent. Figure 2.6 shows him taking part in a reception with other male elders after a curing ritual for a fellow villager, in the company of Buasai (facing him on the left) (May 2011).

kum baan. He is, hence, the main representative of the Party in the village and in the whole *kum baan*. His daughter married the present *chao süa*, the descendant of the first settlers who is in charge of the village shrine, as discussed on page 132 [219, 252].

Phèèngsoon, the present deputy chief and former chief of the village (2004–2008), is the younger brother of Phoonsai, a general of the National Army who settled in Vientiane and passed away in 2016. Phèèngsoon also held high responsibilities at the *taasèèng* level, and was charged in 1988 to collect data in relation to the territorial limits of villages – this is why he knows the history of the different places well [73, 103, 252].

The next-ranking deputy chief, Khamphian, is quite rich by local standards. He married the daughter of Ua, the late elder sister of *Naai baan* Bunsoon, who was a renowned medium [153]. Khamphian has received political education in Muang Èt, an important step to prepare him as a leader for the coming years.

To go back further in the past, Thoongsôm (born around 1940), who was *naai baan* during about two decades (from circa 1971 to circa 1993), also has a very good political pedigree: he served as a soldier in 1959, then engaged in the police at the provincial level, where he reached a high position (*naai hooi*). He learned Marxist–Leninist theory at the basic level during a residential seminar in the region. He held the position of *naai baan* during the collectivization period. He has been chief of the Party at the subdistrict level (*hua naa phak khéét*) and, after he quit his term as *naai baan*, he became leader of the Village Front (*Neo Hom*), the mass organization for the elders, for ten years [36, 103, 107, 262].

These cases have been presented in some detail to demonstrate that local leaders have substantial kinship ties, and long experience in the state, the Party or the defense apparatus. This concentration of good political pedigrees has

Figures 2.7 and 2.8 Thoongsôm, when he was a young revolutionary staff (in the 1960s–1970s) and in June 2011. Uniforms and awards of honor ostensibly show the status of a person in relation to state authority, but embodied dispositions, such as self-command, calmness, and eloquence, are even more central to status. Thoongsôm exemplifies all these features.

allowed Houay Yong to secure a predominant position in the micro-politics of the valley, as evidenced by Buasai's leading position at the subdistrict level.

The state is an everyday reality in Houay Yong. It is embodied by the presence of state officers, such as those people we have mentioned, but also of mass organizations, such as the Women Union, the Youth Union, and the Lao Front for National Edification. The state is also represented through employees such as village guardians, teachers, or health officers. It speaks through the national TV. It has specific places, such as the school, the health center, the central place of the village with its boards of achievements (see pages 110–111), and the communal hall. It is made visible on the outside wall of each and every house of the village, on which, since 2017 or 2018, is affixed a blue identification plate similar to the ones visible throughout the country. The capacity of these 'banal' institutions and artifacts to create a national identity should not be underestimated (Billig 1995).

The village hall is an important public space in Houay Yong. All official meetings are held there. The households are invited to send one representative to attend, usually the male household head. This is seen in Figure 2.10, a picture shot during the meeting for the inauguration of the new school building, in June 2011. About 60 household heads came to the invitation, among which were only

44 *The setting*

2 or 3 women. In Figure 2.9, one sees the place where speakers take the floor. Symbols of state authority are displayed on the wall: pictures of Kaysone and Souphanouvong, the two founding fathers of the revolutionary nation, but also a map of the world, a poster with flags of the world, another one on the national army, and a few certificates of village achievements. The desk of honor is decorated with flowers. The contractor in charge of building the school takes the floor with the microphone while the provincial officer who came specially from the provincial capital (Sam Neua) for the occasion completes the text of the discourse he will deliver, explaining to the villagers how important it is that they follow the road to development. The only villager who took the floor during the meeting was Buasai, the head of *kum baan*. Note also, in Figure 2.10, the presence of notebooks taken by many villagers because of the official character of the event.

This banal meeting has been described as demonstrating that the state is not a distant reality, but a very concrete one, performed through bureaucratic routines involving the whole village. We can describe such village hall meetings as a "*dispositif*," a French word (sometimes translated as "dispositive" or "device") used by Michel Foucault to describe an integrated set of materialities, ideas, and rules producing specific relationships between people.[14] Very clearly, the village hall in Houay Yong is the place where the dichotomy and the relationship between the people and the state authorities is given form, with the authorities speaking from the table of honor, behind the paraphernalia of the Lao State, using the rhetoric of knowledge, development, kinship, and solidarity, and facing the audience of villagers who listen carefully and take notes about the topic. Everyone knows his or her role and follows the patterns of interaction observed in similar circumstances, notably on TV national broadcasts. The register of gestures, speech acts, and bodily attitudes is not very different in this village event and in the official gatherings repeatedly presented by the national channel on the daily news.

Even if the state is essentialized as a distant reality in representations and discourses, it is also made present through such 'state relations' (High and Petit 2013; Petit 2017) that pervade everyday life in Houay Yong as elsewhere. This everyday presence appears in the following chapters, when discussing the inter-village rivalry for achievement boards (see pages 110–111), the semantics used to describe the ritual post (see pages 155–156), and the influence of monumentality in the village (see pages 177–185). The state is of central concern for the Tai Vat. It is definitely part of their world.

Notes

1 The ridge of mountain on the east of the village is called *San Ta Tom* on its northern side and *San Ta Kôm* on its southern side; beyond the crest of this ridge is the territory of the village Houay Lom. Northeast is the mountain *Phuu Sôôt*, beyond which is the Tai Dam village of Ban Sot. The mountain northwest of Houy Yong is *Phuu Kup* [65, 66, 75, 80].
2 From Xiang Kho, following the 6A Road, it is possible to reach the provincial capital, Sam Neua (about 120 km from there). One can reach also Sam Neua from Muang Èt, going south on Road PR3201, but the road is currently poor.

The setting 45

Figures 2.9 and 2.10 The communal hall, front scene and back scene, during the inauguration ceremonies for the new school (June 2011).

46 *The setting*

3 In the 1930s to 1940s, Nasan was a very small village of around seven families, including some Tai Soi (see page 76). With the policy of regrouping villages after the 1975 national revolution, the population from Houay Louang was relocated to Nasan: nine Tai Dèng and seven Tai Vat families were concerned. Some of the latter eventually moved to Houay Lom (see pages 147–148). The 42 households settled in Nasan are ethnically balanced between Tai Dèng and Tai Vat [82].

4 See Evans (2000) about Navan and the relationships of its Singmun inhabitants with the Tai Dam of Ban Sot.

5 Houay Yong, Houay Lom, Nalèng, Pakfèn (see Map 2.1). Three villages, Nasan, Ban Lung, and Ban Sé, have a mixed population including Tai Vat [2, 24]. We should further include Thongnamy, in Bolikhamxay Province, and Nam Mo, in Xaisomboun Province, as villages of recent resettlement (see page 110).

6 See Cầm Trọng (2004: 194–195) for the etymology linking Muang Vat to the Lao origins of its first settlers, coming from a Buddhist country (*vat*, temple). The toponym was first Vietnamized as Việt Châu, then as Yên Châu in 1822.

7 Interestingly, the only mention about Tai Vat in the academic literature related to Laos is from Grant Evans, who worked in the late 1980s to early 1990s in the Tai Dam village of Ban Sot, only 5 km north of Houay Yong. He makes the distinction between Tai Dam and Tai Vat, who intermarry, and presents the Tai Vat as "a localized group of Tai Dam from Muang Wat in Vietnam" (Evans 2000: 278). Such a taxonomy, with different levels of identity among the Tai populations, has already been commented on by Moerman in his seminal article on Lü ethnicity (Moerman 1965). Subgroups included in the generic category of Tai Dam by my informants are Tai Vat, Tai Dam (in the narrow sense), and Tai Saan; some people mention Tai Phiang and Tai Hai as well [56a, 60, 63, 191]. See also Lissoir (2016: 25–30) on the flexible extension of the ethnonym Tai Dam.

8 Moerman (1965), Barth (1998 [1969]), Jenkins (1997), Evans (2000), Brubaker (2004), and Scott (2009).

9 Raquez went on: "The Tai inhabit Muang Èt since five or six generations, according to the elders. … They originate from Muong Mouei" (Raquez 1905: 1328). Mường Muôi is the name of a former important Tai Dam polity in the district of Thuận Châu, in the Vietnamese province of Sơn La (see Map 3.3; Cầm Trọng 2003).

10 A "*fête du serment*" (festival of the oath). See Tappe (2018: 60) on that 'invented tradition.'

11 The word "animism" has progressively waned from the anthropological lexicon due to its evolutionary connotations and its mind/body dichotomy. The concept has been revived recently with a new perspective, to refer to systems creating alterity, relationship, and eventually life in a world where humans and non-humans share agency; such systems coexist with world religions throughout southeast Asia (Sprenger 2016). Although I subscribe to this last view, I use here the word to refer to ascriptive categories distinguishing Buddhists (*satsanaa phut*) from non-Buddhist populations whose religions are directly related to *phii* spirits (*satsanaa phii*). I consequently use scare quotes as a reminder of this specific meaning of 'animism.'

12 Nahit, Nangeun, Nalèng, Ban Sot, Navan [222]. See Map 2.1.

13 The successive chiefs of the village since the 1953 revolution have been listed below, but the dates should not be taken for granted before 1998: they present discrepancies among our informants [13, 36, 90, 103, 153, 215, 217, 252, 262]. The lack of precision is due to: the fact that people often rely on computing, not on dates; the lack of archives; and the flux between various positions in the village council (*khana baan*) and in the subdistrict administration, which creates confusion on the role played by a specific person at a specific time.

 i Thaao Chüang, also called Sèèn Phadii (from circa 1953–1954 to circa 1956–1959).

ii Sèèn Daan (from circa 1956–1959 to circa 1971).
iii Thoongsôm (from circa 1971 to circa 1993), one of our informants.
iv Bunhoom (or Chao Hoom) and Koongsing have replaced each other as *naai baan* several times up to 1998. Bunhoom replaced Thoongsôm, but, after some time, he was injured due to a fall and was replaced by Koongsing, the deputy chief. Bunhoom resumed his function until he was eventually succeeded by Koongsing, who eventually quit the position in 1998 and led a group of migrants to Nam Mo (see page 110).
v Buasai (from 1998 to 2004), one of our informants.
vi Phèèngsoon (from 2004 to 2008), another of our informants.
vii Bunsoon (2008 to the present), the present *naai baan*. In 2018, Bunsoon asked the authorities to quit his position before the official term of 2022, because he felt he was becoming old and had been in the post for many years – he was in fact very eager to take a rest and have leisure time traveling across the country. He was, however, requested to hold on until 2021.

14 See, for example, Foucault (2010 [1975]: 200–201).

3 Traditions on origins

Oral history in a literate context

(Re)constructing history is never simple, whether or not written documents are available. This chapter and Chapter 4 are devoted to this demanding enterprise in the *Huai Yoong* valley, with a focus on the precolonial period in Chapter 3, and on the colonial and postcolonial period in Chapter 4. Written sources are practically silent on the valley. Houay Yong is never mentioned in any book devoted to the history of the region, and its name appeared only once during my consultation of the French National Overseas Archives in Aix-en-Provence. "Houa Yong," as it was spelled, is mentioned on a list of taxpayers dated 1902 (RSL E3, 4/5/1902). I question the silence of the archives on pages 87–91, 112, but for sure it is partly related to the fact that the village did not play a significant role in the major events that happened in the region over the last two centuries.

Despite this dearth of written data about the valley, archives and published sources are helpful for situating the area in the regional context, and elucidating enigmas related to the coming of the Tai Vat into their present location. But the core source on local history will be oral traditions. Consequently, the first sections address the practices of orality and of writing in the valley and in Houaphan at large. After this necessary groundwork, the attention switches to the very contents of the foundation narratives of the Tai Vat.

Historians usually consider oral data with suspicion, and as a second-best choice when written documents are unavailable. The process of interviewing direct witnesses about past events is quite common and accepted in history, but, when the information relates to a period that informants could know only indirectly, historians are more cautious and suspicious about the way to use such data. The methodological warning is all the more important when dealing with oral traditions, that is, stories transmitted from generation to generation which relate to ancient historical events, such as foundation stories, as noted by Vansina (1985: 27–28): here 'objective' facts seem inextricably mixed with the contents of a more ideological nature related to the self-representation and legitimization of the narrator, or of his or her group as a whole.[1] This has not discouraged Vansina to face the challenge and pave the way to historical research in Central Africa.

Unfortunately, in the historical research in mainland southeast Asia, there is more than methodological circumspection: oral history has been most often neglected by historians, to the point of being "untapped," an observation made by Michaud (2010: 190–191) a decade ago but still relevant today. Consequently, oral history has most often been collected and analyzed by anthropologists. Half of the authors mentioned in the state-of-the-art page (page 12) are indeed anthropologists who have contributed to the emergence of the field of historical anthropology, or cultural history, in mainland southeast Asia.

The debate on oral history in southeast Asia has been given a new impetus by James Scott's much-discussed book, *The Art of Not Being Governed*. Scott supports the idea that upland societies in southeast Asia have developed a wide range of technologies and institutions to escape inclusion into the lowland states. He considers the use of oral history, and the rejection of writing, as part and parcel of these anti-state mechanisms (Scott 2009: 220–237). Using oral history would allow people to reformulate their historical traditions and adapt them to changing contexts, a very convenient technology in these societies that developed various strategies to escape the grasp of the state. For example, changing a foundation story to fit with a new political alliance is easier when it is supported by oral accounts rather than by old manuscripts, or inscriptions engraved on a stele.

In line with Scott's model, the villagers of Houay Yong use oral history to speak about their past. This is not an obvious option. Almost all the inhabitants of Houay Yong are able to read Lao, with the exception of some elderly women who never attended school. Even during the Second Indochina War, a primary school was active in the village, or rather in the forest for fear of bombing. The writing culture is even conspicuous in some contexts, mostly for activities related to the state, as appeared in the use of notebooks in the communal hall during the meeting mentioned on pages 43–45. In the home, writing appears on various diploma, certificates related to land rights, lists of people affixed to a phone number, etc. Until a few years ago, some male elders could also read the Tai Dam script, which uses letters based on an Indian model similar to Lao (Finot 1956: 986–988; Cầm Trọng 2003; Le Failler 2014: 440). Currently, the only person able to do so is Thoongsôm (see pages 42–43).[2] He owns manuscripts written in old Tai script, and has an almanac (*soo* in Tai Vat language) to distinguish propitious and non-propitious days for engaging in different activities, and to provide prescriptions related to various issues. He made a version in Lao script. He also owns a book with Tai mourning prayers, and documents with genealogies from his Vietnamese home region, Yên Châu. Thoongsôm is not only the owner and user of old manuscripts: he is also, to my knowledge, the only villager who writes and conserves notebooks with historical and cultural observations that he gathered in the past, when he held responsibilities at the village or subdistrict level; questioned about the spirits addressed during a territorial cult (*đông khuaang*, see pages 142–143), he checked in a small notebook where he had listed six names on one page, long ago [262]. Interestingly, apart from this occasion, Thoongsôm does not rely on his manuscripts when he recounts history.

50 *Traditions on origins*

Figures 3.1 and 3.2 In Figure 3.1, Thoongsôm compares a recent paper block almanac calendar from Vietnam with his old almanac written in Tai. Figure 3.2 shows his book of prayers for mourning ceremonies, in Tai script (June 2010).

More broadly, no one, in Houay Yong, relies on written support when discussing history – with some reservations for Thoongsôm, as explained above. The situation was different in Muang Van, the present seat of the subdistrict. When we inquired about Muang Van's history, it turned out that written documents were referred to much more than in Houay Yong. We were told about manuscripts that unfortunately disappeared due to flooding in the 1970s, or about an elder who had a book reporting a detailed history of the village. When we eventually interviewed that man (in a formal meeting with village authorities), he sometimes consulted a notebook where he had written notes, especially to provide us with the list of the successive chiefs (Figure 3.3) [113]. However, most of the conversation went on without looking at that notebook.

To put it briefly, written documents are used to support – at least, symbolically – historical narratives in Muang Van whereas, in Houay Yong, history relies quasi-entirely on orality. This difference is not easy to explain because the villagers of both places share similar reading and writing competences. But they are different in other aspects. First, Muang Van has been an administrative center since at least the colonial period; at the time, it was the center of an administrative unit (called *phông*, canton, or *taasèèng*) under the authority of Xiang Kho or Muang Èt, depending on the period. Second, Muang Van

Traditions on origins 51

shelters a Buddhist temple (*vat*). These two elements – the acknowledgment as an administrative center and the presence of a temple – are both linked with written culture, which may explain the stronger reliance on texts observed in Muang Van.

Despite this stronger literacy background in Muang Van, no informant seemed to rely seriously on written texts during the discussion. What seemed important was not so much the content of these texts as the fact that assertions were based on them, which provided authority to the speaker.[3] In this respect, the difference between Muang Van and Houay Yong is a shallow one: from a pragmatic point of view, the narration of history follows broadly the same patterns in the two places.

Such observations put at stake Scott's argument about the gap between the regimes of orality and written culture. The supposed stability Scott attributes to written culture, which would impede the strategic transformations of history, versus the lability of orality, is a tempting hypothesis but it does not take into account the practicalities of production, conservation, access to, and use of written texts. The royal chronicles of Laos – as well as the national(ist) historiography that followed – are characterized by a constant process of rewriting to legitimize the current order (Lorrillard 1999). Texts may be produced, but not conserved or not used, or not used in relation to history. They are above all artifacts, belonging to specific owners, who can employ them in different ways, with no specific concern for their contents, or simply keep them secret, or hoard them as a piece of evidence about their authority. The dichotomy proposed by Scott is too sharp: it should be more nuanced and take into account the practicalities of written culture, a dimension explored by the New Literacy Studies movement, which questions such great divides and explores the vernacular forms of literacy as situated in local contexts (Street 2001). His argument holds true only if the actors acknowledge writing as the central element of legitimization in relation to history, and if they would commit to the conservation and public display

Figure 3.3 The collective interview in Muang Van [113]. The presence of notebooks and written documents is conspicuous, contrasting with our fieldwork experience in Houay Yong (June 2011).

of the archives. This is apparently the case in neither the local context of Houay Yong nor the surrounding area.

The legacy of manuscripts and the history of Houaphan

The issue of regional and local archives should be raised here, which requires a short presentation of the history of the province (Monpeyrat 1904: 126–130).[4] Etymologically, *hua phan* means "the head of a thousand"; it was a title for hereditary chiefs of some importance, whose rule applied on a large population; by extension, *huaphan* signified a large polity. The chronicles of the Lao kingdom of Lan Xang report that, in the middle of the sixteenth century, King Setthathirat invaded the whole region which remained under royal vassalage for a century and a half – as shown below, local archives allow dating of the early influence of the Lao kingdom to the reign of Setthathirat's father, Phothisarat. When the Lan Xang kingdom was divided in 1707, the region was attributed to the king of Luang Prabang, but was conquered by the kingdom of Vientiane under the reign of Chao Anou (1805–1828).[5] After the destruction of Vientiane by the Siamese (1828), it fell in the early 1830s into the orbit of two powers at once: the kingdom of Luang Prabang, allied at the time with Siam, and the Vietnamese court of Huế. The political landscape was extremely shaken due to Chinese invasions and local rebellions in the 1870s. The Siamese took direct control of the region in 1886, until they handed it over to France after the signature of the Franco-Siamese Treaty (3 October 1893).

Throughout these periods, the different *huaphan* principalities, the number of which varied throughout history, were also collectively referred to as *huaphan*, in the plural sense, as attested by the ancient long name of the region: *hua phan thang hok*: the six *huaphan* (Monpeyrat 1904: 126). Their number was raised to eight under the Siamese, a figure that would evolve again during the French colony (Map 3.1).

The polities that exerted political tutelage on Houaphan throughout history – Lan Xang, Luang Prabang, Vientiane, Huế, Siam – all relied on writing and produced chronicles. One could presume that under such conditions, texts would be a strong support of historical memory in the whole region. However, wars and pillages wreaked havoc from 1872 to the 1890s, leading to systematic plunder and destruction throughout the area. "The annals conserved in the Buddhist temples have been partly destroyed during the Chinese invasion of 1872. What was left was removed by the Siamese" (Monpeyrat 1904: 127).

Indeed, the largest known collection of these documents is presently conserved in the National Library of Bangkok (Phimphan 2000; Lorrillard 2015: 24–28). The library notably holds 28 territorial charters (*kongdin*), listing topographical boundaries of polities in Houaphan.[6] They are dated from 1541 to 1862. Of these, 22 written on textile support have been published by the National Library of Thailand (Phimphan 2000). The document numbered 16 in this edition relates to "Muang Sop Èt," most probably the former name of Muang Èt – *sop* meaning, in northern Lao language, the confluence of two rivers, as for the

River Èt and the River Ma joining in Muang Èt. The chart was issued under the authority of King Phothisarat (1520–1547)[7] who reigned in *Chantabuulii*.[8] Phothisarat endows a lord, Phanyaa Kamphônnyathai, from *Müang Khuaang*, with the duty to govern the territory of Muang Sop Èt. Afterwards, the chart lists quite precisely the names of villages, mountains, cliffs, brooklets, and ponds that bound the territory. Surprisingly, Houay Yong, Muang Van, or other toponyms in the vicinity of the *Huai Yoong* valley do not appear in the list. It is possible that the present toponyms are different from those that were used in the sixteenth century, when the charter was written, or that the *Huai Yoong* valley was not a dependency of Muang Èt, but of Xiang Kho, for which no territorial chart seems to be conserved in the National Library of Bangkok. The document ends by listing good rules of governance and taxes (Phimphan 2000: 153–156).

Such charts and other old manuscripts largely disappeared from the region in the last decades of the nineteenth century, which impeded the development of a local acquaintance with archives. The production of written documents was given a new impetus by French colonization, as evidenced by the archives of Aix-en-Provence that conserve some manuscripts in Lao script. This substantiates the

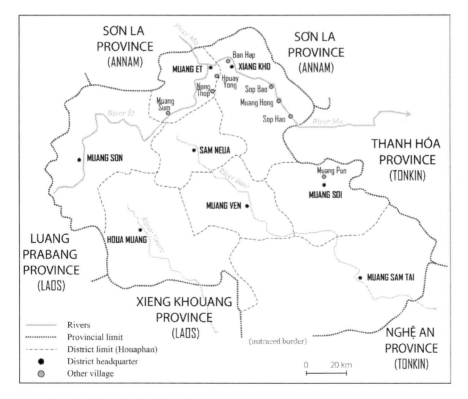

Map 3.1 The eight principalities of Houaphan under the early French regime.
Source: "Carte de la Province des Houa Phans", by Wartelle, RSL E4, 3/12/1911.

literacy of local authorities in that early period. Literacy was indeed a political privilege: Bobo, a French military officer and one of the very first Europeans to live in Muang Èt in the early 1890s, observed that only the chiefs (among the Lao and the Tai) and the male members of their families could read (Bobo 1898: 512). Only one woman (the wife of a senior chief) could read in the whole province, presumably as a consequence of such learning usually taking place when young men became temporary monks as part of their education.

The document appearing in Figure 3.4 is a good example of this written production. It demonstrates how written culture was instrumental, among the local authorities of Houaphan, in validating a certain version of history and influencing political decisions in the colonial system.

Before giving the translation of the document, elements of the specific context should be provided. After the French took over the control of Houaphan from the Siamese in 1893, its administrative status became an issue: should it be attached to the *Résidence Supérieure* of Laos or the *Résidence Supérieure* of Annam? As mentioned above, the Houaphan local authorities used to pay a tribute to both Luang Prabang and Huế during most of the nineteenth century, so there was no decisive argument for one option or another.[9] The main argument used by the authorities of Annam was their need to control directly the mountains where unrest and rebellion could put a risk on the *mise en valeur* of Vietnam, the central component of French Indochina. The authorities of Laos insisted rather on the cultural proximity between Houaphan and the Lao civilization. This led to the division of Houaphan into two halves in 1896, with four principalities coming to Annam and four to Laos.

On 26 July 1898, Monpeyrat, the French Government Representative in Houaphan, sent a letter to the *Résident Supérieur* in Luang Prabang, in which he argued for the urgency to reunify the different principalities of Houaphan (RSL E3, 26/7/1898). He based his assertion on the cultural unity of the region, its history, and a critique of the fallacy of the arguments used by the local authorities of Annam. But a most convincing part of his demonstration consisted of two documents, handwritten by the local authorities of the four principalities administratively attached to Laos at the time (Figure 3.4). Below is the translation of that document Monpeyrat forwarded to the colonial authority in Luang Prabang:

> Phaya Thamma Vong Sa, Phya Palat, Phya Kham, *Thao Khoune* [that is, local authorities] Lao and Thai of Muong Sone; Phaya Saya Vong Sa, Phya Houa Phane, La Sa Kouane, *Thao Khoune* of Muong Houa Muong; Phaya Si Volonat, Thao Kouane, Phya Boune, *Thao Khoune* of Muong Sieng Kho; Phaya Pham Vi Sai, Phya Houa Phane, Phya Palat and *Thao Khoune* of Muong Het
>
> To the *Commandant Supérieur du Haut Laos*
> Mr. High Commander,
> We are honored to address to you the following claim.
> In the beginning, the Hua Pan Thang Hoc [that is, the six *huaphan*, the old name of the polity] were a dependency of Luang Prabang and all the

Traditions on origins 55

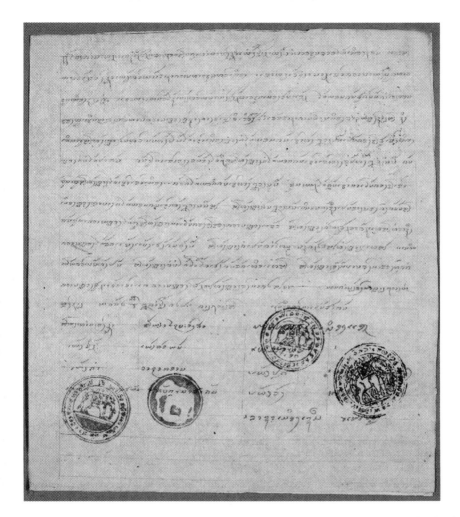

Figure 3.4 Letter addressed to the *Commandant supérieur du Haut Laos* by the local authorities of Houaphan asking for the reunification of their territory. The stamps are respectively, from left to right, those of the *huaphan* principalities of Muang Son, Muang Hua Muang, Muang Èt, and Muang Xiang Kho (RSL E3, 26/7/1898).

Credit: Archives Nationales d'Outre-Mer (France).

eight principalities ["*uiens*" in the text, a French transcription of the Vietnamese word "*huyên*"] were united.

When the king of Vientiane took the *huaphan*, the eight principalities came under its authority.

When we were a dependency of Annam, the eight principalities were jointly dependent. Later on, when we were given back to Luang Prabang, the eight principalities belonged once more to Luang Prabang. The eight principalities were together as brothers.

Since we have become your servants, we have always been faithful to you.

But since the eight are separated, we are in a deep sorrow and endure it painfully. For since the beginning, the *huaphan* have always been united. This is the reason why we allow us to address you this claim.

Made on the 8th of the waxing moon, 8th month of 1260.

(27 June 1898)

Then comes a list with the names of the signatories, in which the names of Phya Vong, of Muang Van (the village close to Houay Yong), and La Sa, of Muang Sum (see Map 3.1), are added to the names of the senders referred to at the top of the document. The document is stamped with the official seals of the four districts.

I have tried to retain the sophisticated rendering of the French translation of the original Lao version. Monpeyrat, whose grandiose style was apparently appreciated by the French authorities at the time, had certainly a common interest with the local dignitaries. He must have discussed with them the opportunity to address a letter to the highest French authority in Laos, and the arguments to use in the letter: the evidence of a shared long-term history; the strong link between the principalities ("as brothers"); their faithfulness to the French authorities; and the emotions of sorrow triggered by their undesired division. Such a letter, duly red stamped and formally certified by Monpeyrat, must have been a strong piece of evidence in the debates opposing the French administrators about the status of the province. It is a very telling example of the link of written culture, political agency, and historical narratives by the end of the nineteenth century. It has probably played a role in the final decision to reunite Houaphan under a single administration in 1903.

As shown by this document, Muang Van was involved directly in this long negotiation: the name of Vông, who was the head of the canton at the time, appears in the third column, on the penultimate line. It appears as well on a similar document dated 9 July 1898, also annexed to Monpeyrat's letter, where the authorities of Xiang Kho and Muang Èt utterly reject their possible inclusion into Annam proposed by some colonial authorities.

Oral history as a male performance

Narrating history is a men's prerogative in Houay Yong. It is a topic they enjoy debating when they meet together. The usual word used to speak about history is *pavat*, the meaning of which is quite close to 'event-driven history,' or 'chronicle,' in western languages. *Naai baan* Bunsoon explains that men enjoy having conversations (*sônthanaakan*) on history, with the idea of exchanging information; only men are interested in history, according to him, because they are involved in politics and have ideas on that topic. Women, he went on, prefer to speak about family, children, the husbandry. They "have no knowledge" (*boo mii kwaamhuu*) about history [250].

I was fortunate to capture an improvised conversation on the history of the village (Figures 3.5 and 3.6). It took place during a meal following a mourning ceremony a month after the funerals [87]. The main orator was Phèèngsoon, the deputy-chief of the village. Four other male adults or elders (including Bunsoon), plus our team, were sitting in a circle next to him. Phèèngsoon explained how the Tai Vat settled in the village of Houay Lom, fleeing an angry female spirit (see pages 66–67). The conversation went on about the resolution of old land disputes between the people of Houay Lom and Nasan, and ended with a discussion on the extension of the rice fields of Ban Kang and the displacements of that village (see Map 2.1). It was a six-minute conversation (which ended when the table with dishes was set in the middle of us by our hosts) but the five guests took the floor eighty times altogether, with only a tenth of the comments being short approvals. The two longest uninterrupted speeches reached twenty and thirty seconds, but, apart from them, most interjections were made of one or two short sentences, with many overlaps – this was a nightmare for the ensuing transcription, especially as the narration was filled with extremely domestic details that were absolutely out of reach for non-local people.

The five partakers nodded their agreement, gave complementary information, and clarified or repeated some of the preceding sentences. Each of them contributed with specific elements; Phèèngsoon had a leading role only during some parts of the discussion. Thaabun, already mentioned before, was not in the circle, but leaning against a wall, about two meters from us: he could not refrain from intervening at some point too. The discussion also evidenced intertextuality: some interventions of Bunsoon relayed information from an interview we made in Houay Lom in his presence five days before [71]; he duly mentioned the name of our informant, Koongvaa.

In short, it was an extremely lively conversation, with a lot of hand and head gestures to sustain the communication (see Figures 3.5 and 3.6). There was no expression of disbelief or contradiction; rather each participant aimed to add his own contribution to the joint narrative. They all tried to display competence on the topic, which is part of performing one's adult male status in the local society. At some point, when Phèèngsoon had taken the floor, one of his female relatives called him for some duty in relation to the organization of the meal; he dismissed the request, answering that "we are still working" (*hao nyang mii viak no*). There was neither humor nor disrespect in his answer: such a collective recollection was indeed "work," based on the village standards.

History has never been presented as a women's concern by anyone – including women. This is reputedly a men's domain, as argued by Bunsoon during his explanation above on the way people discuss history. We have been referred to women when discussing domestic religion, mediumship, household production, or current migration, but never about history, or territorial cults. We tried to interview women on those issues, among which were elderly women and mediums: they seemed to have little knowledge on the topic, and their account

 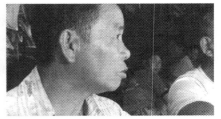

Figures 3.5 and 3.6 Screenshots from the improvised historical recollection. Phèèngsoon (Figure 3.5) raises his finger, one of the many non-verbal components of the conversation. It is a typically male sign of authority – I have seldom seen Tai Vat women using it. Note the presence of people around, who sometimes listen to the conversation like the three women behind Bunsoon (Figure 3.6) (May 2011).

was never organized in structured narratives similar to those of male elders in charge of such traditions; at least, they professed to know little and eventually referred us to men. I eventually asked in 2018 which woman could have any kind of historical knowledge, and I was referred to Mèèthao Leua. That woman, aged over 70 years when we interviewed her, was indeed knowledgeable, mostly about territorial cults, but this was largely due to her being the widow of Phongsai, also called Koongvan, the last ritual leader of the *dông khuaang* inter-village ritual (see pages 142–143) [242]. Her late husband, the son of a former *naai baan* of Houay Yong, was the head of the Cultural Unit at the subdistrict level; he is mostly known as a famous composer of *khap* – traditional, non-melodic songs, partly improvised; Mèèthao Leua used to sing some compositions of her late husband, because she had a more pleasant voice than him (Lissoir 2016: 87–90). During her interview, Mèèthao Leua turned out to also be much knowledgeable about the history of her family, explaining in detail the dramatic circumstances that made them leave their village in Vietnam in 1952 or 1953, a story she was told by her mother (see pages 104–105).

The other stories we could hear from women were of a similar biographical type: articulated with the life of the informant or her family, and largely devoid of reference to ethnicity, ancient or recent polities, office holders, genealogies, or political struggles. Despite this, women are obviously informed about event-based history, as evidenced by their attention to our discussion mentioned before (Figure 3.6). But they do not play an active role in the public discussions on history, and are not invited by men to do so. The basic fact that men and women usually eat separately when there is a collective meal (see Figure 1.5) explains how the sense of history is shaped differently according to gender: as women do not participate in the *sônthanaakan*-type discussion on history, they do not develop competence in that topic – although they probably develop different forms of knowledge among themselves, which should be investigated as such.

Figure 3.7 Nguan (right) performing a *khap* song accompanied by Somvang, a talented player of the mouth organ (*khèèn*). Nguan is currently the most popular *khap* singer in the village, and has a leading role in the artistic unit of the subdistrict (Lissoir 2016: 96–102). Although *khap* songs are not aimed at relating history, they may allude to some episodes of it. This is one of the rare public occasions where women relate historical events in Houay Yong (June 2010).

Hence their knowledge of history appears in less explicit ways, for example when discussing recent migration or religious issues (see pages 113, 169), or in *khap* songs, the contents of which are poetry that can sometimes evoke episodes of the group's history.[10]

All these elements contextualizing the production of history in Houay Yong were important to avoid a naive interpretation of local statements about the past. History is narrated in specific contexts, by specific people (usually elder males [*phuu nyai*], acknowledged as competent historians by the community) and for a specific audience. To be plausible, a narrative must certainly be reminiscent of the past as it was experienced, or told by other villagers: the audience would certainly not adhere to a version of the past that seems to be unbelievable based on what people know, or too different from other versions they had heard previously. I never came across a case of contestation of a specific account: juxtaposition and aggregation are the standard, rather than overt disagreement. There is little room for pure invention in the process, but history is always entangled in the narratives of local actors, who speak about the past from their present condition, in the present time, with the present stakes, as argued by Vansina in the quote reported in the introduction (see page 6). Some events that might displease or shock the current audience, or trouble the present-day order, might be silenced, understated, euphemized, or reformulated. The role of the authorities – moral and political – in reaching this consensus is difficult to assess, because no warning against alternative versions was ever observed: we never came across gossip, for example, that would question the mainstream version. Contrariwise, events that confirm the legitimacy of the orator's group will presumably be given emphasis, and progressively structure the core of a narrative.

The foundation narratives

The foundation story of Houay Yong is an excellent example to test these assertions: it contains many objective elements of the ancient history in the valley, as I demonstrate by comparison with archives, but the narratives must also be approached as statements on the moral and political order of the past and the present. I present here four summarized accounts and one extended historical narration relating the foundation of Houay Yong and Houay Lom, the two neighboring Tai Vat villages of the valley.[11] The narratives on the history of these two villages should not be separated because they are intertwined, referring to the same origins, even if the migrants settled in two different places.

Narrative a

The first version dates back to 2010 and was told by Thaabun – the actual setting of the interview appears in Figure 1.9. I start by his account because we were repeatedly directed to him when inquiring about history in Houay Yong. Thaabun was born around 1938 and died in March 2018. He successively held three different names in his life: Looi as a child and young man; Koong Ngian as a married adult; and Thaabun as an elder [262]. Such changes complicated much our research, but are not unusual in Tai Vat society. Thaabun was a direct descendant of the Tai Vat pioneers who settled in Houay Yong in the late nineteenth century. He was presented to our team as holding the title of *chao kôk chao lao*, "master of the foundation and of slashing the forest," which was reportedly transmitted patrilineally in a lineage of the first settlers. In fact, it turned out after his death that this title was perhaps just a way to honor Thaabun – the expression is a generic name referring to the descendants of the first settlers of a place. As Thaabun was considered in the village as the most knowledgeable and the most legitimate holder of the historical traditions related to the foundation, he was given that honorary title, which has not been transmitted to anyone since his death. This question is discussed on pages 132–133.

Their ancestors were Tai Dam living in Muang Vat (*Müang Vaat*), or *Èm Chao* (Yên Châu in Vietnam, in the Vietnamese province of Sơn La), in the "land of the Tai" (*din Thai*). Before the coming of the French, the region was invaded by Chinese (*Haan Chiin*) armies, especially the Yellow Flags (*khüa lüang*) and the Red Flags (*khüa dèèng*). At the time, four brothers lived together in Chièng Sàng village (see Map 3.2): Phuu Hüaang, Phuu Thèèng, Phuu Uu,

Traditions on origins 61

and Phuu Vèèng. The first three left their home place to settle in this valley. Phuu Hüaang and Phuu Uu are ancestors of the present inhabitants of Houay Yong and its hamlet *Naa Kuu*, whereas Phuu Thèèng is the ancestor of the people living in Houay Lom. Phuu Vèèng remained in Vietnam. Thaabun evaluates the time of their coming to three centuries or three generations; he also says that his own grandfather was born in Vietnam. When their group came here, about 60 families of Tai Soi and Lao were already living in Houay Yong, where they had built the paddy fields. They lived together. After some time, the Tai Dam became more numerous, and the Tai Soi decided not to argue but to leave the place. They went back to their home place, Muang Soi, to rejoin their relatives [8].

Narrative b

Bunmaa is the *chao süa* – the man in charge of the village rituals (see page 132) – of the hamlet of *Naa Kuu*, a dependency of Houay Yong on the northern fringe of the village. I explain later about his account of the creation of this hamlet in the twentieth century (see page 126), but what follows concerns the history of the main village of Houay Yong. I interviewed Bunmaa three times: the first in 2010, in the presence of *Naai baan* Bunsoon [42], the second during the annual ceremony conducted on the *Naa Kuu* village shrine, in 2012 [142], and the third during a casual visit in 2018 [245]. Although it would be interesting to present the three versions in detail, for the sake of fluidity I take the first interview as a frame, and briefly present the elements that appeared in 2012 and 2018.

Long ago, there was a war. Seven families fled from *Èm Chao*, in Vietnam. At first, they settled in *Naa Soo*, on the heights of the present village of Nahit (close west to Muang Van, see Map 2.1), in an area that was later to be used to hide from the French or from the "Japanese fascists" (*faasit Nyipun*). Afterwards, they resettled in Houay Yong, which was already occupied by Tai Soi. Ethnically, the latter were not Tai Dam like the people from *Èm Chao*: they were "*Lao – Thai khao*," "Lao, White Tai" ('white' possibly in the sense of Buddhist, here). They had a Buddhist temple (*vat*) on the place where the school is currently built. The Tai Vat from *Èm Chao* multiplied to the point of being in competition with the Tai Soi, who were less active. At some point, soon after the liberation from the Japanese (1945–1946), the Tai Soi definitely left the place (see pages 99–100).

During the 2012 interview, Bunmaa introduced the story of the four brothers, explaining that he got it from Thaabun (see above). He mentioned the names of the four brothers: Vèèng remaining in Vietnam, Thèèng separating to create the village of Houay Lom, while Hüaang and Uu settled in Houay Yong. Eventually, Hüaang, or a descendant of Hüaang, moved away to create *Naa Kuu*.[12] The story goes on as in the first narrative, with the seven families settling in *Naa Soo*, and afterwards moving to Houay Yong because space was lacking in *Naa Soo*.

62 *Traditions on origins*

The third interview (2018) provides a different, three-layer chronology regarding the population of the place. The very first inhabitants of Houay Yong were, in fact, Lao,[13] who had built the Buddhist temple. Later, Tai Soi people came to settle, and the Lao left the village, hiding their Buddha statues in mountain caves. Eventually, the Tai Vat came and progressively mixed with the Tai Soi. Competition ensued until the departure of the Tai Soi.

These successive narratives are interesting in their differences. Family relations, ethnic assignations, and chronology seem to change with time, displaying the lability of oral narratives within a few years.

Narrative c

The third account moves us to the close village of Houay Lom, the history of which is closely related to that of Houay Yong. The narrator is Koongvaa, an elder from Houay Lom. We interviewed him in 2011; his son and the *naai baan* of Houay Yong, Bunsoon, were present and added small comments to the exchange [71]. Koongvaa belonged to the lineage of the founders of the village (*chao thin chao thaan chao kôk chao lao* (see page 132), but held no specific status. With 77 years of age, he professed to be the oldest inhabitant of the village, and the last of his generation – unfortunately, he died in the following months.

After the episode about the departure from Vietnam, I reproduce long quotes from the interview due to the interesting contents, but also to give a better idea about the lexical, narrative, and dialogical nature of the recording, and to make the reader aware of the kind of raw and often ambiguous material produced by such interviews.

Figure 3.8 Koongvaa during his interview (June 2011).

The grandfather of Koongvaa was called Èèng Phuan, who was among the first settlers; the latter's son was Baa Meeung, whose son was Baa Fèèng, the sons of whom were Baa Buun and Baa Toom, the first of whom was the father of our informant. Èèng Phuan lived with his fellows in *Baan Booi*, a village of Yên Châu district in the province of Sơn La. At the time, there was a war with the *Haan Khüa Lüang* (Chinese Yellow Flags), although Koongvaa does not know more about that. This prompted the departure of a group of families, including the family of Èèng Phuan. The refugees settled first in the area of Nahit, as already reported in Narrative b.

Koongvaa: At first, our ancestors settled in the village named *Koonkham*, next to Nahit. They came and settled there. They also built the paddy fields of *Naa Ngeun* and *Naa Ngiu*. *Naa Ngiu* is on the south side [the right bank of the river Ma]. One of our ancestors built the paddy fields in the vicinity of the brooklet *Huai Hiit*, which are named *Naa Soo*. It's like that.

At the time, there were a couple of spirits (*phii*), husband and wife. Such powerful spirits! These people living in the forest [the villagers], they said that those spirits were really powerful. And they wanted to hurt the people.

One of our forefathers was a very strong man. He killed the male spirit. Yes, he killed him, the spirit died. True or not, we do not know, but the spirit died.

At nightfall, the wife spirit roamed the place, crying, looking for her husband. There were only four or five houses over there. The people wondered what was going on.

Eventually, the lord (*aanyaa*) of Muang Van – *aanyaa* was a title during that period of extortion, he was called like that at the time – the *aanyaa* addressed those people: "You are afraid that the spirit will harm you; you have just escaped from the war, but you are afraid that the enemies could see you. As *aanyaa*, I will bring you to hide in the valley over there. And if the situation becomes better, when peace comes again, you will become my subjects (*khônnam, khônkuaang*), it's like this."

64 *Traditions on origins*

ຈຶ່ງໄດ້ເທຍຫ້ອຍລົມເປັນຄົນພວງອາຍາບັ້ນນະ. ອາຍາຮ່ວມມາ
ມາຢູ່ບັງປ່າດົງຊົງກົດ. ບັ້ນະ ມາຢູ່ແຕ່ 5 ເຮືອນມາທຳທິດມາຢູ່ແຕ່
5 ເຮືອນມັນແຜ່ອອກດອກ.

And then, the people of Houay Lom became the subjects of this *aanyaa*. The latter invited them to settle in this thick jungle forest. There were just five families at the time. Their number increased progressively.

ອຳພອນ: ພໍ່ເຖົ້າຈື່ເບາະ ພະຍາຕອນນັ້ນຊື່ຫຍັງ?

Amphone: Grandfather, do you remember the name of the *phanyaa* lord at the time?

ກອງວາ: ພະຍາເມືອງທວັນ ເຜັນເອັນເພັຍເຖົ້າ.

Koongvaa: This *phanyaa* lord of Muang Van was named Phia Thao.

ອຳພອນ: ເປັນຄົນລາວເບາະຫຼືຄົນຝຣັ່ງ?

Amphone: He was Lao or French?

ກອງວາ: ຄົນລາວ ຄົນເມືອງທວັນເຮົານີ້ລະ.

Koongvaa: He was a Lao from Muang Van.

ອຳພອນ: ແຕ່ວ່າເວລາມາຢູ່ມາຮັດຄົນຂັ້ນຈັກປີ?

Amphone: How many years did you stay in Nahit?

ກອງວາ: ບໍ່ໆ ຄົນກະໃດມີແຕ່ 4-5 ປີບັ້ນດອກ.

Koongvaa: Oh, not so long. It lasted four or five years.

ອຳພອນ: ຕອນທຳຮັດມາຢູ່ຫ້ວຍລົມ ເປັນປ່າ ບໍ່ມີໃຜມາຢູ່ກ່ອນ?

Amphone: When you settled here in Houay Lom, was the place still a forest? There was no one before?

ກອງວາ: ບໍ່, ບໍ່ມີໃຜ.

Koongvaa: No one.

ອຳພອນ: ເວລາມາຢູ່ທຳຮັດຖາງປ່າຖາງດ້ວຍຄົນເອງບໍ ຫຼື
ມີຄົນມາຊ່ວຍ?

Amphone: When you settled in the place, did you slash down the forest by yourselves or did other people come to help you?

ກອງວາ: ບໍ່ໆ ຖາງດ້ວຍຕົນເອງ ບໍ່ມີຄົນມາຊ່ວຍ ລັກສະນະ
ວ່າຢູ່ລຸ່ມຊື່ງມາ ມາລີ້ຊື່ງ

Koongvaa: We slashed by ourselves, no one helped us. It's just like …. We just came to stay below, just to hide.

ອຳພອນ: ແລ່ວອັ້ນ ຕອນທຳຮັດທີ່ມາຢູ່ຫັ້ນ ເນາະ ອັ້ນ
ຕອນພວມຂຶ້ນປ່າຫັ້ນ ປ່າດົງ ເຂົາໄດ້ເຮັດພິທີກຳຫຍັງ ບໍ່ ເຮັດຮີດ
ເຮັດຄອງ ເຮັດຜີເຮັດຫຍັງ ບໍ່?

Amphone: In the beginning, when you settled in the middle of that thick forest, did you carry out ceremonies, rituals, or anything?

ກອງວາ: ເອີ! ເຊີ່ມຢູ່ທຳຮັດ ບໍ່ເຮເຮັດຮີດເຮັດຄອງກະເທີ
ເຮົາກໍ່ທນິ ໃໝມາແຕ່ ເປົ້າປູ່ຍ່າຕາ ມູນເຊື້ອ ແມ່ນ
ຢູ່ຫາງເຊີ່ນຫາລະບໍ. ເອີ! ມາຢູ່ບັງໝອດອະນະ ເຂົ້າມານີ້ນ່າ
ໝວດ 5 ຄອບຄົວ ເປັນປູ່ເຖົ້າແກ່ ລະລົ້ມຕາຍມາ ຈຶ່ງ
ເປັນລ້ານເປັນຄຳ ບ້ານເຮົານີ້.

Koongvaa: Ah! When we had just arrived, we did nothing along the traditions. We had just escaped; our ancestors were in Sơn La. Those who settled here, the five families, were our ancestors. After they died, they became the Laan, the Kham [Laankham, the protecting spirit of the Tai Vat] of our village.

(Later on:)

Traditions on origins 65

Amphone: After setting up in Houay Lom, did you have relationships with other villages, as Houay Yong or places around Nasan or Houay Lom?

Koongvaa: Of course, we kept contact with Houay Yong. They were our relatives. There was one elder brother …. There were two elder brothers who settled in Houay Yong. Those people were brothers at the time. The old men Koong Ngian [the former name of Thaabun, the narrator of narrative 1] and Koong Eun [the former name of Thaao Chüaang, see Figure 5.15], they were our relatives.

Amphone: Was this village built before Houay Yong or was it the other way around?

Koongvaa: Our village was built first. There were two steps for the peopling of Houay Yong, my son. The first comers were the Tai Soi, who originated from Muang Soi.

Amphone: So, if we compare the foundation of this village of Houay Lom [by your ancestors] and the settlement of Houay Yong by the Tai Soi, who came first? The Tai Soi came first, right?

Koongvaa: Yes. The Tai Soi village was built first.

Naai baan **Bunsoon**: The Tai people [the Tai Vat] have come together, haven't they?

Koongvaa: Yes, we came all together.

Naai baan **Bunsoon**: One of the groups founded the village here; the other founded the village there.

Koongvaa's son: The two brothers parted away. The elder settled in Houay Yong, the younger in Houay Lom.

Koongvaa: The paddy fields over there belonged to the Tai Soi.

Narrative d

Koongthéé, the current *chao süa* of Houay Lom, is a younger relative (*noong*) of Koongvaa. He told a very similar story in 2014 [196]. His great-grandfather came together with eight families from Chiềng Sàng village, in the current district of Yên Châu. At first, the eight pioneer families settled in Nahit, where they built paddy fields. When they cultivated swidden rice fields, they were afraid of a spirit (*phii*) and they shot him with a gun. Unfortunately, his wife cried for him and looked for him, which terrified the Tai Vat refugees. They informed the *phia* (lord) of Muang Van, a Lao Buddhist called Phia Kham, who hid them from the spirit in the thick forests of *Huai Lôm* stream. There were already Tai Soi, a subgroup of Tai Dèng, living in the place, but fewer than in Houay Yong. They had no *vat* temple as in Houay Yong. Due to a war that was raging in Vietnam at the time, other families left their place of origin to settle with the eight pioneer families, gradually creating a new village. Later on, the relationships with the Tai Soi became tense, because the two groups competed for the village leadership. The Tai Soi eventually left the place (see pages 99–100).

Later in the conversation, which included different people, the narrative of the four brothers was added (see Narrative a), but with no mention of names. One of the brothers eventually settled in Houay Lom, two settled in Houay Yong, and one remained in Vietnam.

Narrative e

Our last narrative comes from Phèèngsoon, the former chief and current deputy-chief of Houay Yong. His narrative is, however, mostly about the foundation of Houay Lom. As already mentioned on page 42, Phèèngsoon held responsibilities at the subdistrict level in the 1980s and was in charge of collecting information on land issues in different villages. This is the source of his knowledge about the foundation of Houay Lom. He narrated the story twice. First, during an unsolicited discussion with four other elders around a table in 2011, an exchange already presented in its pragmatic aspects on pages 57–58 [87], and, second, during an interview in 2018 [252]: Phèèngsoon was sitting with the political leader Buasai and *Naai baan* Bunsoon in front of the latter's house, in the kind of informal meeting people often have in the morning before proceeding to work. I was puzzled by the history of the killing of the *phii* spirit that he related in 2011, and asked for an expansion of it, which explains why the second narrative is centered on this episode.

His first account relates that seven Tai Vat families came from Vietnam and settled in *Naa Took* and *Naa Soo*, close to Nahit. A couple of spirits threatened them: during the night, they came to eat people. Among the refugees was a hunter. He killed the male *phii*. The widow of the spirit was very angry with the killers, so she annoyed the refugees. The local *phanyaa* lord took the families to the *Huai Lôm* valley to hide them from the spirits. The son of the hunter, called Hoom, Koonghoom, or Cheuang Hoom, founded Houay Louang, a bit upstream from the present Houay Lom.

At some point during the conversation, Bunsoon intervened to relay information he had heard from Koongvaa during the interview made in his presence five days earlier (Narrative c). He explained that there were two ancestors, the elder of whom settled in Houay Yong, whereas the younger settled in Houay Lom, all this happening five generations ago.

The second version I heard from Phèèngsoon is similar to the first but provides more information on the spirits. The seven families who had resettled from *Èm Chao* in Vietnam to *Naa Soo*, on the heights of Nahit, used to dip their fishing nets into a container filled with animal blood, to color the nets and make them stronger. This was carried out it in a small hut. The man in charge of the operation had seen that the spirit came to eat the blood. So one night, he stayed outside the hut, prepared his bamboo musket, and, around 11 p.m. or midnight, he pointed his gun in the direction of the container, and ignited the match cord. The gun shot the spirit, who left the place badly injured, proceeded closer to the mountain ridge, and died. It was a very large spirit (*phii luang*), with a chest as large as two arms' length, and the eye as wide as an upper arm. He was living in *Phaa Boo*, the "cliff of the water source," in the mountains close to the *Huai Yoong* valley.

But the spirit was not alone: he had a wife, a *phii* like him. On the next night, at midnight, she went on looking for him, crying and complaining that, if she would find the killer of her husband, she would kill him. Sometimes she would appear as a tiger or a wild cat. Such *phii* can deceive through their appearance (*phii look kaap*). The villagers could not stay. They went to meet the *phia* lord of Muang Èt. The latter declared that he would protect the seven households and find a place for them. They were eventually resettled into the present place of Houay Lom, presented as a "low" place, difficult to spot by spirits and even by people. Up to the present day, the female *phii* is still hanging around her abode on *Phaa Boo* cliff. There is a cave on top of the cliff, which is always clean as if someone was living there. The spirit kills anyone disturbing her, especially men.

During the conversation, other elements of genealogical nature were added but are not developed here. Phèèngsoon also explained that the story above pertains only to the people of Houay Lom. As for the people of Houay Yong, they were originally three families who resettled directly from Vietnam to Houay Yong, where nine families of Tai Soi were already living. These Tai Soi were similar to Lao people, according to him, and were Buddhist. They originated from both Muang Soi and Muang Pun (*Müang Puun*), a small polity north of the former one (see Map 3.1 and Figure 4.3). Some other participants argued instead that they were Tai Dèng, some of them Buddhist, some of them "animist". They eventually left the place for the benefit of the Tai Vat (see page 100).

The feedback effect and the brotherhood trope

These five narratives relate differently the foundation of the two Tai Vat villages of the valley. However, some tropes are recurring: the migration to flee the war (Narratives a, b, c, and d); the resettlement from Nahit to Houay Lom for fear of the spirits (Narratives c, d, and e); the four brothers settling in different villages (narratives a, b, d); and the contact with the Tai Soi first comers (all the narratives).

It is tempting to use such similarities as a base to validate some specific contents as objective historical facts. Indeed, if narratives were transmitted independently, congruencies would provide a strong piece of evidence for objectivity. However, this does not fit with the transmission patterns of oral history: informants are connected in a network and their accounts are not independent. For example, the two accounts related in 2010 and 2012 by Bunmaa (Narrative b, versions 1 and 2) are different. The second introduces the trope of the four brothers, which was not mentioned in 2010. The narrator mentioned he got it from Thaabun. In the account of Koongthéé (Narrative d), the mention of the four brothers came late in the conversation, as an addition unrelated to the main story. And during the free discussion of the five elders before the meal (Narrative e, version 1), *Naai baan* Bunsoon reported elements from the narrative of Koongvaa (Narrative c) he heard previously with our team.

Let us examine first the trope of the founding brothers. The use of kinship to describe the relationships between the proponents of a foundation story is quite usual, in Laos as elsewhere. It seems related to the capacity of kinship to articulate a relational narrative. Brothers can actually found villages at the same time, but it is much more likely that oral history has shaped narratives so that the genealogy of the reported founders fits with the current political order. It is not surprising that *Naai baan* Bunsoon often took the floor to stress the relationship of brotherhood between the founders of the different villages, because it showcased their unity, much in line with the Lao political valuation of solidarity.

The names of the brothers and the villages they founded vary from one version to another and I do not elaborate on this. More interesting is the distinction between younger and elder brothers that surfaces here and there. At some point during his narration, Koongvaa (Narrative c) mentioned an elder brother living in Houay Yong; his son declared more explicitly that there were two brothers, the elder of whom founded Houay Yong, whereas the younger founded Houay Lom. This version was repeated exactly by *Naai baan* Bunsoon a few days later in his own village (Narrative e, version 1). As we shall see on page 126, the founding ancestor of *Naa Kuu* hamlet is presented by his descendants as a younger brother of the founder of Houay Yong [42], despite the chronological inconsistency of this assertion. In short, in all cases, the preeminence of Houay Yong is acknowledged through the mention of its status as elder brother to the villages of the vicinity. This demonstrates that oral traditions should always be contextualized in relation to their potential ideological function in the local scene: historical accounts are by their very essence loaded with arguments on legitimacies and hierarchies of the local groups (Vansina 1985: 102–108).

As oral narratives are in a permanent relationship of exchange and feedback, leaving little room for the validation of their contents based on their similarities, the main evidence for checking their historical veracity is to confront them with external sources – such as written sources, toponymy, or archaeology. This is not easy due to the paucity of such sources at the level of the area. However, the

Traditions on origins 69

next two sections show that this 'triangulation' remains possible, even for events that happened more than a century ago.

Violence under the Chinese Flags

All the stories assert that the first Tai Vat settlers in Houay Yong and Houay Lom came from *Èm Chao*, or Muang Vat, the current district of Yên Châu in Vietnam, in the province of Sơn La.[14] This seems true from a strictly historical point of view. The present populations of Yên Châu and Houay Yong/Houay Lom share the same ethnonym, "Tai Vat," and basically have the same language and partake in many aspects of their culture; as we shall see, the pioneers settled in Laos kept links with their families in Vietnam, which explains why the latter could come during the colonial period and even more during the First Indochina War. The toponym of Chiềng Sàng (Narratives a and d) is attested to in Yên Châu: it is the name of the Tai Vat village eponym of the present Chiềng Sàng commune (Map 3.2).

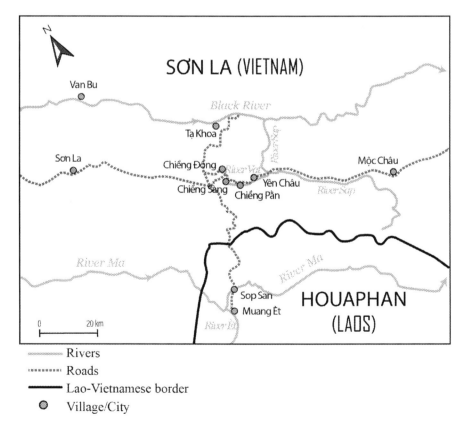

Map 3.2 The cross-border area between the Black River and the River Ma.
Source: map "Réseau routier de Son La", RSL E4, undated.

70 *Traditions on origins*

An early colonial source relocates this migration on a broader regional scale. Bertin, the commander of the military circle of Van Bu (on the Black River, see Map 3.2), was commissioned to the area of Houaphan in the last months of 1893. His exploratory mission took place just after the signature of the Franco-Siamese Treaty (3 October 1893), which marked the end of the Siamese claims over Houaphan. He wrote a 23-page report that constitutes the very first European monograph on the region (GGI 9211 [1893–1894]). It contains interesting observations on history, the local political system, and the different groups ("races", as was commonly said in this era) living in the region. After the Lao, who hold the leadership in most places, come the "*Thaïs*", who are concentrated in the valley of the River Ma – that is, the present districts of Muang Èt and Xiang Kho. Bertin explains that this group is made up, first, of populations who have been living a long time in that valley and, second, of:

> *Thaïs* who have been chased away from the province that holds presently the name of *Sip song chu thaï*,[15] which corresponds to the circle of Van-Bu. Chased away, did I say, by the fear of the pirates, or by the exactions of unpopular chiefs who have been imposed upon them.

The motivation for resettling into the valley of the River Ma mentioned by Bertin – the fear of the (Chinese) pirates and the chiefs they imposed – is echoed in the oral narratives collected in Houay Yong and Houay Lom. They evoke the disruption caused by Chinese invaders, more precisely, according to Narratives a and c, by the Yellow Flags and the Red Flags. Here again, external sources confirm the plausibility of this explanation.

In *Imperial Bandits*, Davis describes the "culture of violence" that characterized the highlands of North Vietnam after the Black Flags and the Yellow Flags came from South China (Davis 2017: 22–49; see also Mignot 2009). These armies were linked to the kingdom of Yanling, crafted in the 1850s in the Chinese province of Guangxi. The Yanling kingdom has often been presented as a component of the contemporaneous Tai Ping Heavenly Kingdom (1851–1864), for both polities were rebellious to the Qing dynasty, but Davis denies this connection, based notably on the fact that Yanling had no religious agenda whereas the Tai Ping had one (Davis 2017: 33, 122). After Yanling was defeated in 1863, part of its armies reassembled under the Black Flags and the Yellow Flags. The Black Flags were the first to come into the north of Vietnam in 1868. The Yellow Flags came a bit later, and became the rival of the Black Flags for the control of land and trade.

The French explorer and diplomat Auguste Pavie was in direct contact with these different Flags armies during his 1888 expedition. Based on discussions he had with their leaders, he summarizes their successive movements, linked in a domino effect (Pavie 1919: 123–124). After the Black Flags settled on both sides of the Black River in 1871:

> in 1872, the Yellow Flags ... overflowed the right side of the Black River [that is, the major part of Sơn La Province; see Maps 3.2 and 3.3], and

Traditions on origins 71

Map 3.3 Northern Vietnam.
Source: vietnamitasenmadrid.com.

pressed the Red Flags who had come from Yunnan southward; the latter took Xieng-Kham, the major city of Tranninh [Muang Kham, in present-day Xieng Khouang Province, see Map P.1], crossed the Mekong River and looted Nong Khai [in present-day Thailand; see Map P.1]. In 1879, the Black Flags dislodged the Yellow Flags and founded the military positions they hold up to the present [1888] on the Black River.[16]

Muang Vat, the place where the Tai Vat used to live in Vietnam, was massively impacted by the Flag armies, often known under the generic name of Hô. The inhabitants of Muang Vat were indirect victims of the Hô's internal conflicts, and direct victims of their exactions, because their villages eventually became the headquarters of the Black Flags when the latter reconquered the area from the Yellow Flags around 1879. In 1888, Pavie met the old chief of the Black Flags, Ong Ba, in Chiềng Sàng (see Map 3.2), which is precisely the home village of the Houay Yong and Houay Lom refugees according to Narratives a and d. At the time, the Chinese soldiers had settled their camp in that village and in the neighboring village of Chiềng Đông. When Pavie descended into the valley of the River Vat, on 5 May 1888, the situation was apparently calm, but the Tai population was under the yoke of the Chinese, and worked submissively for them (Pavie 1919: 108–115). Pavie thought that the peasants had been asked by the Black Flags to stage normal occupations to impress him about their governance, because the domination of the French seemed inevitable in the short term. The local Tai authorities of Chiềng Sàng came to welcome him and his troop: Pavie was moved by their condition:

> Resignation to all misfortunes seems to be the main factor of their strong embarrassment. They are afraid to see so many people, to have so many masters. After the greetings, they lead the walk, following the customs. They are Black Tai; they have become passive after endless misfortunes, and seem to accept their present condition, being more anxious about what could happen tomorrow.
>
> (Pavie 1919: 109)

The situation at the time was no better in the region of the current research. Concrete memories about the havoc in the *Huai Yoong* valley and the nearby area are profusely reported. The village of Ban Kang, a little upstream from Houay Yong (see Map 2.1), was founded by a returnee whose father had been abducted by the Yellow Flags when he was a child.[17] In Muang Van, the Chinese invaders reportedly destroyed the stupa (*that*) of the local temple ([113], see page 77). In fact, that kind of iconoclastic behavior is usually related to the "Chüang wars" (*seuk Chüaang*),[18] that is, repeated rebellions and messianic movements of the Khmu and related 'Kha' populations that shook the region from 1875 on, and resulted in the systematic destruction of temples and stupas, with the view to finding gold statues or items in them. But the Chinese Flags had a similar destructive behavior, and ruined, for example, the temple of Muang Èt, as well as all the village houses when they occupied the place (Raquez 1905: 1328). The climax of terror was reached between 1875 and 1886, due to the conjunction of the troubles engendered by the Yellow Flags and by the revolted Kha. The Siamese eventually occupied the region in 1886 to secure Houaphan into their sphere of influence, and to bring an end to the anarchy. When the Siamese arrived, Houaphan had already lost a great part of its population, who had emigrated to flee danger and chaos.[19] The Tai Dam inhabitants of Ban Sot, settled along the River Ma a few kilometers north of Houay Yong, report that, when their ancestors came from Vietnam[20] four generations ago, they found paddy fields and big trees at the present location of their village, but abandoned by the former inhabitants who never returned [258].

Starting in 1886 the Siamese occupation did not bring safety to local populations. A few days before his arrival in Chiềng Sàng, reported above, Pavie was in Muang Èt. He was able to observe that the apparent peace hid collusion

Figure 3.9 The ruins of the temple (*vat*) of Xiang Kho destroyed during the late nineteenth-century wars (May 2011).

between the Siamese officers and the Yellow Flags, the former turning a blind eye to the exactions of the latter. The local chief of Muang Èt disclosed this situation of abuses to Pavie, discretely in the evening, for fear of retaliation (Pavie 1919: 102–103).

On the next day (1 May 1888), Pavie traveled downstream on the River Ma, accompanied by the local chief of Muang Èt. At some point he must have passed at the level of Muang Van, on the mouth of the *Huai Yoong* stream, but he mentions no village. In fact, he could see no more villages on the River Ma than on the River Èt, along which he had been traveling during the preceding days: the villages had all been deserted, and their former position could be guessed at only through the presence of fruit trees. When the column reached Sop Sang, about eight kilometers downstream from Muang Van (see Maps 2.1 and 3.2), Pavie was welcomed by the chief of the principality of Xiang Kho, whose domain currently starts precisely in Sop Sang – an interesting case of administrative continuity. The chief of Muang Èt, who had accompanied Pavie up to that point, returned to his home place.

The chief of Muang Xiang Kho explained to Pavie that "the presence of the Hô forces the villagers to settle and live in the forest. Recruiting coolies for transport is difficult in such conditions" (Pavie 1919: 105). This is why he asked Pavie to wait one more day to recruit carriers for his trip to Muang Vat.

These excerpts from Pavie's edited diaries are very interesting. They reveal that, despite various disruptions and the presence of the Hô, the local chiefs of the *müang* were still in place and attached to their duties in their respective territories (as the village chiefs of Chiềng Sàng mentioned earlier, who welcomed Pavie according to etiquette), and were able to voice their concerns to him. They also attest that, despite appearances, the region was not wholly deserted: the thick forests on the mountain slopes and in the adjacent valleys had become home to the villagers who wanted to protect themselves from the abuses of the Hô – and probably of the Siamese as well. The chief of Xiang Kho declared he could find coolies to help Pavie during his trip, and he managed to do so: this is a piece of evidence that he still held authority within the population, and had probably retained relationships with the villagers hidden in the forests. All this shows that the local societies displayed resilience when facing the disorders of this troubled era. The literature has usually underscored the disastrous effects of the invasions and other troubles in the region from the 1870s onwards; this should in no case be underestimated, but nor should it create a blind spot for the reorganization capacities of the local societies to face the hardships of the period.

If the general context that prompted the departure of some Tai Vat families to the *Huai Yoong* valley is clear, it is more challenging to provide a date for their leaving. In any case, it must have been after 1872, the earliest date provided for the settlement of the Yellow Flags on the right side of the Black River, and for their pushing of the Red Flags further south (Pavie 1919: 123–124). Both Yellow Flags and Red Flags are mentioned in the oral traditions we collected and, even more tellingly, there is no mention of the Black Flags who settled later, in 1878 or 1879. The period between 1872 and 1879 is hence a most plausible time for their migration.

One can be more precise. The refugees – presented as moving in groups of three to eight families in the oral traditions – must have chosen a safe place for their settlement: there is no benefit to leaving a dangerous place to settle in an insecure location. But narratives mention that the refugees settled first in the area of Nahit, the village presently west of Muang Van (see Map 2.1), and moved afterwards to either Houay Lom (Narratives c, d, and e) or Houay Yong (Narrative b). The stories refer to the paddy fields of *Naa Soo* or related areas close to the River Ma, which the refugees constructed themselves. This episode does not seem to have any legitimizing purpose – the current inhabitants of Houay Yong or Houay Lom have no land pretensions in that area – and is hence plausible. Building paddy fields on such a place, close to the banks of the River Ma, could testify that the region was safe at the time of the Tai Vat's arrival. This must correspond to the years preceding 1875, which was marked by an explosion of violence. That very year saw the departure of mandarins related to the court of Annam from the *müang* of Xiang Kho, due to the arrival of the Yellow Flags – it marked the definite end of Vietnamese presence in the region, to the benefit of Siam. The year 1875 is also the year when the terrible Kha/Khmu revolt expanded from the east to the west into the province, as mentioned above.

The Tai Vat must have come a few years before this explosion of violence. This would explain the following: why they moved to that area (it was peaceful at the time); why they settled closer to the River Ma (there was nothing to fear at the time); why they started to build paddy fields (a labor-demanding, long-term enterprise no one would launch during a period of unrest); and why they had to stop their construction after a few years and hide upstream of the *Huai Yoong* (to protect against the vagaries of the time). The oral traditions explain this last movement referring to the need to hide away during a war, or to the fear of spirits. Although an unknown specific event might have prompted this fear of the angry *phii*, it is tempting to see it as the expression, at a religious level, of the disruptions that desolated the region from 1875 on.

With all this in mind, and based on the fact that the creation of paddy fields by the pioneers in Nahit had been partly completed (which supposes a few years of labor), I argue that the Tai Vat migrants had probably left Muang Vat in 1872, when the Yellow and Red Flags invaded their home region; they settled first in the area of Nahit, close to the River Ma, where they started the construction of paddy fields in what they considered to be their new settlement in the long term; due to the rise of violence in 1875, they had no other choice than to leave the place (and the heavy work they had started) to hide more in the hinterland, in the upstream valley of the *Huai Yoong*.

The earlier inhabitants: Tai Soi and Lao

All narratives mention that, when the Tai Vat pioneers settled in the *Huai Yoong* valley, the place was already occupied by people usually identified as Tai Soi. This has been reported in various other contexts, as in this book's introductory vignette – which credits the Tai Soi as having built the collective rice fields (*naa luam*) (see pages 3–4, [142, 217]). The narratives describe the settling of the Tai Vat pioneers among the Tai Soi as a peaceful one, even if the departure of the latter from the valley in 1945–1946 hints at a conflict between the two groups, which is discussed pages 99–100.

76 *Traditions on origins*

The Tai Soi are usually described as being Tai Dèng (Red Tai), as in Narratives d and e. "Tai Dèng" is an ethnic label referring to a large group of populations who were historically concentrated in the Vietnamese province of Thanh Hoá, east of Houaphan (Boutin 1937: 93; see Map 3.3).[21] However, they are also sometimes referred to as Tai Khao (White Tai), or as being "like Lao." "Tai Khao" certainly does not refer, in this context, to the well-known ethnic group concentrated around Lai Châu in Vietnam (Michaud *et al.* 2016: 385), but presumably refers to the Buddhist religious identity of the Tai Soi. Some people hold the view that there were two different groups, Tai Soi and Lao, settled in Houay Yong and its vicinity: I elaborate on this issue at the end of this section.

The Tai Soi of Houay Yong reportedly came from the principality of Muang Soi (*Müang Sôôi*, see Map 3.1), as their very name suggests.[22] Muang Soi is an ancient polity, allegedly created in 1777 to become the sixth component of Houaphan, on its eastern border (Boutin 1937: 71).

The Tai Soi of Houay Yong, or at least some of them, were Buddhist: their temple (*vat*) stood on the place formerly occupied by the primary school, an area called *San Kadii*, "the heights of the temple,"[23] up to the present. Some bronze objects, including the feet of a Buddha statue, axes, and vessels for alms (*kup baat*) were discovered on the spot when the road was broadened in 2011. Gold has sometimes been found when building houses in Houay Yong: the Tai Soi supposedly buried it in the foundation grounds of their houses. They had a cemetery situated on the lower side of the path adjoining the present Tai Vat cemetery [90, 110, 111, 244]. They are also credited as having hidden Buddha statues in mountain caves during the wars of the nineteenth century (see page 167).

About 60 Tai Soi families lived in Houay Yong in the past, and the land belonged to them, according to Thaabun (Narrative a). Their presence is also attested to in other villages of the valley. In Nasan, between Houay Yong and Muang Van, a Tai Dèng elder, whose family came from Vietnam, reported that Tai Soi founded the village [82]. He said they settled in the *Huai Yoong* valley because of a war raging in their home region. Sèèn Hoom was the first chief of the place, and was succeeded by Sèèn Thia, then Thao Oon. After the war (1945–46), people were asked to settle back in their place of origin, and the Tai Soi left. So after three generations of Tai Soi chiefs came two Tai Dèng chiefs.[24] In the words of our informant, some Tai Soi were Buddhist ("*Phuu Lao*"), some not, that is, they just worshipped spirits ("*Phuu Thaï*"). Unlike in Houay Yong, there was no temple in Nasan village.

The presence of Tai Soi is also mentioned in Ban Kang: an elder of the place reported that the whole valley used to be called "*Müang Yoong*" in the past – an important piece of information that will be analyzed on pages 163–166 – and belonged to Tai Soi; tamarind trees were planted by them and can still be seen today, as evidence of their former presence [76].

The presence of Tai Soi in the village of Houay Lom is less clear. Koongvaa seemed to refute it (Narrative c). But the present *chao süa* of Houay Lom and Houay Louang both acknowledged the presence of Tai Soi in the past (Narrative d). They say that Tai Soi were already in the *Huai Lôm* valley when their ancestors settled. Tai Soi were, in their view, Buddhist Tai Dèng. They were less numerous than in Houay Yong village, where they were concentrated and had their temple.

Tai Soi are hence reported as being all along the *Huai Yoong* and *Huai Lôm* streams. However, no villager in the valleys presents him- or herself as such. The only place where we found someone who identified himself as Tai Soi was Muang Van. Vông, an elder of this village, declared he was a Tai Soi (based on his ancestors' place of origin) and a Tai Dèng Buddhist (based on the local definitions of ethnic and cultural identity) [113]. Although he insisted that the story of his group is unrelated to the story of the Tai Soi formerly settled in Houay Yong, his interview demonstrates the long-term presence of Tai Soi in the present district of Muang Èt, and their intense mobility. Long ago, about 50 families of Tai Soi lived in *Kèng Sung* (halfway between Muang Van and Muang Èt). Then some of them went to *Sop Phia* (closer to Muang Èt). Afterwards, some families went in the direction of Luang Prabang Province,[25] whereas others settled back in Muang Van, where they erected a high stupa, or in Muang Hom (close to Sop Bao, in Xiang Kho district). The grandfather of Vong's grandfather, five generations ago, settled in Muang Van. The Haan (the Chinese) eventually destroyed that stupa, an assertion that in any case situates the Buddhist Tai Soi in the area well before the 1870s.

The presence of Tai Soi in the area of Muang Èt in an early period of the nineteenth century is perplexing. What were Tai Soi doing so far west from their original area? Fortunately, the archives and published colonial sources provide substantial information about the district of Muang Soi. One of the reasons for this colonial concern is related to the long-term conflict between the Tai Dèng and the Lao over the control of the polity during the precolonial and colonial periods. The origin of this situation is reported by Martin (1899: 490), a French missionary who traveled from Thanh Hóa (in Vietnam) to the neighboring districts of Muang Soi and Muang Sam Tai, on the eastern border of Houaphan.[26] Martin interviewed the chief (*phanyaa*) of Muang Soi in March 1899. The grandfather of the latter was a trader born in Annam, who quickly grew rich trading with Muang Soi. He developed a close acquaintance with the *phanyaa* of Muang Soi and eventually married his daughter, becoming like the intendant of the palace. The Lao of the region felt bitter about this situation, accusing the Tai (obviously the ethnic group of the informant's grandfather) of having encroached on their authority. With the help of the Siamese, they forced the Tai away from the place. Afterwards, the Lao ruled Muang Soi for over 60 years.

At the time when the Chinese Flags invaded Houaphan (that is, in the 1870s), the interviewee of Martin was the chief of a small *müang* in Thanh Hóa. He took advantage of the situation: he gathered partisans, allied with the Chinese, and managed to expel the Lao from Muang Soi, re-establishing the Tai as masters of the place, and taking the title of *phanyaa* for himself. This 'revenge' coup can be dated, thanks to other sources, to September 1880.[27] The Tai Dèng *phanyaa* whom Martin interviewed in 1899 had held that position since that coup, despite the protests of many Lao dignitaries.[28]

78 *Traditions on origins*

As for the first coup, which resulted in the rejection of the Tai Dèng from Muang Soi, it would have happened more than 60 years before the second coup according to Martin – which would mean around 1820.[29] This seems incompatible with the mention of the help of the Siamese mentioned by him. Indeed, the first presence of a large Siamese army in Houaphan dates to 1831. When the Siamese destroyed Vientiane in 1828, Houaphan remained out of tutelage for a few years. The Annamese kingdom, formerly allied with Vientiane, had views on Houaphan. To impede this annexation, the Siamese and the kingdom of Luang Prabang (vassal to the former at the time) joined in a military expedition to regain control of the region (Boutin 1937: 71; GGI 20724, 18/10/1894; Monpeyrat 1904: 129). As this is the only mention of a Siamese army in the region before 1886, and in consideration of the insistence of Martin's informant on the long period ("more than 60 years") that elapsed between the two coups involving people actually separated by two generations, and in light of the fact that Martin's piece of evidence is a first-hand interview, I contend that the first coup in Muang Soi was carried out during the campaign orchestrated by the coalition of the Siamese and their allies of Luang Prabang in 1831 – or not long after, in any case.

To come back to Houay Yong, now, I hold that the Tai Soi who settled in the *Huai Yoong* valley and on the stretch of land between Muang Van and Muang Èt are most probably the Tai Dèng victims of the coup carried out in 1831 by their Lao rivals, who took advantage of the presence of the invading army. The Siamese and Luang Prabangese certainly shared affinities with the Lao against the Tai, especially if the latter were coming from Annam, the main political rival of Siam at the time. This fits with all available information, with the fact that these Tai Soi refugees were able to build the rice fields in the *Huai Yoong* valley before the coming of the Tai Vat (in 1872 or soon after) and to build a stupa in Muang Van. Such constructions must have started long before, during a peaceful period.

The successive back-and-forth movements of the Tai Soi mentioned in the narrative by Vông, in Muang Van, hints at the fact that their resettlement was not an easy process. There must have been negotiations and possibly frictions with the local authorities of Xiang Kho, who controlled the area of Muang Èt at the time; it probably took one or two decades before their situation was stabilized. This must have applied to those who settled in the *Huai Yoong* valley as well, whose installation could have happened years or even decades after 1831.

An issue remains: why were these Tai Dèng Buddhist, and not 'animist' as most of their fellows in their home region? Some informants say that there were both Buddhists and 'animists' among the Tai Soi population of Houay Yong (Narrative e). Other information points to the fact that the ancient population of Houay Yong was made up of Tai Soi and Lao. This is the opinion expressed by Thaabun (Narrative a). Thoongsôm said in an early interview [106] that, in the 1940s, there were *Phuu Thai* (Tai Vat), *Thai Khao* (Buddhist Tai, that is, Tai Soi), and *Phuu Lao* (Lao) living in Houay Yong. In a recent interview [262], he argued that the *vat* temple in Houay Yong was not built by the Tai Soi, but by

Lao people from Muang Vat, who hid in the valley during the war with the Chinese (that is, in the 1870s to 1880s).[30] Another opinion is expressed by Bunmaa (Narrative b, version 3): the *vat* of Houay Yong must have been built by Lao people who left the place when the Tai Soi, that is, Tai Dèng 'animists,' came.

This is confusing. However, taken together, the opinions of Thaabun, Thoongsôm and Bunmaa converge on the presence in Houay Yong of a group of Lao, distinct from Tai Soi. One might suppose that, when the Tai Soi came into the region, they settled in a Buddhist context, and adopted elements of the dominant religion of the Lao. Maybe they had to, as a sign of their submission to the Lao families in the place. Could they have been prisoners captured by the Siamese army after the latter's intervention in Muang Soi, and left in the region during their return trip, along the River Ma and the River Èt? The issue remains open.

The 'autochthonous' Khmu

There is no evidence on how the Tai Soi and the Lao concretely settled in the *Huai Yoong* valley. Archeological research in the area, or the archives on Houaphan conserved in the National Library of Bangkok, could shine new light on the question. The Tai Soi and the Lao were probably not the first inhabitants of the place. Throughout the province, Khmu and related groups (such as the Pong) are credited as having been the first comers, who had been subdued by the Lao since the sixteenth century (Raquez 1905: 1308–1402; RSL E4, 1/3/1925; Boutin 1937: 69–70, 94–96). Bunsoon mentioned in a casual discussion that, when Ban Kang was resettled upstream of the river, the Tai Dam pushed the Khmu, who occupied the area until then, upland; the Khmu moved back to their "home village," Nong Thop, southwest from Houay Yong (see Map 3.1) [51, 75]. The villagers of Ban Kang confirm this version [254]. I was eventually able to meet a leader of those Khmu [256]. The villagers of Nong Thop were resettled in 2010 to Nangiu, on the provincial road PR3201 south of Pakfèn (see Map 2.1). The interviewee asserted that their ancestors were "born here" and did not come from somewhere else. This was the unique occasion on which I heard someone professing autochthony in the course of my field research in Houaphan. He went on to say that, in the past, the Khmu village was in the same area as Houay Yong and Ban Kang; there was no border, the population was limited, and there was a lot of space to do *hai* and *naa* (swidden and irrigated agriculture) – "there was solidarity." So even if the evidence is shallow – such assertion seems to refer to the twentieth rather than the nineteenth century, and points to the recent ideology of the harmonious multiethnic state – one can presume that the forefathers of these Khmu already occupied part of the valley when the Tai Soi resettled in the early nineteenth century.

Political and religious subjectivities

This chapter has discussed oral traditions of origin. Even if information was scanty, even if oral testimonies on ancient events often remain dubious, the triangulation with independent data provided by the literature proved useful, to the point of providing a tentative chronology for the twofold settlement of the valley, by the Tai Soi (and Lao) first and then by the Tai Vat. Of course, new data could put my argument to the test, but, based on the information at hand, it seems the most plausible way to include all the information available in a coherent system. However, this long discussion to unfold the chronological argument led us far away from the ideological and symbolic functions of oral traditions that were highlighted by Vansina, and were briefly discussed when analyzing the "founding brothers" trope (see page 68).

To redress this imbalance, I conclude the chapter by elaborating on the political and religious subjectivities that appear in the Houay Lom narratives. They all relate the episode of the spirit's anger and the help provided by the lord of either Muang Van (Narratives c and d) or Muang Èt (Narrative e). This lord holds the title of *phanyaa*, or *phia*, or *aanyaa*, the last designation being the most typical Tai word. This provides a clue to understanding the way elders of the 2010s portray the ancient political order. The *aanyaa* political figure mediates the resettlement of the refugees: he acts as a protector against the wars and the spirits, and as a broker for land, in exchange for the refugees' political allegiance. He commits to protecting the refugees if and only if they accept becoming his servants, his subjects (*khôn nam, khôn kuaang*, Narrative c).[31] Asked about the meaning of *"khôn kuaang,"* "the people who depend," Bunsoon explained that this word means political subjection in the sense of being under the control of the *aanyaa*, who gets direct benefit from the situation, but also being under his protection, and receiving food from him when needed [260]. He went on to say that the *aanyaa* has to *liang khao*, take care and provide food (rice), especially for the poor. Up to this point, the story seems to value inclusion into the local polity, in a way reminiscent of Thomas Hobbes's *Leviathan*, wherein people subject themselves to a sovereign authority in exchange for the protection of their life and their goods.

However, the moral evaluation of yesteryear's political power is not so simple. In the same interview, Bunsoon also commented on another expression Koongvaa (Narrative c) used to introduce the *aanyaa*: *"aanyaa beung khuut hiit,"* literally, the *"aanyaa* who looks after and extorts." He explained that, in the past, the authorities like *aanyaa* or *phia* had no salary and relied only on people to eat. This meant that, when the upper level of authority required the payment of a tax, the lower level in charge of its collection would ask more: "if the head of district asks for 5 or 10 piasters (*man*) per capita, the head of *taasèèng* asks for 15, and the head of village collects 20." When a family did not have enough to pay, they had to sell their cattle, or even their cooking pots; this is why some families fled to other areas, whereas some others could be chased away by the local authorities for the same reason. Bunsoon also explained that those authorities were corrupt: when they had to settle a case, their judgment was favorable to the party who paid most, even in the case of cattle theft. He then contrasted this situation with the present one, because the current authorities are very eager to protect the people (*pasason*) and treat everyone on an equal footing [260].

Interestingly, we see through these mentions that the Tai Vat incorporate the state into their traditions of origin. More globally, their relationship with the state can certainly not be reduced to a proclivity to escape state control, along the "Zomia" anti-state traditions described by Scott (2009). This view does not do justice to the capacity of highland societies to negotiate their relationship with larger polities, their inclusion into modern states, and their access to related resources (Petit 2015; see also Jonsson [2014] for a critique on Scott's argument on "escapism"). Joining a political structure is not denounced here as alienating: it is, first of all, a way of generating security and protection from danger. It does not elude, however, criticisms on the state agents, as the moral comments on "exploitation" attest in the words of our informants.

Another fascinating dimension in the Houay Lom foundation narrative is the reference to the power of the spirits. The couple of *phii* who interfere with the refugees are described in chilling terms: bloodthirsty, giant sized, spiteful, changing their appearance, eager to kill. They are also located: they roam a specific area and live on a distinct cliff, where the widow spirit occupies a cave until the present. The refugees from Yên Châu could just escape them, going to a place that was presented as "low" so that the widow spirit could not spot them. Evidence is lacking for a broad interpretation – no similar story has been reported in the region, to my knowledge – but general comments can be made based on this episode: a territory can host spiritual presences; the spirits live in the mountains above human villages; they are dangerous; they need to eat; they have feelings, and live and die like men and women. Such observations are generic, but they are indicative of the relationships people have with their territory and with the spirits attached to it, which are unpacked in Chapters 5 and 6.

Notes

1 All narratives are interpretations, of course. However, degrees of 'objectivity' – in the sense of a proximity with the original event – can be assessed notably in relation to the chronological and spatial sequence of facts, the identity and actions of the protagonists, and so forth. This remains the base of any historical approach, to be elaborated on with the subjectivities governing human agency.
2 The situation is very different among the Tai Vat of Vietnam as I observed between 2010 and 2014 in Yên Châu. Tai language and writing were taught at school until 1972–1973, after which Vietnamese language alone was used for education. Some male elders still have books and manuscripts in Tai, and can write using this script. Old boards for public health information still display their message written in Vietnamese with a Tai translation underneath. But this is, along with paper block almanac calendars that are popular for choosing propitious days for ceremonies, one of the last public manifestations of this script.

3 This remark echoes the interpretation given by Kilani (1994) about the use of manuscripts by the inhabitants of the Tunisian Oases, who own ancient books but do not make them available for public reading.
4 See also Tappe (2015, 2018) for a recent integrated overview of the history of Houaphan.
5 Monpeyrat (1904: 127). According to Boutin (1937: 71), that conquest took place in 1791.
6 See Bouté (2011: 64–66) on similar territorial charts granted by the Lao kings to the Phounoy of Phongsali.
7 Phothisarat is the father of King Setthathirat (1548–1571). For the chronology and the history of the reigns of these two kings, see Le Boulanger (1930: 72–90) and Stuart-Fox (1998: 74–82).
8 *Chantabuulii* is the old name of Vientiane. Phothisarat gradually shifted the seat of power from Luang Prabang to Vientiane during his reign. The central district of the present capital holds that name, usually spelled "Chantabouly" nowadays.
9 Tappe (2015) has analyzed this complex period, highlighting the multiplicity of intervening parties and the alliances they made to promote their interests: the high officers of colonial administration in Hà Nội, Huế and Luang Prabang; the colonial authorities based in Thanh Hoá (for Annam), Muang Èt, and Muang Son (in Houaphan); Cuvelier, a military officer who had economic interests in keeping the west of Houaphan in the sphere of Thanh Hoá; Catholic missionaries, whose vicariate straddled different polities; and, of course, the local Lao and Tai authorities. Indeed, the colonial state was not a monolithic structure, and the local authorities had some room for communication, negotiation, and strategic alliances with different segments of the administration (Tappe 2015: 382).
10 Lissoir (2016: 89–90) evokes only two *khap* with a clear historical content, both composed by Phongsai, the late husband of Mèèthao Leua, but potentially interpreted by female singers: one about a Chao Faa revolt of the Hmong against the government, and another about the division of the district of Xiang Kho in 1997. But these are rare occurrences by comparison with the many other topics appearing in these songs.
11 Parts of this chapter have already been discussed in Petit (2015), with much less detail. A few excerpts from this publication have been reproduced here.
12 Note, compared with Narrative a, the twist between the villages founded respectively by these two brothers.
13 He names them "Lao Luang" (the main Lao) or "Lao Lum" (the lowland Lao).
14 Pavie uses alternatively the names "Wat," "Muong Watt," "Muong Wat," "Yên Châu," and "An Chau" to describe that specific area (Pavie 1919: 103, 173, 186, 189). *Nam Vaat* is the name of the river that runs through the region, from which the names of the polity (*Müang Vaat*) and the ethnonym (Tai Vat, *Thai Vaat*) have been derived.
15 The "twelve principalities" (*Sip song chu thai*, *Sip song chao thai*, or *Sip song châu tai*) is a geographical term referring to the aggregate of the ancient Tai polities mostly centered along the Black River in Tonkin. They have often been presented as a polity or a federation, which is unsubstantiated. Their number varied from ten to sixteen through history (Le Failler 2014: 45–47; Cầm Trọng 2004: 190–199).
16 Davis (2017: 70–72) and Le Failler (2014: 86–87) confirm this flux and reflux of the Black and Yellow Flags in Sơn La's territory, but provide slightly different dates: 1872 or 1874 for the invasion of the latter, and 1878 for the reconquest by the former.
17 Chiaobun, an elder who claimed to be 82 years old when we interviewed him in 2011, narrated the story of the village [75, 76]. This child abducted by the Chinese was named Koonghôông. He was brought by them to the region that would eventually become Sơn La province, in Vietnam. After some years, he married there and had children. After his death, his son Sèèntaang settled back into the *Huai Yoong* valley, where he thought his father came from. He formed a small village with other Tai Dam returnees from Vietnam. As he was wealthier, he became their leader, the *naai baan*,

and the founder of the place (*chao kôk chao lao*). At first, Ban Kang was close to Houay Yong, and was its dependency. Later on, it moved upstream and became autonomous. Nowadays, Ban Kang, officially called Ban Kang Houay Yong, remains a small Tai Dam village, with 288 inhabitants and 45 families reported in 2014, originating from various places. Its population does not result from a big flux at a precise period, but from constant immigration [2, 64a, 179, 248, 253].

18 The wars of Chüang have been analyzed at length by Proschan (1998). A Khmu informant in Nangiu, where his group has been resettled from Nong Thop (see page 79), still remembers the violence of this period: he compares those Khmu with the messianic movement of Chao Fa among the Hmong. The Khmu of the Chüang wars used to kill a lot of people, usually by cutting off their heads; they were reputed to put children into mortars to kill them [256]. Bunsoon adds that these Khmu came from China, and became insects after their life – due to their terrible behavior, one might presume [255].

19 GGI 9211, 10/12/1893; Monpeyrat 1904: 129–130; Boutin 1937: 71; Proschan 1998; Tappe 2015: 372.

20 I do not follow Evans when he dates the foundation of Ban Sot in the 1930s: the village was already well established in 1902, as evidenced by the census for gun owners reproduced in Figure 4.1. The *naai baan* of Ban Sot mentioned Muỗi Nọi, *Siang Peuk* as the place of origin of the three brothers who founded their village. Muỗi Nọi is in the district of Thuận Châu, province of Sơn La (see Map 3.3).

21 My informants confirm that Tai Dèng – at large – do not originate from Houaphan, but from *Müang Mot* and *Müang Dèèng* in Vietnam [113, 196, 222, 235].

22 The smaller polity of Muang Pun, close to Muang Soi, has been mentioned as well (Narrative e).

23 *Kadii* is a variation of *kudii*, or *kutti*, the dormitory of the monks (Reinhorn 2001: 20).

24 Sèèn Hoom (second of the name) and Sèèn Chau.

25 This might be confirmed by the existence of a village called "Ban Tai Soï" on the River Èt, upstream from Muang Èt in the direction of Luang Prabang (GGI 20770, 1895–1899).

26 I thank Oliver Tappe for bringing my attention to this source. These events are also described, with less detail, in a hand-written monograph drafted in 1896 by Monpeyrat (GGI 26509, 8/6/1896). Bobo, who was the military authority of Muang Èt in 1894 (GGI 20724, 18/10/1894), published a version of this monograph in 1898, followed by a book by Monpeyrat in 1904. It is difficult to know who wrote the original text.

27 See Mironneau (1935–1936: 774). The date 1880–1881 is also given by Proschan (1998: 193) who mentions the alliance of Kha, Red Tai, and Yellow Flags against Lao people in Muang Soi and the neighboring areas.

28 The pre-eminence of the Tai Dèng went on during the colonial period: they were very reluctant to allow the resettlement of the Lao who had fled and were refugees in different areas of Houaphan, or even in Vientiane, and intended to come back to their place of origin, from the mid-1890s on. The situation was even complicated due to the conversion to Catholicism of segments of the Tai Dèng population, whereas the bulk of Lao remained Buddhists. Eventually, the French administration tried to balance the rights of the two groups, providing each of them with dignitary positions. The situation was very tense until the 1930s at least (GGI 20724, 3/4/1895; Bobo 1898: 571–572; RSL E3, 1/6/1904; RSL E4, 2/8/1909, 1/3/1925, and 22/3/1930; Mironneau 1935–1936: 770–772).

29 Monpeyrat wrote in his 1896 manuscript that it happened "about 30 years ago," which would mean around 1866 (GGI 26509, 8/6/1896). But it seems less informed than the first-hand account presented by Martin.

30 Still, according to Thoongsôm [262], the Lao of Muang Van would have built a stupa (*that*) in the vicinity of Ban Kang during that period; it was destroyed a few decades

ago and replaced by a paddy field (presently named *Naa That*, "the paddy of the stupa"). Thoongsôm also argues that the Tai Soi were wandering people who used to live for long periods in the area; their name "Tai Soi" would not reflect their place of origin but their place of destination, which is a surprising etymology acknowledged by no one but him.

31 Bouté refers to ceremonies of allegiance that linked the chiefs of village to the *phanyaa* in the prerevolutionary regime (Bouté 2011: 33). Even if the link between the Tai Vat refugees and the lord of Muang Van or Muang Èt is not described in such a formal way, ceremonies of allegiance were promoted by the French from the mid-1890s in Houaphan, due to their reinvention by the colonial officer Monpeyrat. The latter set up the "*fête du serment* (festival of the oath) … a bricolage of European and indigenous practices of political ritual" analyzed in detail by Tappe (2018: 60).

4 From the French colony to the present

Chapter 3 dealt mostly with conjectures – those of my interlocutors but also my own: we tried to make sense of fragments and echoes from the past. I aimed at substantiating a plausible history based on heterogeneous information from oral and written sources, as well as from the landscape and toponyms. The period beginning with the French presence provides a very different scenario. Colonial archives and literature have produced extensive documentation since the first presence of French state agents in Muang Èt, in late 1893. Even if there were very little information pertaining directly to the *Huai Yoong* valley, the profusion of data on the province would allow the casting of a generic pattern that must have applied throughout Houaphan. In the first section of this chapter, our interviews in Muang Van, the polity into which the Tai Vat pioneers were incorporated, link the local history to the colonial regime at large. The second section analyzes different aspects of the colonial time as they appear in the archives; it also discusses the blank spots and foci of colonial attention. The archives conserved in Aix-en-Provence in relation to Houaphan do not cover the period after 1940 well, but direct testimony is still available for this period – this was especially true when we began our research ten years ago. Oral information will, therefore, come again to the forefront in the last five sections which address the different periods from the decline and fall of the French colonial empire to the policies of development implemented since the turn of the millennium.

Muang Van: the local seat of power in a nested polity

Informants from Muang Van present their village as the oldest one in the area, created sixteen generations ago [81, 113, see pages 50–51].[1] It had its own local chief (*phia*), chosen among the six founding families – the leading one being the lineage founded by a certain Loo Van Nooi. The origin of those founding lineages is unclear,[2] but, interestingly, the name Loo Van Nooi sounds like Tai Dam names in Vietnam, and denotes belonging to the Loo aristocratic clan (see page 144n8).

Muang Van was a subregional seat of power. The elders of the village did not report any precolonial authority on surrounding villages, despite the fact that this relationship has been acknowledged by our informants in Houay Lom, when they related about their settlement in the 1870s (Narratives c and d). Archives confirm Muang Van's position of authority in the precolonial past. In the nineteenth century, when Houaphan was under the vassalage of Luang Prabang, it used to be divided into six principalities (*huaphan*), as explained on page 52. The lower basin of the River Èt and the middle basin of the River Ma made up the principality of Xiang Kho. After the Siamese occupied the area in 1886, they redrew the political map of the region. For strategic reasons, they elevated two former secondary *müang* to the rank of a full principality (*huaphan*): Muang Èt and Muang Ven (not to be confused with Muang Van). When Muang Èt was elevated to this status, it was consolidated with two lower-rank *müang*, one of which was precisely Muang Van, also detached from Xiang Kho.[3] All this proves that Muang Van was already an established polity before 1886.

With the French colonial rule starting in 1893, the political structure installed by the Siamese did not change a lot. The French took over the local system of "*phanya*" lordship. Muang Èt (spelled "Muong Het" in the French archives) was elevated, from October 1893 to January 1897, to the seat of the colonial administration for the whole province, before Muang Son replaced it in 1897.[4] In 1904, Wartelle proposed its disappearance as a district and its inclusion into Xiang Kho as a mere canton (RSL E4, 20/7/1904), a proposal that was officially endorsed in 1911 (Boutin 1937: 72). I do not discuss in detail the varying status that Muang Èt held until it regained the status of a full district in 1997 (see page 40).[5]

According to the elders of Muang Van, their village was the seat of a colonial administrative unit called *phông*, placed under the authority of a *phia phông*. The *phia phông* were not people born in Muang Van; rather they were appointed by the French authorities settled in Muang Èt.[6] They were in charge of applying the French rules on taxes, justice, or recruitment for the army, or as coolies or labor force, as discussed in the next section.

The *phông* was made up of eight villages: Houay Yong, Houay Lom, Muang Van, Ban Kang, Nasan, Nahit, Nalèng, and Ban Sot. Yesteryear's authority of the *phia phông* of Muang Van is acknowledged in Houay Yong [90] – this is not very different from the present-day situation: Muang Van is currently the administrative seat of the *kum baan*, the main authority of which is Buasai, from Houay Yong (see pages 41–42).

Still based on the interviews in Muang Van, the villages controlled by the *phia phông* of the area were each represented on a committee, the *kum pèèt*, literally "group of eight" representatives of the villages. This indicates that there were two authorities based in Muang Van: the *phia phông* and the representative of the village Muang Van. The "group of eight" resorted to the *kum sii*, a "group of four" people who were the close colleagues of the *phanyaa* or *phia phông*, who was himself the head of this three-level hierarchy. When a deer was killed, the *phanyaa* was supposed to get a better share than the *kum sii*, who were themselves supposed to get a better share than the *kum pèèt*.

As it appears from this description of the system of positions, the local society was highly structured. It has often been described as a feudality (Maspero 1950 [1929]: 25; Condominas 2006 [1980]: 302–308), or a system of vassalage, which in my view captures the multi-layered system of allegiance quite well, involving many incumbents, who could rise or fall along the ladder of the hierarchy. Besides the high positions at the top of the polity, there were also a lot of secondary titles, such as *thao* or *sèèn*, which were awarded to leaders in charge of, respectively, one or two *tao*, that is, a group of ten houses (Bobo 1898: 572). In our interviews, the title of *sèèn* was reported for village chiefs in Houay Yong (see page 46n13), Ban Kang (see page 82n17), Nasan (see pages 76, 83n24), and Pakfèn [257].

Such a system of vassalage supported the structure of nested polities in the whole region, or in the kingdom, considering that the king of Luang Prabang was acknowledged as the head of the polity.

The colonial regime from 1893 to the 1930s

A colony seen from the road

When heading for the archives conserved in Aix-en-Provence, I expected to find substantive information on Houay Yong under the colonial regime. This was all the more needed because this period elicited few comments during my interviews, and remained a gap between the two foundation events passionately related by the villagers: the migration from Vietnam during the Chinese invasions and the First Indochina War that triggered the second migration wave. I thought there would be maps, or sketches showing the location of the different villages in the *Huai Yoong* valley, lists of successive chiefs, minutes on successions, statistics on the economic activities, a survey on the ethnic groups living in the valley, and reports on the Japanese occupation and the expulsion of the last Tai Soi in 1945–1946. Nothing of this sort appeared, despite consulting several hundred documents related to the province of Houaphan. As already explained on page 28, I found out only one mention of the village, in a provincial census of gun owners dated 1902, with the view to raise taxes (Figure 4.1).

Let's try to see the glass half-full. This sole mention has at least two implications: first, the village already held that name at the time; second, Houay Yong must have been quite important in the microregional context for the number of gun owners (three people) is similar to the one reported for Muang Van, the seat of the canton; there are also two gun owners in Ban Sot, in the eastern adjacent valley, but no other village of the present subdistrict is mentioned in the list. The names of the gun owners of Houay Yong, "Sène Bane, Khouang Thay, Khouang Thy" are very interesting: even if the second and third names did not appear during our interviews, Sèèn Baan has been mentioned independently by Thaabun and Thoongsôm among the earliest chiefs of the village.[7] This is another piece of evidence that oral history can be reliable for events that took place over a century before. *Sèèn*, as mentioned above, was a title awarded to people in charge of at least 20 houses, which provides basic demographic information. Whether Sèèn Ban was a Tai Soi or a Tai Vat cannot be determined from the name alone.

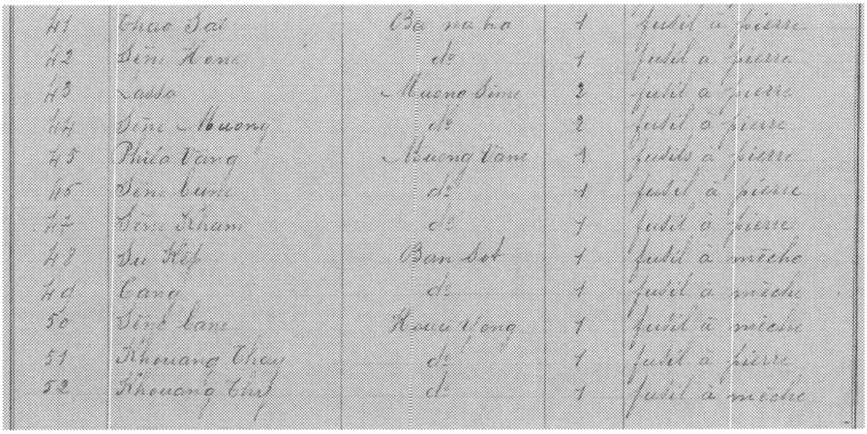

88 From the French colony to the present

Figure 4.1 The 1902 census for gun owners, by Wartelle. Detail of the second page for the district of Muang Èt. Muang Van, Ban Sot, and Houay Yong (spelled Houa Yong) appear on lines 45–52 (RSL E3, 4/5/1902). Credit: Archives Nationales d'Outre-Mer (France).

It is possible that further research in the archives will provide more results, but I doubt there is much more to find. My reading progressively revealed that colonial reports referred mostly to villages on the passable roads of the province: administrators rarely ventured on inland tracks. The only mention of a French administrator who in all likelihood ventured into the *Huai Yoong* valley concerns Wartelle, the officer who consolidated the list of gun owners. In his administrative inspection of April 1902, he reported:

> From Muong het (Muang Èt), I went to Mg vane (Muang Van) on the song ma (the River Ma); I vaccinated,[8] people seem to be happy and do not complain, the road is passable and well maintained, I visited the few villages that depend on it [on Muang Van], I have also seen silkworms, I see that it propagates and I appreciate this. Still on the road along the song ma, I visited Sop sane [Sop San, the last village on the road before entering Xiang Kho district].
>
> (RSL E3, 5/4/1902)

Unfortunately, Wartelle does not mention the names of the villages depending on Muang Van that he visited, but, as most of the dependencies of Muang Van are concentrated in the *Huai Yoong* valley, one can guess that he came up the stream. It is plausible that his visit in April 1902 explains why, a month later, in May, the name of three people from Houay Yong appeared on the list of gun owners concerned with taxation. Evasion of taxes was certainly the norm in the hinterland, but the coming of a colonial officer made them more difficult to

Figure 4.2 Spinning the silk in Nasan (May 2011).

dodge. Wartelle's observation about silkworms is also interesting, because some villagers of the valley raise these insects on a limited scale up to the present day, and still spin the silk manually as I was able to observe in Nasan and Houay Yong in 2011; four families of mostly elderly people still raise silkworms in Houay Yong [259].

Such out-track inspection is very uncommon among the reports I consulted, and this April 1902 survey by Wartelle in the hinterland cantons is an exception. Another exception is the 1925 inspection in the district of Sam Tai by Lagreze, who acknowledged in very relevant terms the lack of information on the hinterland: "between Xieng-Mene and Xieng-Poune, there are no fewer than twelve villages that are not reported on any map"; "some villages I went through had never been visited by a European" (RSL E4, 1/3/1925). This is a fascinating statement given the previous 32 years of French rule. But, apart from these rare instances, most administrative inspections[9] followed the roads and rivers, as appears in the itinerary followed by Foropon in 1926 (Figure 4.3).

Besides their focus on the on-the-road villages, colonial officers also had a perception of the local society framed by the administrative structure of the colony: the significant units were the districts (*müang*), that is, the four to eight principalities (*huaphan*) that made up the province, depending on its successive reorganizations. There is a lot of information in the archives about Muang Èt and Xiang Kho, because both used to be district headquarters – and even, for Muang Èt, the seat of the provincial administration for a few years (see page 86). State officers sometimes also mention villages that shelter the headquarters of a *canton* (subdistricts; *taasèèng*), such as Muang Van, but the villages depending on them

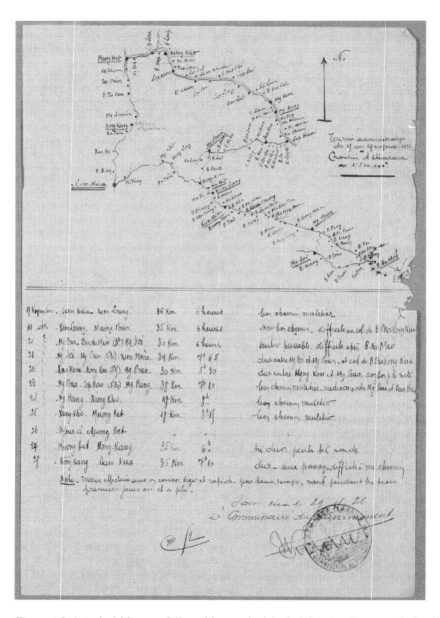

Figure 4.3 A typical itinerary followed by a colonial administrator, Foropon, during his inspection tour of November 1926, along the roads and the rivers of the Province (RSL E4, November 1926). Muang Èt ("Muong Het") and Xiang Kho ("Xieng Kho") are underlined on the upper left of the map; Muang Van appears in between. Note the remarks on the quality of the roads in the last column.

Credit: Archives Nationales d'Outre-Mer (France).

From the French colony to the present 91

are rarely mentioned, except when building a road that passes through them, when there are economic activities such as a mine or a plantation, when disobedience is reported, or when there is a criminal or judicial problem. Hence Houay Yong, positioned on a track to nowhere (from the colonial perspective at least), remained 'under the radar' of the French administrative reports during the whole period.

Despite this frustrating result, archives and published colonial documents provided a lot of information on the province at large: on administrative (re)organization, demography, economy, ethnic categories, mobilities, law and courts, conflicts inside the colonial establishment, and, of course, precolonial history, as attested throughout Chapter 3. Let us examine successively the information available on demography and ethnicity, on taxes, trade, and administrators' conflicts, on infrastructure, and on religions.

Censuses and ethnicity

The first census of the population of Houaphan was taken in 1896 by the French administrator Monpeyrat (GGI 26509, 8/6/1896). In Table 4.1 the data devoted to Muang Èt and Xiang Kho are presented, compared with those of the whole province.[10]

Table 4.1 shows the interest the early colonial administration devoted to ethnic categories, an interest manifest since the very first report on the region (GGI 9211, 10/12/1893). Strangely enough, it fails to record any Black Tai (Tai Dam) for the district of Muang Èt. This demonstrates, I guess, not so much a mistake of the administrator as the fluidity of ethnic self-identification – the contextual switches across the identity of Tai Dam, Tai Nüa, and Lao have been discussed at length on pages 36–38.

Another census was made by the administrator Macey in December 1899 (RSL E2, 22/1/1900). It gives more elements on the subdivisions of Muang Èt, because the three cantons of the district are detailed.[11]

Unfortunately, the names of the six villages making up the canton of Muang Van in 1899 are not reported. Based on the list of gun owners presented before, the villages of Muang Van, Ban Sot, and Houay Yong must have ranked among the six.[12]

The figures of the table are interesting in different aspects. First, between 1896 and 1899, the population of the district fell from 2214 to 1649 people. This change might be related to various reasons, including epidemics, the translation of the provincial seat from Muang Èt to Muang Son in 1897, or the departure of refugees settled in Muang Èt who returned to their place of origin.

The average population of the villages is very low. For the district of Muang Èt, the average is 45 inhabitants per village in 1896 and only 31 in 1899. The 6 villages of the canton of Muang Van hosted 280 inhabitants in 1899 – an average of 47 inhabitants/village. We can have a raw approximation of the number of families based on the figures for married women, 53, which means that there were on average 9 families/village, each of them composed of an average of 5–6 members. But there must have been disparities, with Muang Van, Ban Sot, and

Table 4.1 The 1896 population census in Houaphan

Uaphan	No. of cantons	No. of villages	Lao	Red Tai	Black Tai	Kha	Meo	Yan	Phuphai and Phuak	Total
Muang Ȇt	3	49	1200	730	–	224	60	–	–	2214
Xiang Kho	6	139	2320	2428	745	316	105	–	65	5972
Province	41	579	15,602	10,443	745	2422	1284	20	2474	32,990

Table 4.2 The 1899 population census in Muang Ȇt

Canton	No. of villages		Total population	Men			Women			Registered	Lame	Monks	Militiamen	Newly installed
	Lao and Phu Tai	Kha and Meo		<18 years	18–60 years	>60 years	Married	Single						
Muang Ȇt	42	4	1193	105	505	31	246	306		457	36	6	4	42
Muang Van	6	–	280	38	79	9	53	101		73	6	–	–	12
Muang Sum	6	1	176	18	62	7	30	59		49	13	–	–	12
Total	54	5	1649	161	646	47	329	466		579	57	6	4	66

Houay Yong probably hosting more inhabitants than the other places if we base on the census on gun owners.

These considerations are in line with all other figures available for the province at the time: the dispersion of the population was extreme, and soon became a preoccupation for the administrators who tried to regroup people in larger units: the administrator Wartelle urged, in 1911, to reconfigure villages into units of at least 40 *"inscrits"* (registered villagers) (RSL E4, 3/12/1911).

The administrative definition of an *inscrit* is very clear in Table 4.2: an adult male aged between 18 and 60, who is not lame, or a monk or militiaman. For example, out of 79 males aged between 18 and 60 in the canton of Muang Van, 6 were lame, which gives a total number of registered villagers of 73. Interestingly, the statistics show that there was no monk in Muang Van in 1899, despite the presence of Buddhism before the 1870s (see pages 76–79). The category of *inscrits* was central for the administration, because it defined who had to pay taxes and provide labor (*corvée*) for the state.

Taxation, mandatory labor, and administrators' conflicts

The issue of taxes and forced labor is possibly the aspect of the colonial regime that surfaced most often during interviews. In Muang Van, people still remember the hardship of these duties, and the way they were enforced by the French, via the *phia phông* [81, 113]. Each family had to supply work from 10 days a year to 15 days a year; they had to provide a young man as a soldier and to pay taxes (5 piasters [*man*]/adult male). This system of taxation had a side effect: families tended to remain grouped, because mandatory labor was calculated per household unit. One informant remembers that his household sheltered up to five married couples to reduce the impact of mandatory labor on their daily lives.

The documents on taxation I found in the archives referred mostly to the early period. The administrator Monpeyrat describes clearly the system as it was implemented throughout Houaphan in 1898 (RSL E3, 2/8/1898 and 14/11/1898). The personal tax reached two piasters per registered villager – it was only one and a half piasters the year before. Altogether, the 73 registered inhabitants of the canton of Muang Van effectively paid 120 piasters, the difference with the theoretical amount of 146 piasters being partly explained by 10 percent of the total income officially due to the local authority in charge of the collection. As for mandatory labor (*corvée*), Lao and Tai had to work for free for 20 days per year, whereas the Kha and the Meo had to work for 10 days. There was a possibility of redeeming this charge through payment. The problem, explains Monpeyrat, is that only one half of the population is concerned: the numerous relatives and close acquaintances of a local authority induced the latter to exempt them from forced labor. As a consequence, only the villagers who had no privileged link with the authorities worked effectively, facing overload due to the exemption of the authorities' *protégés*. Some people worked probably as much as 80 days during 1 year.

Monpeyrat pleaded that the inconsistencies of the system should be taken into consideration; he asked for a better remuneration of the local authorities, and a reduction in the number of labor days to half. His successor – and personal enemy – Macey completely reversed the trend (RSL E2, 2/11/1901). In 1901, Macey learned about three chiefs who had not collected the taxes in their respective villages. He put them in jail and fined them 500 piasters each. All their property, including their cattle, their horses, and their pigs, was seized and sold, but the amount was not sufficient to pay the fine. The chiefs of the different districts of Houaphan sent a collective letter imploring clemency for their colleagues, a letter Macey transmitted with satisfaction to the *Résident Supérieur au Laos*, suggesting that the latter accept the request for clemency because the present case had been a successful example for everyone. Besides being strict on the payment of the personal taxes, Macey was also infuriated by the lax attitude of Monpeyrat on trade taxes, and again imposed heavy fines on the authorities who did not collect them properly (RSL E2, 31/12/1900).

This discussion brings to light at least two elements. First, there were fierce personal oppositions among colonial administrators. Tappe (2015) has already discussed the fissures of the colonial administration based on the conflict between officers who interfered in the acknowledgment of the border between Laos and Annam. The archives I consulted are replete with letters of denunciation between officers: Montpeyrat tried to annihilate all the work done by Wartelle, and took measures to back his own "brother-in-law" against the "brother-in-law" of Macey, both of these French administrators having local concubines in the princely families of Houaphan (RSL E4, 11/9/1911). Such affairs were apparently frequent, and effected by the local authorities: the head of Muang Son "gave his daughter to a European [very probably Montpeyrat] and feels free since then to do whatever he wants and to lodge complaints against all those who displease him" (RSL E2, 11/6/1899). Through such affairs, apparently frequent, the Europeans were enmeshed in the local arena, a point redressing the balance of agency between the colonized and the colonizers.

Second, the archives show how unpredictable tax imposition and forced labor must have been for the local population in Houaphan during the early colonial period. People were very differently affected, depending on their acquaintance with authorities, the year, and the French administrator in charge of the province, whose attitude could range from sensibility to brutality. There were also differences in imposition between the provinces, which triggered mobility of the villagers (GGI 20671, 24/9/1896). The uncertainty and frustration that probably resulted explain why this aspect of the colonial regime has been so vividly remembered up to the present time. This issue, which has already surfaced in the comments about greed and corruption of yesteryear's authorities, appeared in the discussion on the oral traditions of origin (see pages 80–81).

Economy and trade

Colonial economy and trade elicited interesting comments. During the first half of the twentieth century, people from Yên Châu brought cropping material and salt to the village, and bartered them for rice, chicken, ducks, or rubber[13] [19].

This lends credence to the continuity of the links the refugees' descendants kept with their relatives and acquaintances in Yên Châu. The trip between the two places took two days at the time, compared with the two hours needed nowadays on a motorbike. It must have been facilitated after 1935, when a road replaced the former track to link Houaphan to Sơn La via Sop San (RSL E4, 12/1/1935). Interestingly, this road followed the itinerary taken by Pavie in 1888 (Pavie 1919: 105–108), which attests to its old age.

Besides this short-distance trade network, long-distance trade also appeared in my informants' comments, and even more so in the archives: in fact, the whole region was involved in long-distance trade, on a west–east axis, stretching from Burma to the Vietnamese coast via Luang Prabang and the River Ma. In December 1894, the French administrator Hardy wrote:

> Two caravans, each strong of about twenty Laotian traders from Muang Èt and Xiang Kho, have departed at a few days' distance, with important loads of gum benzoin [*benjoin*, a resin used for perfumes] and lac [raw shellac, a resin produced by insects]. They were heading for Nam-Dinh [in Vietnam, see Map 3.3], using rafts to flow down the River Ma.[14] Eight days ago, about thirty traders from Xiang Kho departed for Burma, where they will exchange silk for opium and different items made in that country. They will go through Muong Ngoï [Muang Ngoi, see Map P.1] and Muong Saï [Oudomxay]. No trade movement of such importance had been observed for long. We hope this will start a regular trade between Houaphan and its neighboring regions.
>
> (RSL E2, 4/12/1894)

Explaining the preference people have trading with the maritime provinces of Vietnam, such as Nam Định, compared with the provinces of Annam to the north, Hardy explains that villagers from Houaphan "are sure to find in the provinces close to the sea all they need: salt, mats, copper saucepans, cups, European fabrics, Chinese crepons, etc." (RSL E2, 4/12/1894).

During a lively conversation, *Naai baan* Bunsoon, of Houay Yong, and the *naai baan* of Ban Sot, close to Muang Van on the River Ma, evoked this long-distance trade [258]. In the past, the River Ma was larger than it is today. People used to boat down the river to reach the sea in Vietnam, and buy salt – it was a rare condiment in the past, which was used economically. Some people, especially the wealthy, could also travel on a horse. The trip took one or two months. This went on until the 1950s, more precisely until salt became more easily available in shops. As for trade to the west, the two *naai baan* evoked the destinations of Muang Noi and Luang Prabang. This last trade concerned mainly opium, and was very lucrative for some villagers. However, it was very dangerous, and the travelers used to hire men at arms to protect them from assault by other traders.

The region was also visited by traders coming from faraway places, as noted, for example, by Monpeyrat in 1898:

> Traders from Luang Prabang have come to buy the wax and the gum benzoin of the last harvest. A caravan from Burma coming from Xieng Thong[15] has arrived in the *huaphans* of Muang Èt and Xiang Kho. They have brought English cloth and cotton fabrics, and buy in return all the spun silk available.
>
> (RSL E3, 5/10/1898)

A Chinese yearly caravan is also reported as following the River Ou and the River Èt, passing through Muang Èt and Xiang Kho, before heading for Xieng Khouang (Raquez 1905: 1326).

The trade of local products attracted a Frenchman, M. Roux, who settled in Muang Èt in 1895 or 1896 to buy gum benzoin, raw shellac, and cardamom (RSL E2, 15/12/1894; RSL E2, 25/4/1896). But his presence apparently did not last long.

The general pattern of this trade is clear: local products are sold for opium, salt, and manufactured products of European, Chinese, and Vietnamese origin.

If manufactured products and salt are the usual imports into the highlands of Laos, opium deserves more comment. The casual mention made by Hardy in 1894 related to a very early period when control of that product was not strongly enforced. Opium quickly turned out to be of great concern for the administration, which struggled to impose a monopoly on its trade. The profits were potentially huge. The selling price of refined opium reached 25 piasters for 1 kg in Houphan; in 1896, the monthly consumption in Muang Èt alone was 200 *taels* (about 7.5 kg, for a *tael* of 37.6 g), for a value of about 188 piasters (RSL E2, 14/8/1896 and 28/7/1899). The archives contain widespread mentions of the generalized consumption of opium in the 1890s. Monpeyrat even tried, with some success, to grow opium in the provincial experimental garden of Muang Son, to investigate its cultivation outside the mountain environment (RSL E2, 1/9/1897; RSL E3, 13/4/1898).

The high value of opium encouraged illegal traffic. The Lü of the Golden Triangle were active in this smuggling:

> Two Lü caravans, trading contraband opium, arrived some time ago on Houaphan territory. One of them was arrested, the opium was seized and the transaction compromise reached 300 piasters. The other caravan escaped pursuit, managed to reach Tran Ninh [Xieng Khouang] and eventually Annam.
>
> (GGI 20672, 7/1/1899)

Anyway, the trade went on for decades, and some villagers of Houay Yong took part in it [258]. In the mid-1930s, the missionary Mironneau, established in Muang Soi, declared that:

the main trade of Houaphan is the smuggling of opium; it is bought in the north of Siam, in Upper Burma, in Yunnan, and it sold to the Annamese. Poppy is also cultivated in the province, but mostly for the local consumption, which is quite high. Actually, the transport and smuggling of opium is left free.

(Mironneau 1935–1936: 713)

The main regional products for export mentioned in the early archives are silk, wax, natural rubber, cardamom, gum benzoin, and raw shellac. As already reported above, Wartelle observed that the inhabitants of the dependencies of Muang Van raised silkworms – it was therefore a contribution by the villages in the *Huai Yoong* valley to international trade. As for the other products, raw shellac merits some development because it positioned the village of Muang Èt in the network of international capitalism. Raw shellac, or stick-lac, is a resin produced by an insect, *Coccus lacca*, which was used notably for making colorants and wood finishes. Its trade was already important in the late 1890s: during Macey's investigation on unpaid taxes, he reported that, in the vicinity of Muang Èt, for one and a half days, he was able to spot four groups of three to five traders passing by, with a total of 80 kg of raw products; they were going to Takhoa, on the Black River in Vietnam (see Map 3.2), to exchange it for salt; all of them professed to be ignorant about taxes (RSL E2, 31/12/1900). Interestingly, this shows that, if long-distance trade was mainly concentrated along a west–east axis, middle-distance trade on a south–north axis with the province of Sơn La remained a possibility for common people, as confirmed by what our informants said in Houay Yong on the coming of Vietnamese merchants to their village.

The production of shellac soon became an international business in French Indochina. A French company, Gomme-Laque J.B., was established in 1921, and started the production of raw shellac in Muang Èt: in 1925, there were two European settlers working in the 120-hectare concession of this company, planted with specific trees for raising the insects that produce raw shellac.[16] It was apparently the main plantation of the company. In 1928 and 1933, the archives report tense relationships with the villagers of Muang Èt and villages upstream on the River Èt, because the employees were requested to kill buffaloes sidetracking into the plantation, which could damage the trees. The company closed its activities in 1953.[17]

In Houay Yong, a few families still collect raw shellac and sell it for a very modest price of about US$2.5/kg to Vietnamese traders. The name of this black product, *khang*, is also the name of the insect. To initiate the production, the producers take such insects and put them on the trunks of trees of the species *fen*, or *phèn*. The insects climb up the tree and produce raw shellac (probably as feces) around the upper branches. People eventually cut these branches and collect the raw shellac attached to them [258].

Blind spots

Obviously, colonial archives can provide a lot of information on economy, trade, and taxes – an observation already made by Michaud (2015) in his research on French military archives about the highlands of Tonkin. This is in sharp contrast to other domains: hygiene and health, for example, appear only as an intermittent concern in Houaphan, addressed especially during the epidemics at the turn of the century. The main problem was cholera, with epidemics mentioned in the province in 1896 and 1898; the problem must have been structural, because Wartelle reported in 1904 that "the epidemic of smallpox has come to an end, and – exceptionally, there was no cholera in Xiang Kho this year" (GGI 20671, June 1896; RSL E3, 1898; RSL E4, 27/6/1904). In 1927, there was one European medical doctor in Sam Neua, and two dispensaries under construction, one of which was in Muang Èt; in 1937, the health dispensary of Muang Èt was the only one in the province outside Sam Neua (Foropon 1927: 37; RSL E4, April 1928; Boutin 1937: 118).

As for education, it appears even less in the documents. An elementary school was active in Muang Èt in 1928, but in very poor condition; it hosted about 50 pupils in 1931 and 46 in 1941 (RSL E4, April 1928; 8–15/3/1931; RSL F6, 1941–1942). No other school was reported in its vicinity.

Religion was not a common concern either. Buddhism attracted little attention, except to mention the presence of monks during a festival (RSL E2, 1/12/1896a), or when they appeared in censuses, as in Table 4.2. The lack of any mention of Christian missionaries in Muang Èt or Xiang Kho is not due to administrative negligence: they were absent from the place – which incidentally deprives our research of a rich source of information (Michaud 2007). The only mission in Houaphan was settled in Muang Soi, and sheltered from one to five missionaries who were not at all appreciated by the French secularist officers; they opened a school, but their action remained very local.[18] As for the 'animist' religions, very little information is devoted to ancestors or territorial spirits – the former are evoked in a guide for travelers (RSL E4, 3/4/1926) and the latter appear in a document mentioning the buying of a buffalo for an annual ceremony, as well as in a description of the sacrifices and prohibitions related to the spirit of an iron mine – both references falling outside our areas of interest, Muang Èt and Xiang Kho (RSL E4, 1904–1906 and 1/3/1925).

The Japanese invasion (1945) and the departure of the last Tai Soi

If colonial rule was only sporadically challenged in the region from 1893 to 1940, things changed utterly with the Second World War. A new cycle of violence and migration was triggered, three generations after the invasions of the Chinese Flags. Despite its proximity to the present, the period between 1940 and 1953 is largely undocumented in the archives related to Houaphan that I consulted in Aix-en-Provence. Whether the documents have disappeared, are conserved elsewhere, or are still in Laos remains unclear. Oral history will hence come to the front of the research again.

The events that happened at the end of the Second World War have to be contextualized based on the French Indochina scene at large. In March 1945, just before the end of the Second World War, the Japanese took direct control of Indochina, despite the neutral status they had acknowledged for the territory up to then (see page 101). Our informants in Muang Van remember that serious fighting took place between French and Japanese in their area in 1945. Some French soldiers were publicly humiliated and tortured after the Japanese victory, their heels and nose being pierced to chain them. French troops came back afterwards, and fighting resumed, but against the Vietminh this time, because the First Indochina War had begun [113].

The departure of the last Tai Soi from Houay Yong is consistently related to the short Japanese period (see pages 4, 61, 76). Why then, and not before or after? Whatever happened, the turmoil between 1945 and 1946 offered opportunities for settling disputes, and the Tai Soi eventually suffered the consequences of the whole process.

The reasons I was given to explain their departure evolved with time. In 2010, Thaabun explained that the Tai Soi started to move back to Muang Soi a few years after the arrival of the settlers from Muang Vat; they did so because they simply wanted to go back to their place of origin [8, 90]. The same year, Bunmaa (the narrator of Narrative b, page 61) and *Naai baan* Bunsoon (see his narrative, pages 3–4) reported that the Tai Soi did move away to their place of origin willingly, with either small groups of families gradually leaving [42] or a whole group leaving together [51], because they could not cope with the industrious way of life of the Tai Vat, who created new canals for irrigation, new fields, and new ponds. "The Tai Dam get up early and come back late. So early that when they leave, they hit the dog [on the road, because it is still dark], and when they come back home, they hit the frog [for it is already the night]" [42]. This lively expression of *Naai baan* Bunsoon illustrates once more the self-perception of the ethnic group as active and hardworking, compared with the former inhabitants of the valley.

However, some elements of these early narratives point to a more antagonistic process. At some point during the interview, Bunmaa [42] mentioned that there had been a struggle (*too suu*), although it was difficult to understand who struggled against whom. He also said that, by the 1940s, there remained only six or seven Tai Soi families; during or just after the Japanese occupation (1945), a chief of district asked them to leave the valley and go back to their place of origin, which they did after having deconstructed their temple.

In 2014, the *chao süa* of Houay Lom and Houay Louang had a similar version (Narrative d): the Tai Vat and Tai Soi were not on friendly terms because the two groups competed for the title of village chief. This is why representatives of the two groups went to meet the head of the district in Xiang Kho, to settle their problem. They did so two or three times, without any result. They eventually turned to the *phia* officer in Muang Van. He asked the two parties about their belongings in the place. The Tai Soi mentioned that they had built the rice fields (*naa*), and the Tai Vat said that they had planted the fruit trees, and made the gardens. The *phia* of Muang Van declared that the Tai Vat had done more than the Tai Soi, which prompted the *chao müang* of Xiang Kho to order the Tai Soi to leave the place for the benefit of the Tai Vat. I was puzzled by this explanation, because the final decision of the authority is counterintuitive: creating rice fields seems much more important, in terms of both labor and territoriality, than planting fruit trees. So why was the decision taken in favor of the Tai Vat?

In 2018, I discussed my confusion on that episode casually with Bunmaa [245]. He reiterated that the Tai Vat were so active that the Tai Soi could not cope with that situation. But he added something new: state officers wanted to organize an election in the village so that there would be only one authority. This raised a conflict and, eventually, the Tai Soi left the place. The reference to an election appeared soon after, and independently, in the narrative of Phèèngsoon (see pages 66–67). An election of the village chief was about to take place, and the Tai Vat were dishonest: they bribed the head of district (*phia*) so that he selected the newcomers for the position. Eventually, the Tai Vat got it, and the Tai Soi thought that they would be unable to win any case afterwards, so they moved away. This statement was made by Phèèngsoon in the presence of Bunsoon and Buasai, the two main political figures of the village who attended the interview: they did not confirm Phèèngsoon's assertion, but did not deny it either.

The reason why Phèèngsoon disclosed this collective secret remains partly obscure. It puts at stake the consensual version that was provided earlier, and could endanger the legitimacy of the Tai Vat leadership in the area. Maybe, after nine years of research, our presence was judged to be harmless to the well-being of the village community. The reported bribery took place 70 years ago, during the former regime, and no Tai Soi has ever reappeared to claim any right: the risks are low. It is noteworthy that the declaration was made by one of the three top leaders of the village, in the presence of the other two. I think that our team's repeated stays in the village, the high position of our interlocutor, and the presence of his fellow *phuu nyai* (big men) were instrumental in this revelation about an issue that had perplexed me for years, as my interlocutors had probably remarked.

The First Indochina War (1946–1954)

To come to the First Indochina War, some elements of the history of northwest Vietnam, especially in Sơn La Province and Yên Châu District, are needed to clarify what happened in Houay Yong, because a large resettlement of Tai Vat from Vietnam to Laos happened during that period.

During early colonial rule, the French established a prison in the town of Sơn La. Such a remote place seemed ideal for the detention of prisoners, especially the revolutionaries and communists struggling for national liberation. The bulk of them were Kinh, the core population of the Vietnamese lowlands. The French expected that sending them to a Tai region would be the best way to cut them off from any social support. What they did not expect was that these prisoners would eventually constitute a very active cell of the Communist Party, and be instrumental in the creation of a larger movement, the "Tai Association for Saving the Homeland," the influence of which went well beyond the walls of the prison.

In March 1945, the Japanese organized a coup against the French Vichy authorities in Indochina. The confusion that ensued allowed 200 prisoners, all belonging to the Communist Party, to escape from the prison. With the help of some Tai they had won over the revolutionary cause, on 22 August this movement launched an insurrection in different places (including Yên Châu) against the Japanese troops, who surrendered a few days later. The Chinese troops of Chiang Kai-shek took control of the place on 31 August. The August Revolution had been short, but it had a deep impact on minds. The nationalist revolutionaries – grouped under the Vietminh movement – were afterwards able to retain some influence, even after the French reoccupied the area in February 1946. The final stronghold of resistance of the Vietminh included Yên Châu. It was disbanded in January 1947 and the struggle went on through guerilla warfare.[19]

To stop the extension of the Vietminh into northwest Vietnam and to set their Tai allies against them, the French, in 1948, proclaimed the autonomy of the Tai Federation within French Indochina. However, many Black Tai, including those of Sơn La Province, sided with the Vietminh, who had been able to convince them of the cause of independence, taking advantage of various frustrations left behind by the colonial regime, and playing on the Black Tai's antagonism with the White Tai elites favored by the French, who had acknowledged the latter's leader Đèo Văn Long as head of the Tai Federation. The local influence of the Communist Party cell created in the prison in Sơn La and the insurrection in the province in 1945 are among the other factors explaining why many Black Tai of Sơn La sided with the Vietminh.[20]

From spring 1948 to winter 1950, the revolutionary movement was headed by the Sơn La–Lai Châu Administrative and Resistance Committee. Through propaganda and guerilla warfare, the movement embedded those provinces into the larger Vietnamese national struggle for independence. The southern third of Sơn La, including Yên Châu District, was for the most part under the control of the revolutionaries. The new administration tried to implement measures taken by the government of the Democratic Republic of Vietnam (DRV), but it was uneasy due to the difference with the lowland setting. There was much violence at the time: former pro-French elites, and members of their family, were murdered if they did not side with the revolutionary regime; the Vietminh allied with those who had switched alliance; conscription and labor demands by both belligerents depleted villages, so that shortages and hunger often broke out (Lentz 2019: 26–60).

In the course of 1950, the Tai Federation took advantage of the strategic concentration of the DRV troops in the northeast of Vietnam to reoccupy the whole northwest. Officers of the DRV fled, often to Laos. The people in some reconquered areas, notably in Yên Châu, were concentrated in large settlements ("*gros villages*") for their control. Many escaped to settle back in their villages, and many went on helping the Vietminh despite the critical situation (Lentz 2019: 60–63).

The tide turned again, for the fifth time, in 1952. From 7 October to 10 October, 30,000 soldiers and carriers of the People's Army of Vietnam crossed the Red River and headed to the northwest region. In a few weeks, they had reconquered most of the territory, including Yên Châu. A new cycle of suffering began, marked again by conscription, labor recruitment, and hunger, plus much bombing by French airplanes of fields, buildings, and roads. Junior and senior executives, from the Kinh majority, came more and more involved with the administration of the place, in a perplexing alliance with the Tai "feudal" elites (Cầm Trọng 2004: 322; Lentz 2019: 64–132). Anyway, the DRV was able to consolidate its position in the province and develop a logistical network, which turned out to be of primary importance for the final victory of Điện Biên Phủ (May 1954) that would expel conclusively the French from the area, and sound the death knell of their colonial empire (Lentz 2019: 133–203). Ironically, the stratagem to seclude Kinh revolutionaries in the faraway prison of remote Sơn La, in the Tai social context, literally contributed to the fall of a world power that would never recover afterwards.

To turn to the situation in Laos, the country had, of course, been much affected by the situation in Vietnam. Unfortunately, the sources on Houaphan during the First Indochina War are much scarcer than those on the neighboring provinces of Vietnam: there is nothing like the detailed monograph of Lentz (2019) on the northwest region, and I could not find relevant archives at Aix-en-Provence. The Lao nationalist movement during that period was the Lao Issara, which occupied parts of Houaphan province from 1946 on (Stuart-Fox 1997: 71). The Lao Issara eventually transformed into a government, the Pathet Lao, which began to organize revolutionary activities in the Laos–Vietnam border region in 1951 (Stuart-Fox 1997: 78–81). In fact, these revolutionary activities were largely fueled by the Vietminh. For example, from 1948 to 1950, the armed propaganda teams of the Sơn La–Lai Châu Administrative and Resistance Committee were active not only in Vietnam, but also in Laos (Lentz 2019: 27).

The very last years of French presence in the vicinity of Muang Èt were marked by a progressive militarization to counter the growing influence of the Lao Issara and the Vietminh: the French built barracks in Muang Èt, on the top of the hill where a telecom antenna is currently erected [113]. The French soldiers used to patrol on a path on the ridgeline between the *Huai Yoong* valley and the provincial road PR3201, which allowed radio signals to be captured. The path connected the fortified position in Muang Èt to an airport in the south, in *Nong Thaam* village – this was explained to our team during a walk in a mountain area south of Houay Yong [246–247]. When French soldiers came to the villages, the inhabitants had to provide support for them [106]. The Vietnamese soldiers hid in the forest during the daytime, coming out only at night; some of them came to Houay Yong to have discussions with the Lao Issara; the French learned at some point that Vietnamese soldiers were in Houay Yong and came to the place; a Vietnamese soldier who tried to escape was killed by them [215]. At some point, maybe in relation to this last episode, people were jailed in Sam Neua [262]. Sèènbun, the last chief (*phanyaa baan*) of Houay Yong under the former regime, had been appointed to this position because his brother was the head of *taasèèng* (subdistrict) of Muang Van: he had to satisfy the demands, especially of food, made by both the Lao Issara and the French; he was like a "bird with two heads" (*nok soong hua*), able to deal with both parties to avoid problems [217] – a posture adopted by many Tai Dam chiefs in Vietnam as well (Lentz 2019: 56). Being a chief was indeed extremely dangerous at the time: Phia Kham, the *phia phông* working in Muang Van, was assassinated in 1952 [81].

After the northwest campaign of October 1952, the People's Army of Vietnam had regained most of the former Tai Federation territory. Troops were secretively positioned along the border with Laos. In April 1953, a major offensive was launched under the command of General Giap. Two divisions of the People's Army of Vietnam were involved, not including the tens of thousands of carriers necessary for the supplies.[21] It was a massive success: in a few days, it secured the Lao provinces of Phongsali and Houaphan. The aim of this campaign was officially to assist the revolution in Laos. But as Hô Chi Minh wrote to his army, "By helping the people of an allied country, it means we are helping ourselves." Giap was, for him, thinking in geostrategic terms: it is not by chance that the two 'liberated areas' formed a buffer area for the ongoing war in the northwest, and were instrumental in the fall of Điện Biên Phủ in May 1954.[22]

Informants in Muang Van remember how the French were eventually defeated after a battle with the Vietnamese in their village [113]. Sèènbun, the *phanyaa baan* of Houay Yong, resigned from his function to avoid any problem, because he had been authoritative and feared retaliation. He was not killed afterwards, but his family left the village, and his descendants currently live in Nalèng, a few kilometers east of Muang Van; it is difficult to determine if this is the consequence of a political measure or not [217, 233]. Old inhabitants of the *Huai Yoong* valley also remember the first independence festivities that were organized by propaganda groups of performers, who went from one village to another after the victory [76].

The influx of refugees in Houay Yong (1951–1953)

The detailed description of the events that occurred in northwest Vietnam during the First Indochina War had a specific aim: to provide the background of the massive migration that impacted Houay Yong and Houay Lom heavily. The two villages had to host refugees from Yên Châu who fled the fighting, or the political turmoil ignited by the revolutionary war. These refugees took advantage of the historical and familial links between their region and the two Tai Vat villages to settle in the latter. Other villages of the valley with little or no Tai Vat population, such as Nasan, Ban Kang, and Muang Van, were largely spared from this influx of migrants: this supports the idea that ethnic links between the Tai Vat of

Laos and those of Vietnam were still very effective at the time. In fact, the links between them had remained active after the coming of the first settlers, notably through trade (see pages 94–95).

We have seen that beginning with the August 1945 Revolution in Sơn La, the area of Yên Châu had been taken over no less than five times up to 1952. Some people moved from Yên Châu to Houay Yong probably as early as the French reconquest of February 1946. Thoongsôm explains that, after the defeat of the Japanese in Yên Châu where his family lived, the French gathered people together to determine who had collaborated with the enemy (and, one may presume, with the Vietminh who were active in the area until January 1947), and burned the houses of those who had; he links his family's move to Laos with these events, explaining that, after the death of his father, in 1946, his mother married a man from Houay Yong and settled in the village with her children. Our informant Bunheuang's brother-in-law had married a woman of Houay Yong in 1949; this is why his family eventually resettled there in 1953, when they fled the conflict [34, 36, 106, 191].

To give a more contextualized idea of the way people remember this period, I leave the floor to Mèèthao Leua (see page 58). She was very young at the time, but she learned the story from her mother [242]. Her family was living in Bản Ngùa, in the current commune of Chiềng Pắn. Her father, who carried food for the (Vietminh) army, was shot dead. His own brother, who was a soldier, gave the bad news to the home village. There was no car at the time, so people carried the corpse back to the village in the middle of the night. It was raining and there was thunder. On the same night, the close village of *Baan Booi* was attacked, because it was suspected of helping the Vietminh – Mèèthao Leua thinks that assault could be linked to the death of her father. Two people who tried to escape were killed. Her family prepared chicken and food to make a ceremony to clear the sky. The thunder struck many trees around the village.

The departure of Mèèthao Leua's family apparently came later. It happened during "the year with much bombing." There was nothing to eat and the poverty was terrible, which explains why many people left, always during the night-time, to settle in Laos, where the bombing was much less severe. Her family was late in quitting, compared with many others who had already settled in Houay Yong.

Mèèthao Leua's account movingly reveals many dimensions of everyday life during the conflict: the massive recruitment of local soldiers and carriers for the army; the contiguity of the belligerents; the toll of death on families; the intensification of bombing; the hunger and poverty; the embeddedness of rituals with the war's violence; and the flow of refugees to Laos. It is difficult to date the events – tellingly, the belligerents are poorly identified in her account – but the departure can be dated 1953, crossing the references to bombing and to the late arrival in Houay Yong.

The sources used by Lentz have abundant reports of the flux of Vietnamese villagers to Laos during the different periods of the war, and even after it. Statistics are sometimes available: in Mộc Châu (the district directly east of Yên

Figure 4.4 Mèèthao Leua in the cottage next to her fields, interviewed by Sommay. Similar to other elderly women in the village, she wears traditional clothes most of the time (November 2018).

Châu), 6,000 out of the 17,000 inhabitants left the place between 1950 and 1952, heading largely to Laos. In February 1953, a Lao revolutionary official complained that there was not enough food and clothes for the numerous refugees from Sơn La who had resettled in Laos (Lentz 2019: 100–101; 123).

According to the villagers of Houay Yong, the influx of refugees became intense between 1951 and 1953, the last year being the apex of the movement. Previously, there were about 35–40 families in Houay Yong; about 30 families of refugees settled between 1951 and 1953 [19, 26]; Thaabun speaks of 70 families [90]. Out of a sample of 25 households surveyed in 2010–2011 (see page 25), at least 4 household heads were born in Vietnam; the father of 3 of them and the father-in-law or mother-in-law of 4 others settled from Vietnam during the early 1950s.

Usually, refugees moved in groups of one to three families, sometimes guided by a relative already living in Houay Yong. When they arrived in Houay Yong, they cultivated swiddens on the slopes of the mountains. But after two or three years, when it became apparent that they would stay permanently, they were given access to the communal rice fields, based on the size of their family.

Informants acknowledge the war as the main reason for leaving Yên Châu, but sometimes in an indirect way, or with secondary reasons. Koongvaakhuu, father of *Naai baan* Bunsoon, was among these refugees (see page 41). He and his relatives, seven people altogether, left their home place in 1953 for two reasons according to his children: the taxes were high and war was raging [42, 43, 154]. Another informant said that the Viet soldiers warned the population against bombing and induced them to go [34]. This narrative about a movement induced by authorities is also supported by migrants coming from Houay Yong currently living in Thongnamy [55]: according to them, the local authorities reminded the Tai Dam that, although they were living in Vietnam, they had Lao customs, which induced them to move to Laos. They also mention the role of Chao Phèènkham, the leader of all Tai Dam according to them, who was working with the French against the Vietminh; he asked the Tai Dam to leave for Laos in 1952–1953. This is why so many Tai Dam moved to the present zone of Xaisomboun, which was at the time part of the Xieng Khouang province, in Laos [55]. In fact, Chao Phèènkham was the title given to Đèo Văn Long, the White Tai ruler of the Tai Federation mentioned on page 101, or to one of his major deputies (Le Failler 2014: 438).

An elder of the village of Ban Hap, in Xiang Kho District [235], gives an overview of the situation in the district at large. He explains that many Tai Dam and Tai Vat fled Vietnam during the period; they took refuge in many villages along the River Ma Valley, on the Lao side of the border. They usually moved in small groups of two or three families and spread out across many villages before they re-concentrated, in a second phase, in specific ones such as Houay Yong. Apart from the dangers of the fighting, many people fled because of the coming of Kinh (or Viet) people into their region, which was another consequence of the conflict. Many people considered that they were, culturally and linguistically, closer to the Lao, and left their home region with this consideration in mind. This elder also mentions that some refugees had collaborated with the French, and tried to disappear, settling in tiny villages of remote valleys.

Let us try to disentangle the information at hand about the motivations of the refugees. Among the different reasons provided by our informants to explain what triggered the movement, some of them are obvious: people fled the war, the conscription, the taxes, and hunger. However, based on these blatant motivations, how do we explain why very few people came back when the fighting came to an end, in 1955? If the conflict had been the sole reason for moving, one would guess that people would come back after its resolution – which did not happen.

The explanation referring to the growing presence of the Kinh and their cultural difference with the Tai is interesting, but seems to be unsubstantiated. At this early stage of the 1950s, the Kinh certainly had no view to clear out and settle in large numbers in the area. According to field researches carried out in Yên Châu, the first settlement of Kinh farmers from the Red River lowlands took place in 1963, when a group of 30 pioneers came from Hưng Yên Province and settled in the district (Ha Thi Hong Lan *et al.*, 2011). This followed the resolution of the third National Meeting of the Vietnamese Communist Party, in 1960, to reshape the demography of Vietnam and relocate the productive forces between the different regions, which eventually prompted, from 1961 to 1998, the migration of 2.8 million people outside their province of origin; it affected the Northwest Highlands strongly, as discussed by Andrew Hardy in his book *Red Hills* (Hardy 2003). With this chronology in mind, I believe that the Kinh presence referred to in the interviews is overemphasized, or is a retrospective look into the past about a current concern. The presence of the Kinh was not an important factor to prompt the flux of refugees in 1952 and 1953. However, the Kinh became more and more numerous with time, and are currently present in all villages, and in all village or commune boards: their presence has become an everyday reality in Yên Châu, and the Tai have lost most of their leadership at the regional and local levels. This might explain why their relatives or neighbors currently settled in Laos, who are not confronted with a similar issue, sometimes justify the former generation's migration to Laos in cultural or ethnic terms, based on a comparison with the current situation of the Tai in Vietnam.

It is also possible that some refugees were direct collaborators with the French, as mentioned by the elder from Ban Hap, which could explain the small numbers of those who came back to Yên Châu after the end of the conflict. The bulk of them had no strong link with the earlier regime, but they possibly feared retaliation for their behavior or, simply, they found out that the situation was easier in Laos, due to the presence of relatives, the availability of agricultural land, and their cultural and linguistic proximity with the Lao ethnic majority in Laos.

Whatever the motivations of the refugees, the movement stopped in April 1953, when the offensive led by General Giap took control of Houaphan. I never heard any mention of refugees after 1953.

The Second Indochina War (1955–1975)

After the capitulation of the French in Điện Biên Phủ (May 1954), the First Indochina War came to an end in July 1954 with the Geneva Agreements: Vietnam was divided into North and South Vietnam, Laos and Cambodia gained full independence, and the Pathet Lao was acknowledged as an official faction in the reunification of Laos (Zasloff 1973: 45; Stuart-Fox 1997: 84–85; Michaud *et al.* 2016: 149). But peace did not last long, because the Second Indochina War started in 1955.

During this period, Houaphan was under the firm control of the Pathet Lao government.[23] The former *phanyaa baan* were replaced by *naai baan* as village authorities. As the Pathet Lao government was allied with the North Vietnamese regime, the issue of the Vietnamese Tai refugees in Laos eventually surfaced. There were very few returnees after 1954. In Houay Lom, where 20–40 families had taken refuge during the peak of the conflict, only 3 families settled back to Vietnam in 1955, after the Vietnamese government explained they could come back safely: the refugees considered that the living conditions and the possibilities for doing *hai* and *naa* (swidden and irrigated rice fields) were better in Laos [71]. The social, cultural, and political arguments advanced just above page 106 should also certainly be taken into consideration. According to the elder from Ban Hap mentioned above [235], in the early

1960s, when it appeared that most refugees would not come back, the Vietnamese and Lao authorities had discussions and the former announced that those who wanted to stay in Laos could do so with the exception of those who had committed offenses – that is, mainly, collaborators with the French, who had to go back and be judged. According to this elder, a few people were convinced of this, were repatriated, and never came again.

During the whole Second Indochina War, young people of Houay Yong had to enlist in the revolutionary army for a period of three years; some of them did longer [36, 40, 44, 71, 181]. The memory of this period is very fresh because all families were concerned, and most male elders (as well as some women) have been soldiers. They keep their old uniforms and wear them when pictures can be taken (Figure 4.5); their old military caps are still used in everyday life.

Young women had positions as nurses or workers in the Pathet Lao institutions; some supplied the army on the front, or fought as soldiers. Villagers had to provide food to the soldiers in the mountains. There was no fighting precisely in Houay Yong, but there was some in Muang Van (with a severe bombing in 1964 [113]), Muang Èt, and Xiang Kho. Fortunately, also, Houay Yong was spared from bombing, but the school had to be relocated in the forest, because of fear of the conflict: General Vang Pao's 'secret army,' supported by the CIA, was active in the region [44, 113]. In all the villages, people had to live in the

Figure 4.5 Somphan, a Houay Yong veteran, displaying his military awards and uniform (June 2010).

forest, as was reported in Nasan.[24] Some of them dug underground shelters to hide from the bombing, notably in Muang Van [113]. Bombing was much less severe than in regions such as Xieng Khouang, resulting in little unexploded ordnance that could be cleared rapidly after the conflict [247].

I have not inquired about the participation in fighting, which seemed a sensitive issue. An important aspect to highlight is that the village was, as was the whole province of Houaphan, on the 'good' side of the revolution, which gave its population a political pedigree still relevant and valuable today, but sometimes despised by those who think that the people from Houaphan benefit from government advantages. Another point is that being preserved from bombing and the other aftermaths of the war is nowadays often attributed to the power of the local spirits [241], a fact showing the strong connection between secular and spiritual concerns among the Tai Vat.

The end of war with the proclaiming of the new regime in December 1975 was, of course, a relief.

From the revolution to the present

During the war, Houaphan Province sheltered the capital of the Pathet Lao government, in Viengxai (see Map P.1). The administration was moved to Vientiane after the end of the conflict, but the province retained a privileged status, and is still referred to as "the cradle of the revolution." As a 'safe' zone, Houaphan was chosen to host prisoner camps after the war. Some villagers remember the soldiers coming from the former Royal Lao Army who had to build a road leading to Vietnam, while their officers had to follow "seminars" (*samana*) of political reeducation [62].

A collectivization policy was adopted after the 1975 revolution. Even if this reorganization of the village production system entailed a drop in the production of rice, here as elsewhere (see Evans 1990), it is remembered as a tough but not a tragic period; a villager, who was a policeman at the time, even regrets the passing of this system. Another revolutionary policy was the campaign against "beliefs," which is described on pages 167–169.

During the 1980s, the regime progressively left the cooperative system off and relaxed the prohibition on rituals. In 1986, the Fourth Congress of the Lao Communist Party adopted a new strategy of market economy under state control (Évrard 2004: 16; Pholsena and Banomyong 2006: 27). The economic openings induced by this new policy were mostly visible in the lowlands and benefited the remote province of Houaphan only marginally. The period was also one of resumption of international relations for Laos, which stimulated the elaboration of development projects under the aegis of foreign or international agencies. In 1991, the World Health Organization supported the building of a two-kilometer canal on upstream *Huai Yoong* to irrigate new paddy fields in the south of the village, and an American agency helped to build a small dam on the stream [41, 50].

In the highlands, the most influential post-1986 policy was related to stopping swidden cultivation (*hai*) throughout all mountain regions of Laos. Officially endorsed in 1989 (Évrard 2004: 16, 20), it has been implemented since the middle of the 1990s and resulted in the resettlement of many highlanders from areas where irrigated agriculture was not an easy option. Situated in a small valley, Houay Yong can hardly provide enough paddy fields for the whole population. Emigration was officially encouraged, and ten families left the village in 1998 to settle in Nam Mo (see Map P.1), in the present Xaisomboun province, under the leadership of the former *naai baan* Koongsing. After that, in 2000, five families departed for a new village opened to migrants in the mid-1990s in the province of Bolikhamxay: Thongnamy (Petit 2006, 2008a). If migration to Nam Mo was not a big success, migration to Thongnamy – which was not organized by the state authorities – turned out to be much more attractive. Currently, about 60 families originating from Houay Yong have settled there, draining possibly one third of the total population. From around 2005 on, the population of Houay Yong decreased steadily due to a third flux: teenagers and young adults leave more and more to go and work in the capital, Vientiane (Petit 2015). The consequences of emigration are many. The pressure on land has been alleviated in the village; a demographic gap has appeared for the generation aged 15–30 years, and remittances have created a new economy that allows families to build new houses or buy new commodities (Petit 2020).

The changes are really noticeable in the village's appearance. In 2011, Houay Yong received the title "cultural village" (*baan vatthanatham*), a status provided by district authorities to villages that present a series of criteria linked, according to the *naai baan*, to the respect of ethnic traditions,[25] and then the title of "developed village" (*baan patthanaa*) in March 2013, based on criteria of economic and social development. Other achievements (such as those of model healthy village, criminality-free village, etc.) are listed on blue panels displayed on the official billboard at the center of the village (Figure 4.6). These are important sources of collective pride. *Naai baan* Bunsoon, for example, declared proudly that Houay Yong had more boards than the other villages of the valley, including Muang Van, the seat of the *kum baan* [215]. As already explained (see pages 41–43), Houay Yong holds the leadership at the subdistrict level, and its authorities are keen to keep this first rank through the receipt of accomplishment boards and similar certificates from the district authorities. This observation is in line with Holly High's view that such official titles are usually a reward provided to villages that are in line with the regime policies and have strong connections with the local state; they are a clear advantage for attracting further development projects from the state, or from international cooperation.[26]

Archives, the colonial order, and the transborder connections

Before concluding this chapter, the most archive-oriented of the present book, I would like to consider more generally the use of archives and colonial documents in my research. As already explained, Houay Yong appeared as such only once in the archives, on a census document. Archives were not useful for detailing the microlocal context of the mountain valley, but they provided the basis for a regional frame on which local information could be checked, or given

From the French colony to the present 111

Figure 4.6 The boards of achievements in the central place of the village (June 2014).

a wider meaning. Colonial documents turned out to be most useful to understand the context of the successive waves of migration – the Tai Soi and the Tai Vat – that peopled the valley in the nineteenth century, as discussed in Chapter 3. Similarly, the role of Muang Van as a local seat of power was more precise when our field data were consolidated with written sources. As for the changing structures of the administration, the system of taxation, and the economic activities, the archives provided more details than the memories of our informants. Other domains well covered by the archives are communication and justice, which I did not investigate much because they had no direct link with the research conducted up to now in Houay Yong.

Overall, on all those domains, the confrontation of oral data with colonial written sources allowed a "play on scales" (Revel 1996), that is, an inducement to consider a same reality under different optics. For example, the current literature on the First Indochina War focuses on the successive offensives and counter-offensives that eventually led to the fall of French Indochina – itself a landmark of the fall of European colonialism across the world, and of the rise of a new world system based on the Cold War. But, at the other end of this continuum, the micro-histories of the villagers who fled in the thousands from Vietnam to Laos remain completely unexamined by the literature. This consideration could be extended to Chapter 3: although there are more and more scholarly contributions on the successive invasions and fighting in the region since the 1870s, little is known about the efflux of refugees, the influx of new settlers, and the reorganization of the local society to cope with the situation of violence that lasted for almost two decades. The oral testimonies triggered by our research produced original information on these historical processes. Things can also be seen the other way round: using archives and colonial documents ensured that our monographic approach, concentrated on first-hand oral research in a few villages, did not regress to localist complacency.

Blind spots also appeared in the archives: they must be reported, because negative findings are also findings. I mentioned on page 98 that religion, education, and health were not major concerns for the colonial administrators. This is even more obvious with kinship, marriage, domestic life, village ceremonies, death, or microlocal politics. All this corroborates that the French did not interfere much with the intimate aspects of the local society: law and order had to be respected, taxes had to be paid and labor provided, but the administrators were not interested in the other dimensions of the villagers' lives, or did not report them in the archives. Such a shallow colonialism – which could be punctuated by brutal affirmations of violence – is related to the limited presence of the French. Based on the census of 1936, Houaphan Province had a total population of 57,031 inhabitants, out of which there were only 10 Europeans, who were probably concentrated in the provincial center of Sam Neua (Boutin 1937: 117). As I have argued, hinterland villages were rarely visited by colonial officers, and what happened below the canton or district level largely escaped their control. This certainly empowered local authorities, which, thanks to French backing, held a direct and extensive authority on their subordinate villagers, as noted recently by Tappe in the same province (Tappe 2015: 381; 2018: 65, 67). The governance of Houaphan can hence be described as a clear instance of indirect rule, with all the room for maneuver this situation can cover.

This matches very well with my interviews in Houay Yong and neighboring villages, which rarely mentioned the presence of Frenchmen, but insisted on the pyramidal structure at the bottom of which lay their village society. For example, I repeatedly asked Thaabun, the local historian, about the structure of the old polities. His answer seemed uninteresting at first, but I consider now that it reflects properly the distant relationship people had with the colonial state through lower administrative intermediaries. Thaabun said [8]:

> The French were organized as lieutenants, captains and commanders; or as head of the district or of the province. But we did not know what they did: it was their job. We followed their political and administrative system. The province rules over the districts, the districts rule over the villages, and that's it. For instance, they recruited soldiers or workers: families having children above a certain age sent them to serve in the French army.

Indeed, villagers had no concrete interactions with the upper levels of the colonial administration. The chief of canton in Muang Van must have been their usual contact with this structure; "and that's it," as Thaabun concluded. Here again, compared with an overall appraisal of the French colonial rule in Laos, investigating the issue of the colonial relation at the microlocal level obliges reconsideration of this reality through the casual experience of a remote village in a mountain area.

This chapter, as well as Chapter 3, has highlighted the strong historical links between the *Huai Yoong* valley and the Tai Vat core area in Yên Châu. It is a very striking example of the way connections between resettled families and their area of origin have been kept active for 80 years (from around 1872 to

1952) and provided a favorable ground for a new wave of migration three or four generations later. It is tempting to see this through the lens of a cyclic history, and some Tai Vat use this reference when discussing their present mobility. For example, Mèè Chét, who belongs to the five pioneer households who settled in Thongnamy in 2000, explained their migration through a comparison with the group's ancient history [155]. She underscored that the patterns of migration followed by the pioneers who left Vietnam to settle in Houay Yong were exactly the same as those followed by the migrants who left Houay Yong to settle in Thongnamy (Petit 2015: 419). The parallels between yesteryear's migrations and the current pioneer fronts evoked on page 110 are a central element of the group's subjectivity. More broadly, her interview gives a good idea of the way people use past events to give sense to their present and their future, through homology (as in this case), causality, contrast, and other figures that would require more attention.

If the connections between the villagers of Houay Yong and Yên Châu have been strong in the past, their intensity has apparently declined in the present day, although they are still active on a limited scale. There are still family visits in the two directions. Recently, Thoongsôm traveled with his grandson Chuang to Yên Châu, to allow him to get to meet his relatives over there [250]. Sometimes, people from Houay Yong access hospitals in Vietnam thanks to their relatives in Yên Châu, who provide them with their identity documents. When Houay Yong was not yet supplied with public electricity, Buasai (the main political leader) and Khamphet (the head of the Soldiers Union) went to Yên Châu to investigate the possibility for this Vietnamese district to electrify Houay Yong [44]. Unfortunately, the local authorities did not answer positively, contending that Yên Châu District was twinned with Xiang Kho, not Muang Èt.

Despite the limited link villagers of Houay Yong presently hold with their old-time relatives in Yên Châu, the latter area remains central in their self-representation. If the Tai Vat of Houay Yong could phrase their history in a single sentence, they would simply say that they came from Yên Châu. When they celebrate the New Year *kinchiang*, this reference to the home place is eminently present: Yên Châu is the cultural model to reproduce. During the festival, the villagers of Houay Yong or Thongnamy like watching videos of the dances and songs performed by the Tai Vat of Yên Châu, which from their point of view look more complex, more professional, and more organized than what they do themselves (Figure 4.7).

Such videos offer villagers a central resource to elaborate on their cultural identity. But videos are not the sole vector of this reconnection between the two places, or between the past and the present of the Tai Vat. On the slope of the mountain next to the village, the ancestral spirits brought by the pioneers who fled the havoc generated by the Yellow Flags still have a physical presence. The territorial shrines of Houay Yong (and Houay Lom), located by tradition above the living, incorporate their Yên Châu origins into the physical and religious landscape of the valley. The next two chapters are devoted to unpicking this complex telescoping of memory, territories, and rituals.

Figure 4.7 The Tai Vat of Thongnamy watching the dances and songs of Yên Châu during the *kinchiang* New Year (January 2005).

Notes

1 The villagers of Houay Yong also acknowledge Muang Van as the oldest village in the close country [75].
2 *Müang Phua* or Xieng Khouang [81]: *Müang Haang*, *Müang Muun*, *Müang Noi*, all places in Vietnam near *Samteu* (Samtai) district in Laos [113].
3 GGI 9211, 10/12/1893; Monpeyrat 1904: 131; RSL E4, 21/8/1911; Boutin 1937: 72; Tappe 2015: 372. The other detached area was Muang Sum, more to the west (see Map 3.1).
4 Sam Neua eventually became the provincial seat in 1905 (GGI 9211, 6/1/1894; GGI 20691, 21/1/1897; Boutin 1937: 72).
5 At some point after 1911, the administrative division of the province was changed again: four of the former principalities held the status of *müang* and three of them received the status of *kong*, a kind of second-rank *müang*, among which was Muang Èt (Foropon 1927: 35). In 1936, Muang Èt lost this status of *kong* to be included again in Xiang Kho, perhaps as a consequence of the formal attachment of the whole province to the Kingdom of Luang Prabang in 1934 (Boutin 1937: 118). Besides all these internal reorganizations of the province, the external borders remained quite stable, except in the early colonial rule, when four of the eight principalities were attached to Annam from 1896 to 1903 (Boutin 1937: 72; Tappe 2015; and see pages 54–56).
6 The elders of Muang Van listed the names of the ten *phia phông* during the French period: Phia Hom Somphuu, P. Kèèo Savatdii, P. Sai Somphuu, P. Sai Somphuu (second of the name), Phia Lüü, P. Phom, P. Bun, P. Phon, P. Kham (killed in 1952), and P. Suvan. Only this last one (Suvan) originated from Muang Van [81, 113].
7 The names of the village chiefs (*phaɲyaa baan*) before the 1953 revolution are difficult to list with precision. A tentative list of names, some of which certainly overlap, would include, in a provisional chronological order: Sèèn Chüaang or Thao Chüaang; Sèèn Baan (also pronounced Sèèn Vaan, and apparently also called Baa Choy); Sèèn Eun; Sèèn Nut; and finally Sèèn Bun, who resigned with the new regime [90, 215, 252, 262].
8 The document does not tell against which illness.
9 The same remark applies to the itineraries followed by early travelers such as Pavie (1919) or Lefèvre (1898), when they traveled to the region of Muang Èt and Xiang Kho in 1888 and 1895.

10 Four decades later, the census of 1936 provided the figure of 22,901 inhabitants for Xiang Kho (including, at the time, the former district of Muang Èt) out of a total of 57,031 inhabitants for the whole province (Boutin 1937: 117–118). The demographic rise is clear, possibly due to the coming of returnees who had fled the violence of the 1870s and 1880s, and/or the coming of new settlers from other districts, or from Vietnam.
11 Muang Sum (*Müang Süm*) is located in the western part of Muang Èt district (see Map 3.1).
12 The three others must be among the five remaining villages out of the list of eight controlled by the *phông* of Muang Van (see page 86 on the organization of that *phông*). Among them, Ban Kang does not fit, because it was created in the early twentieth century as a dependency of Houay Yong, at first (see page 82n17).
13 This rubber comes from native trees and lianas; this trade has been reported since the end of the nineteenth century, and was encouraged by Monpeyrat, who created a nursery in this view (GG1 20666, 11/10/1899).
14 Two years later, Monpeyrat reported the departure of "100 to 150 natives" taking advantage of the temporary navigability of the River Ma to travel to Thanh Hóa Province. It is, according to him, much more advantageous to trade with Thanh Hóa than with Luang Prabang, because salted fish can be found only in Thanh Hóa, and salt is much cheaper in Thanh Hóa than in Luang Prabang (RSL E2, 1/12/1896b).
15 Very probably the town of Kengtung, in the Shan state of Burma bordering Laos (see Map P.1).
16 All this information comes from Léger (2018), who compiled data about this company from different journals of French Indochina, in particular *L'Éveil économique de l'Indochine* (30/12/1923), *Bulletin financier et économique de l'Indochine* (16/1/1925), and *Annuaire général de l'Indochine française* (1925).
17 RSL E4, 1927–8; April 1928; 15/11/1931; November 1933. The enterprise disappeared in 1953, after the region was taken over by the April offensive led by General Giap (see page 103) (Léger 2018, quoting the *Bulletin officiel du haut-commissariat de France en Indochine*, 30/7/1953).
18 RSL E3, 1/6/1904; RSL E4, 27/6/1904, 10/3/1907, 1/11/1911 and 1/3/1925. See Mironneau (1935–1936) to contrast the administrative reports with the standpoint of the missionaries.
19 Ivarsson 2008: 208–210; Stuart-Fox 1997: 56; Cầm Trọng 2004: 289–322; Le Failler 2014: 418–467; Lentz 2019: 23–25.
20 Le Failler 2014: 427–467; Michaud *et al.* 2016: 126–127, 369–370; Lentz 2019: 15–16.
21 Comparatively, the Pathet Lao fighting forces were very limited at the time, amounting to a few hundreds fighters (Zasloff 1973: 69).
22 Deydier 1954: 30, 154; Stuart-Fox 1997: 82–84; Lentz 2019: 70–71, 141–142. The quote of Hô Chi Minh is from Lentz (2019: 71).
23 In 1958, Houaphan was pacifically occupied by the Royal Army, as a consequence of the creation of the first coalition government (Stuart-Fox 1997: 96, 98), but it was reoccupied by the Pathet Lao troops, backed by the North Vietnamese army, as soon as this coalition government collapsed in 1959 (ibid.: 108; Zasloff 1973: 15).
24 The population of Nasan used to live about 150 meters from the present village but, during the war, they hid in a jungle called *Lung*. After the war, they slashed down another area that eventually became the present village [82].
25 Holly High (Projectland: Life in a Lao socialist model village, unpublished manuscript) argues that the important point is not so much the respect of old traditions, but their transformation to fit with the current ideals of development in Laos.
26 See the note above for the reference of High's manuscript.

5 The ethnography of territorial cults

Territorial cults in southeast Asia

Historical memory is in no way confined to written or oral accounts. Landscapes, material culture, and ritual performances rank among other supports for remembering the past, in Laos as elsewhere. I mentioned in the introduction the importance of landscapes in the process of memory making (see also Pholsena and Tappe, 2013). As for artifacts and rituals, their role in the art of memory in Laos has been explored by Grant Evans in his book *The Politics of Ritual and Remembrance* (1998), which unpacks the tense relationship the present regime holds with the revolutionary past. The earlier chapters investigated the production of history based mostly on discursive data: this chapter highlights the importance of materiality and performance in this process. The difference is a question of degree: performativity is an inherent dimension to oral narratives and to rituals; books and notebooks are as material as a shrine; and disappeared rituals can be narrated without performance or material support, as I show.

In line with Chapters 3 and 4, territorial cults are approached in their link with collective memory. In the present day, their main manifestation lies in village shrines, that is, basically, wooden posts and small houses sheltering the spirits protecting the village, which are related to the first settlers, or deceased incumbents of official functions. The presence of such a shrine close to the village, the narratives about its links with the first settlers, and the rituals performed on the place actualize a collective memory for all villagers. Even if the cult is performed by a small group of elders who 'own' their ritual function, attendance at the ceremony is open to every villager and is certainly a strong vector for the collective identity of the village. By comparison with the oral traditions on origins, which circulate in a very limited sphere, territorial cults are addressed to a wider audience. In the last section of this chapter, I go beyond the village-level institutions to investigate the *dông khuaang*, an intervillage territorial cult that disappeared only two decades ago: it is instrumental in providing a glimpse of yesteryear's connections along the valley.

Such cults have sometimes been called territorial cults, in reference to their spatial dimension, and sometimes founders' cults, because they are addressed to spiritual beings linked to the foundation of the place. I use the first term because only the village shrine rituals involve specifically the spirits of founders (the *dông khuaang* addresses a much larger array of spirits), but also because it casts the issue at a supra-village, relational level. The reference to territoriality is intrinsically linked to the concept of boundaries and, consequently, to relationships with the neighboring areas, which is central to my approach.

A much-quoted text on territorial cults in mainland southeast Asia was published by Mus in 1933; its success is due partly to its translation into English in 1975, under the title *India seen from the East. Indian and Indigenous Cults in Champa*. As remarked by Schlemmer (2012: 7), Mus's article is in fact rooted in a longer French tradition of research: the sinologist Edouard Chavanes developed the concept of "gods of the soil" in 1910, and the notion quickly became popular among other scholars working in the region, especially under the aegis of the EFEO (École Française d'Extrême-Orient). Basing his work mostly on archeological and philological evidence, Mus argued that the territorial cults one can observe in different parts of Indochina have two cultural substrata: first, old indigenous cults of farmer societies dedicated to chthonian deities providing well-being and fertility; and, second, Indian religious conceptions that both adapted to and transformed this earlier layer of local practices, introducing statuary, references to Shiva, and new political meanings. Mus advocated for acknowledging the complexity of this ritual complex, which had nothing to do with "primitive" beliefs, as was argued by some researchers of this early period, and for having a comparative approach of those cults throughout "Monsoon Asia," because their presence was attested to from India to Indochina (Mus 1975: 33–34).

Another early text on the topic was authored by Maspero (1950), based on a seminar he presented in 1929 in Tokyo. This text is all the more interesting for the present book because Maspero draws on first-hand data collected during a decade among the Tai, and mostly Black Tai, of northwest Vietnam. Maspero committed to displaying the strong similarity between Tai societies and ancient China, with the intent to show that China's past could be better understood through a comparison with the twentieth-century societies on its southern borders. Here again, as with Mus, the ambition was comparative, but with China rather than India. One of the five cultural/religious institutions Maspero used in his demonstration related to the "gods of the soil," the territorial cults in ancient China and among the Tai. He showed that the two societies share many similarities on that point, the most important being the relationship of the territorial cults with their "feudal" organization. This aspect is considered at length later on (pages 164–166 and 184–185).

Archaimbault, another French ethnologist, did extensive fieldwork in Laos in the 1950s and 1960s, mostly between 1951 and 1956. His texts (Archaimbault 1956, 1964, 1973, 1991, 2014) provide extremely detailed historiographical and ethnographic data on the myths and rituals in the ancient polities of Laos: Luang Prabang, Vientiane, Xieng Khouang, and Champassak. Archaimbault was strongly committed to dealing with rituals and history at once (Lemoine 2014: 163), showing, for example, how the precise contents of territorial rituals in Xieng Khouang could not be explained without referring to the political turmoils of the nineteenth century (Archaimbault 1991: 31, 82). Another obvious quality of Archaimbault's work is its comparative dimension: he stressed the similarities and dissimilarities of rituals and myths not only among the four polities listed above, but also in neighboring areas – including the Tai Dam principalities, for which Archaimbault consulted the archives left by Maspero (Archaimbault 1991: ix). As developed pages 160–161, Archaimbault analyzed the link between autochthony and kingship in a way that is directly relevant for understanding territorial cults up to the present day. Archaimbault worked in a philological tradition turned toward exegesis. His preoccupation with transcription, detail, and exhaustivity left little room for arguments of an anthropological nature. However, his works are replete with information and theoretical intuitions for the reader ready to delve into his elaborated texts, where annexes and footnotes often amount to over two-thirds of the contents. His contributions are, hence, absolutely fascinating, and at the same time somehow elusive.

The Japanese anthropologist Tanabe (1988, 1991, 2000) conducted research in the 1980s and 1990s on territorial cults among the Tai Lü of Yunnan (China), and various populations settled in the Chiang Mai area (Thailand) and in the northern districts of Houaphan – although on a limited scale for the last. Moreover, Tanabe developed a comparative approach based on publications in various languages, including Chinese and Thai. At the heart of his concerns are: the imagination of communities through territorial rituals; the representations of ritual sacrifice; the link between autochthons and invaders that appears in legends and rituals; the political relationships, notably of domination, that the cults animate; and their transformation through history. Tanabe shows very clearly, for example, how the incorporation of the Chiang Mai territory into Siam/Thailand has changed the cult of the city pillar, through Buddhicization, bureaucratization, and heritagization in the age of global tourism; he also discusses the processes of disappearance and partial resurgence of those cults in both Thailand and Communist China.

Another central reference on the topic is *Founders' Cults in Southeast Asia. Ancestors, Polity and Identity*, a collection of articles edited by Tannenbaum and Kammerer (2003). Its geographical range is wide, because it brings to the fore case studies from both continental and insular southeast Asia. The contributors question the very notion of founders' cults, which may refer to a wide array of situations. For example, the spirits addressed in these cults are not always chthonian/autochthonous as one would guess from Mus or Archaimbault: ancestor spirits or non-local spirits can sometimes be the recipients of such religious practices as well. Tannenbaum and Kammerer also stress the adaptive dimension of the cults that have not disappeared despite modernist assumptions about their archaism. The case studies display adaptations to the entrenchment of the state, world religions, migration, or inclusion into the national narrative.[1] Similarly, in his book *Spirits of the Place*, Holt (2011: 232–258) contends that spirits, including territorial spirits, are in no way vanishing from Lao religious culture despite repeated assaults from orthodox Buddhism and varying political regimes: on the contrary, they form the basis of this religious culture, "inspiring" Buddhism rather than being reframed through Buddhicization.

The contributors to *Founder's Cults* were all interested in the stakes of these cults at the turn of the millennium, and in the people's agency dealing with them. By comparison, Mus, Maspero, Archaimbault, and other authors influenced by French ethnology (such as Deydier [1954] and Zago [1972]) focused much more on comparative analyses and religious symbolism appraised over the long term. This perspective aiming at religious comparison was given a new impetus in 2012, in a special issue of *Moussons* edited by Schlemmer (2012), which continues and renews this typically French tradition of research. *Rituels, territoires et pouvoirs dans les marges sino-indiennes* (Rituals, territories and powers in the Sino-Indian margins) resumes with a comparative approach among societies living on the fringes of Indian, Chinese, and southeast Asian polities. Territorial cults in the area, Schlemmer argues, revolve and vary around a common pattern. A link has been established with the powers of the place, often linked to a chthonian presence inscribed in the landscape, but also to other entities (including ancestor spirits). It is perpetuated and reactivated by communal rituals led by incumbents who are often presented as the descendants of the first inhabitants. Schlemmer discusses recurring features of such cults, including their material and symbolic dimensions, their links with issues of legitimacy and fertility, their importance for sustaining a sense of community, and their relationship to local hierarchies and larger political structures.

Last, but not least, territorial cults have been the topic of a workshop organized by Holly High during the Australian Asian Studies Association Conference in Sydney in July 2018. Titled "Stone Masters. The territory cults of monsoon Asia," by reference to the contribution by Mus, it was met with great success, with six successive sessions and twenty speakers. I presented an abstract of Chapters 5–7 of this book. The workshop demonstrated the extension and the vitality of those cults, and pointed to new issues such as their relationship with environmental concerns, state-sponsored heritagization, or processes of 'development,' among others.

Despite the variability of the approaches and concerns of the authors who have discussed territorial cults, most of them share some assumptions that go back to Mus's seminal text. I highlight two of them that are central to my approach as well. The first is that territorial cults have to do with dualism. This appears through various symbolic dichotomies that frame rituals or narratives: sky deities/chthonian spirits; commoners' power/kingship; village/court; peripheral polities/central polity; autochthonous presence/later immigration; female/male; local/non-local; etc. Founders' cults mediate such dichotomies at the symbolic level, resolving oppositions through ritual performance. I elaborate on this issue on pages 156–160.

A second theoretical conjecture left largely unexplored is that territorial cults are – this might seem obvious – territorialized and territorializing. They constitute a common frame, a grammar shared by neighboring communities, who acknowledge their mutual rights and statuses on this basis. As Mus put it:

> the central fact is that each collectivity occupies a limited area, and that in basing its religion upon its association with this area, its cults imply not only

a contract with the soil, but also the recognition of other contracts in the neighborhood.

(Mus 1975: 37 [1933: 383])

In this respect, Mus considers such cults as a "cadastral religion" (Mus 1975: 55 [1933: 378, 396]). This view is echoed (and quoted from Mus) in O'Connor's concluding chapter of *Founders' Cults*: such cults function as a "lingua franca of localism" that "implied the recognition of its neighbors' cults. A shared civility thus underlies ethnic and local boundaries that it leaves otherwise unquestioned" (O'Connor 2003: 282–283). This dimension is certainly most relevant, but has been left unaddressed empirically, because most anthropologists discuss territorial cults based on a *single* village or city. By contrast, I here analyze neighboring settlements, with the aim notably to understand how these cults play a role in settlement fissions, which is often evoked elliptically in the literature, and in settlement fusions, which have been ignored as far as I know. I also discuss a specific territorial cult that used to be performed in Houay Yong until a few decades ago, and involved eight or nine villages of the area, which questions the past and present centralities of the region. In Chapter 7, I broaden the scope in analyzing the diffusion throughout Houaphan of new monuments evoking territorial shrines, the prototype of which is in the provincial capital, Sam Neua. Those different sets of considerations raise, in sum, important issues about the ritual construction of territories on different scales.

Empirically, my main attention has been devoted to the Tai Vat villages in the *Huai Yoong* valley: Houay Yong and its hamlet *Naa Kuu* (which has a specific shrine), Houay Lom and Houay Louang (currently deserted but persisting ritually through a shrine in Houay Lom). Interviews and sometimes observations were also conducted in Ban Kang, Nasan, Nangiu, Pakfèn, and Ban Sot.[2]

The discussion of this chapter needs an introduction, reduced here to a vignette paragraph, to the religious practices of Tai Vat, which are very lively up to the present day. Tai Vat hold rituals in relation to various types of spirits (*phii*). There is no 'conversion' process going on, even though Tai Vat are quite aware of Buddhism, the predominant religion in the country, and have links with it through migrants living in the capital, visits to the district center of Muang Èt, and monks who are sometimes involved in territorial issues in the valley (see pages 166–167). Every house has one, sometimes two, ancestors' shrine(s), made of one or a few planks of wood fixed on a wall (Figures 5.1 and 5.2). The head of the household, or an elder acting as a representative, addresses the spirits through *thaam*, ritual formulas using archaic vocabulary; (s)he offers food and drinks to the ancestors so that they will be pleased and will keep on protecting the members of the household. Beside the spirits of the house, there are many other kinds: spirits of the forest; malevolent spirits bringing bad luck that calls for the intervention of mediums (*moo môt*);[3] spirits of the sky (*faa*) or of 'heaven' (*thèèn*) linked to childbirth and the growth of rice; etc. The village shrines I discuss here come within the broader framework of this religious system: the gestures, prayers, offers, representa-

Figures 5.1 and 5.2 Both pictures were taken in Thongnamy on the first day of the *kinchiang* New Year, during the ceremony addressing the spirits to ask their protection for the family. Figure 5.1 displays the offerings in front of which the medium Mèè Ua is reciting *thaam* prayers. Figure 5.2 shows the domestic shrine for the house spirits (*phii heuan*), at mid-height on the wall, in front of which a male elder leads the ceremony (January 2008).

tions, and divinatory practices that are presented over the following pages are similar to those appearing in the domestic rituals.

The four following sections of this chapter are devoted to the description of the shrines in Houay Yong, *Naa Kuu*, Houay Lom, and Ban Kang. The focus is on their materiality, the spiritual presences related to them, and the system of prohibitions surrounding the place. I then disentangle the role of the different office holders in charge of the institution and describe the communal ceremonies conducted on the shrines, or in relation to them. The whole chapter is very descriptive, because the ethnography of territorial cults has not usually been reported in detail (with the exceptions of Archaimbault [1991] and Tanabe [1988, 1991]); many pictures are provided to give a better idea of their material structure, and of the interactions and the atmosphere during the ceremonies.

This ethnographic material paves the way for Chapter 6, which comes back to the theoretical issues evoked in this introductory section, notably to unpack the theoretical benefits of addressing territorial cults as a "cadastral religion," as proposed by Mus, and to explore the way in which territorial cults are embedded in a hierarchical structure involving the living and the dead. The last section eventually reconnect more directly with the issues developed in Chapter 3 through a reflection on the collective memory embodied in village shrines.

The village shrine of Houay Yong

With the exception of Muang Van, which shelters a Buddhist temple, all the villages in the *Huai Yoong* valley have a ritual post called *lak man*, which can be translated as the post (*lak*) of stability/solidity (*man*) – the semantics are discussed further on pages 148–152. In Houay Yong, it is erected about 20 meters from the village houses, at the edge of a small forest on the western end of the village, at the bottom of the mountain slope. The post is made of a hard wood but not from a specific essence. It is about one meter high, roughly sculpted with a pointed tip, and surrounded by lesser posts. The *lak man* is supposed to remain unchanged and in the same place, under the shade of a big tree over which a parasitic fig tree (*kôk hai*) has developed – the latter is *saksit*, magically powerful. Describing the post, *Naai baan* Bunsoon declared, in 2009: "One does not change it, one does not mend it" (*Boo pian boo pèèng*) [4]. However, as appears in Figures 5.3 and 5.4, the *lak man* was surrounded with cement in 2010, which seems to be contradictory to the former assertion about changelessness. This issue is discussed in Chapter 7, where it appears that further changes happened due to the low quality of the cement.

The function of the *lak man* is to make people remain in the village, and to bring protection and peace (*hôm yén*, "a cool shadow") [4, 91]. In the past, some enemies were about to besiege Houay Yong, but, thanks to ceremonies to the *lak man*, they were obviated, and the *lak man* protected the village from tigers and other wild animals when dense forests still surrounded the area [64a].

Climbing up from the *lak man* of Houay Yong for a two-minute walk on a narrow path winding through a small forest, one comes to a clearing where three

Figure 5.3 The *lak man* of Houay Yong, June 2009, presented by Bunsoon. The *lak man*, in the proper sense of the term, is the post sprouting from the top of the earth cone. Note the post with a wooden plank (for offerings) on its right, the smaller (or lower) posts around, and the big tree providing shadow, on which a fig tree has developed.

Figure 5.4 The same *lak man*, seen from the tree, in June 2010. See Figure 1.3 for a detailed view.

Figures 5.5 and 5.6 The three *thiang seun* of Houay Yong, before and after their enhancement with cement and roofs (June 2009, January 2012). In Figure 5.6, the soil has been cleared from vegetation for the yearly ceremonies; jars of rice beer are prepared for the ritual.

small houses are erected on piles (Figures 5.5 and 5.6). This is the *thiang seun*, the shrine sheltering the village spirits. *Thiang* (sometimes pronounced "*siang*" in Houay Yong) usually refers to the huts farmers use as a shelter in their rice fields. *Seun* is a Tai word referring to ancestor spirits at a collective level, more specifically the spirits of the first settlers and their descendants [239].[4] The place is also sometimes called *phii seun*, referring just to the spirits, not to their houses. The latter are empty and flanked with a ladder leading to the entrance. In front of the entrance is a small forked branch on which, during ceremonies, candles are placed and lit, and at the bottom of which jars of rice beer (*lao hai*) are tied. In 2009, they were made of wood and thatch, but they were shuttered with cement and roofed with corrugated tiles in 2010, at the same time as the *lak man*.

The most important of the three houses seems to be the one on the left. It shelters the spirits of the successive *chao süa*, a position patrilineally inherited by a male descendant of the first settlers. Currently, Vôngkham holds this position. The title *chao süa* refers to the shirt (*süa*) that this office holder has to hand over to the man in charge of the ceremony at the *thiang seun*. The shirt is placed inside the *thiang seun* during the ritual, and given back to his owner after its completion. This is not a specific element of territorial cults: during rituals organized by a medium to cure or protect someone, relatives and friends of the recipient leave a shirt on a pile close to the officiating medium; their bodily souls (*khuan*) stick to the shirts, and will accompany the companion spirit of the medium during its travel into the invisible world, to help it to resolve the problem [211].

The central house shelters the spirits of all the late *naai baan*; sometimes it is specified that it concerns only those who died before the end of their mandate, when they were still in function. They go on with their duty after death. Sometimes, also, this small house is presented as hosting the spirits of all state employees (*khaalatsakan*) [29, 239].

The house on the right side is ascribed to the spirits that the first migrants brought from Vietnam. It is described as Laankham (or *phii* Laankham, or *Chao* Laankham), the name of the most important spirit for the Tai Vat, who is supposed to accompany them wherever they settle. Laankham seems actually to telescope all past generations, being at once a specific spirit and all those who came after him, a principle that applies to other kinds of spirits among the Tai Vat. Hence, we were told that, after their death, some people become Langkham, as if this word was generic [239]. This is evidenced more clearly when we come to the presentation of the shrine of Houay Lom (see page 129).

The village shrine of *Naa Kuu*

At first glance, the extension of Houay Yong as a village is unproblematic. Observed more closely, the situation is more complex, because it can be described as a twin village. On the northern end is a hamlet called *Naa Kuu*, which hosts a specific territorial shrine. A *thiang seun* is erected on the mountain slope above the hamlet; its *lak man* – which is covered by a termite hill except on its top – stands very close to a unique house dedicated to the spirits (*phii seun*). There is also a sacred fig tree (*kôk hai*) close to it, as in the shrine of 'central' Houay Yong (Figures 5.7, 5.8, and 5.9).

The existence of a separate village shrine in *Naa Kuu* is explained by the history of its foundation. Bunmaa, the present ritual authority (*chao süa*) of *Naa Kuu*, reports that his paternal grandfather Phuu Phoom (Chüang Vaan by his formal name) was the younger brother of a former chief of Houay Yong village.[5] Long ago (possibly in the 1920s), this elder brother requested Phoom to create a separate settlement north of the village, beyond the *Nam Boo* brooklet, with the view to extending the irrigated rice fields. Phoom did so, creating a small village with four to seven families that eventually became known as *Baan Naa Kuu*, due to the presence of another brooklet, *Nam Kuu*. The latter provided the water used to irrigate the new rice fields. Its name derives from the *kuu* trees that were abundant on the spot. Houay Yong and *Naa Kuu* were at the time autonomous villages with their own authorities.

Around 1954–1955, Phoom died and a village shrine was built to host his spirit, because Phoom was the founder of the settlement (*chao kôk chao lao*). Soon after, around 1957, *Naa Kuu* was administratively integrated into Houay Yong, apparently due to a village policy of the Lao Issara (the Independent Lao Government). Nowadays, the visitor could not easily see the distinction between the two villages: Houay Yong is an integrated village administratively speaking,

Figure 5.7 The *lak man* of *Naa Kuu* covered by a termite mound (on right), presented by *Naai baan* Bunsoon (in a white shirt, behind Amphone Vongsouphanh). In the background stands the *thiang seun* (June 2010).

Figure 5.8 Detailed view of the *lak man* of *Naa Kuu*. In the foreground is seen the post with a plank for offerings. On the upper right, the pointed top of the *lak man* appears above the mound (June 2010).

with only one *naai baan*, and there is no separation in the building area. But the people still point to the brooklet *Nam Boo*, which is crossed by the main road in the northern part of the village, when asked about the border between the two areas.

One can wonder why the reference to *Naa Kuu* has not simply vanished with the new situation. Why do people still care about a distinction that has disappeared, administratively speaking, for more than two generations? Although it is difficult to answer that question clearly, it can be connected with the continuing ritual identity of *Naa Kuu*: despite this administrative consolidation, the shrine of *Naa Kuu* is still the object of a yearly celebration (see pages 140–141):

Figure 5.9 The *thiang seun* of *Naa Kuu*. The ritual material has been gathered for the annual ceremony (January 2012).

The ethnography of territorial cults 129

the families of the place join together to celebrate this ritual, but they do it separately from the villagers of 'central' Houay Yong. We come back to this issue on page 147.

The village shrine of Houay Lom

Houay Lom also hosts a shrine for the village spirits, on the slope of the mountain north of the settlement, within one- or two-minute walking distance from the road. The spirits of the place are referred to as *chao kôk chao lao*, which means the founding ancestors. Village informants also relate the shrine to Laankham, the collective spirit(s) of the Tai Vat mentioned in Houay Yong (see page 125). In fact, the interview with Koongvaa about the origins of Houay Lom (translated on page 64) already mentioned Laankham. Koongvaa explained very clearly that, after the first settlers eventually died, they became "the Laan, the Kham" for the village. This is a sound piece of evidence that Laankham cannot be equated with a single, specific spirit: it is a more general principle, by which ancestors lose part of their individuality (and their name) to reach a more generic power active at the collective level. Archaimbault (1991: 48–50) reports a similar phenomenon in Xieng Khouang, where Lo Kham, the founder of the dynasty, is a generic name for the successive incumbents.

The *lak man* (Figure 5.10) is here quite different from those of the two villages evoked up to now: it is shorter (a bit less than half a meter), painted blue with white stripes and numbers referring to its carving in 2013 [196, 198]. It is

Figure 5.10 The *lak man* of Houay Lom. The numeral 13 appears on top of it, in relation to the year of sculpture, 2013 (June 2014).

protected by two surrounding lattices of bamboo, and located above the houses of spirits (contrary to their respective positions in Houay Yong). Another difference is that here there are four *thiang* houses instead of three. From right to left, we have first a house for the founding settlers of Houay Lom; it is referred to Thao Phèèng, the late father of Koongthéé (the present *chao süa* of the village), as if he was including all the previous incumbents. The second house is related to the former *naai baan*, and especially those who died before the end of their mandate, and have to go on with their duty – it is attached to the names of Sommay and Thaao Hông. The third is for the ancestors who came with the villagers from Vietnam – the names of Khambaan and Éng Ong are given as the main occupants.

The whole setting is similar to the one presented for the *lak man* in Houay Yong, except that the order is from right to left and not left to right. However, if we refer to the current of the stream nearby (respectively, the *Huai Yoong* and the *Huai Lôm*), the house for *chao süa* is always upstream, followed by the house for the *naai baan* and eventually the one for the spirits from Vietnam.

Another difference is the presence of a fourth house (Figure 5.11), which has recently been added to the left of the *thiang seun* shrine. It is devoted to the spirits of Houay Louang. Its main occupant is the late father of Buaphoon, the present *chao süa* for that village community. Houay Louang was formerly located a bit upstream. Its inhabitants were resettled in Nasan and Houay Lom. The way in which their village shrine was eventually added to the one of Houay Lom is discussed on pages 147–148.

The village shrine of Houay Lom has been located in three successive spots over the last decades, for purely practical reasons, but never far from its present position. It must always remain above the level of the village. Close to the village shrine, but apparently distinct from it, was a very basic shrine made with a few sticks and leaves for the spirits of the forest (*phii paa*): the hunters make ceremonies on that spot to bring good luck to their activity.

Figure 5.11 The four *thiang seun* for the spirits of Houay Lom and Houay Louang. The lattices of bamboo surrounding the *lak man* appear between the two huts on the right, a bit above them (June 2014).

The village shrine of Ban Kang

Although its history is closely related to Houay Yong, Ban Kang has a Tai Dam population, and the two villages cultivate a sense of distinction.[6] The village shrine is very different from those of the Tai Vat: there is only a *lak man*, with no *thiang seun*. The post is planted under a large fig tree (Figures 5.12 and 5.13). With a height of less than 40 cm, it is indented on its pointed apex. The area around cannot be disturbed, or even weeded. The *lak man* has reportedly been the same since the foundation of the village, and has been moved during the three successive locations of the settlement.

The present *chao süa* of Ban Kang is Khamchan, who is over 60 years old. He inherited his position from his father, himself a son of Lan, the third son of the founder of the village, Sèèntang.

The first settlers and the ritual incumbents

As appears clearly from the preceding sections, the village shrines are intimately linked to the families of the first settlers and their patrilineal descent. In this section I disentangle the different statuses and titles related to this domain of symbolic and ritual power, because they can be confusing. Who are the *chao*

Figures 5.12 and 5.13 The *lak man* of Ban Kang, at the foot on the right side of a fig tree (December 2018).

süa, the *chao kôk chao lao*, the *chao thin chao thaan*, and the *chao cham* [26, 70, 130, 141, 217, 239]?

Chao süa means the "chief of the shirt," in reference to the shirt of the incumbent used during the ceremonies (see pages 125, 137, 139). He is also referred to as *chao kôk chao lao*, which means the "chief" of the [human] "foundation" and of the [slashing down of the original] "forest," or *chao thin chao thaan*, which means the "chief of the place – chief of the base." These two titles have, however, a more generic meaning than *chao süa*, because they are also used to describe the first settlers and their descendants at large.

In Houay Yong, Vôngkham (also called Phèèngông) currently holds the title of *chao süa*. He succeeded his late elder brother, Toi, who inherited the position from their father, Sing Nguan (also called Thaao Théé). The latter got it from his father, Koongbannôô (or Koongvannôô), who got it from his elder brother, Süaa, who succeeded another relative (his father?) named Phoom [26, 64a, 239, 260, 262]. The succession is from the father to the elder son; if someone has no son, the position is transmitted to the brother; if there is no son and no brother to take it up, the title of *chao süa* is supposed to disappear. The spirits of the five late *chao süa* are addressed in front of their *thiang seun* house during the ceremonies, as appears on page 135.

A last title is *chao cham*. This refers to the elder who leads the ceremonies for inviting the spirits to eat at the village shrine, if the *chao süa* doesn't lead them, which is usually the case.[7] He can also be called *moo phoon*, a generic word for anyone asking for benedictions on behalf of other people. The *chao cham* officiating in Houay Yong and *Naa Kuu* is Koongbun, half-brother of Thaabun by a different mother [217, 239].

The status Thaabun held in Houay Yong is a confusing issue. He was presented to us – and he presented himself – as holding the title of *chao kôk chao lao* ([129, 130, 239]; see page 60). The title would have been transmitted in his lineage which reportedly held political authority over the village in the past, whereas another lineage held religious authority through the office of *chao süa*. These two related lineages, both affiliated to the Sing Loo clan,[8] are reportedly in a perpetual relationship of the elder brother (*chao süa*) to the younger brother (*chao kôk chao lao*), because their respective founders were elder and younger brothers[9] – another variation of the brotherhood trope evoked on page 68. With the new regime, the *chao kôk chao lao* lost his political authority and was replaced by the elected *naai baan*, whereas the *chao süa* position did not change. However, during our time of research, Thaabun had little prerogatives: he gave general instructions to the *chao süa* about the necessity to undertake ceremonies, and he collected all the food and components needed to carry out the ritual for the *lak man* and *thiang seun*. But, despite this situation, the status of Thaabun turned out not to be an institutional position: after his death in 2018, no one replaced him in this status of *chao kôk chao lao*. His half-brother Koongbun thinks that the latter title was just coined to please Thaabun, because he was indeed a reputed oral historian and had an intimate knowledge of the traditions of the Tai Vat; this is why he was much respected by the *chao süa*, Vôngkham, his junior by many decades, who always referred to him when asked about the traditions of the village.

In summary, the status attributed to Thaabun was possibly an invented, ad-hoc tradition to show respect to this elder, although it might well be a reminiscence of an old partition of political and ritual power in the village or the region. Among the Tai of Vietnam, the political and ritual functions were distinguished and attributed to two different incumbents (Cầm Trọng and Phan Hữu Dật n.d.: 155–156; Cầm Trọng 2004: 233). Whether or not this occurred historically in Houay Yong cannot be ascertained. The important point is, however, the relevance of this dual representation of power, which informed the description of the role of Thaabun and his relationship to the *chao süa*.

As appears from these descriptions, the people in charge of the village spirits are all male adults or elders descending from the first settler families. No woman has ever been mentioned in relation to territorial cults, either as ancestor or as officeholder. Women reportedly cannot make *thaam* prayers for the village spirits, despite the fact that they are often in charge of the rituals at the domestic level, and represent about half of the mediums (*moo môt*) among the Tai Vat of the valley. The situation described in the former capital of Luang Prabang is very different: the post of the city, called *lak man* as in the *Huai Yoong* valley, was under the custody of a female medium. This is in line with the oral tradition reporting that, for the foundation of the city, a pregnant woman committed to become the wife of the post and was eventually buried alive for the foundation of the city (Archaimbault 2014: 198–199; Tanabe 2000: 302). In the same way, in Chiang Mai and Vientiane, women used to play active roles in the territorial cult of the city, notably as a spirit medium, a charge inherited through matrilineage in Chiang Mai (Tanabe 1991: 7, 9, 13, 31; Lévy 1956: 851). The difference with the situation in Houay Yong can be at least partly related to the kinship systems, with the Tai Dam having a clear patrilineal orientation compared with their western neighbors of Luang Prabang, Vientiane, and Chiang Mai, the kinship system of which is bilateral, and matrilineal by some aspects.

The annual village ritual

I turn now to the ceremonies carried out in relation to territorial spirits. I distinguish three kinds of rituals that each has a specific purpose. I describe first a ritual performed every year at the shrine of *thiang seun* and *lak man* in the wake of the *kinchiang*, the local New Year. Thereafter I present the *sén baan*, a ritual conducted sporadically to get rid of all the 'bad things' that have accumulated in the village. And third, I present a disappeared annual ritual that involved representatives of seven or eight other villages that converged on Houay Yong, because the village hosted the seat of the regional *dông khuaang* ceremony to placate the spirits of the heaven, sky, mountains, rivers, soil, and forest with the view to have a good harvest of rice in all the areas that depended on the *Huai Yoong* River.

The annual ceremony for the *thiang seun* and *lak man* is most usually carried out after the *kinchiang*, held at the same time as the Vietnamese New Year (*Tết*), in January or February. On 26 January 2012, directly after the three-day celebration of *kinchiang*, we attended the ceremonies in Houay Yong and *Naa Kuu* [137–142, 239, 251]. The following description is based on that ethnographic observation. I add information from other sources when needed.

Food and objects had to be collected before the ceremony, for which the collaboration of the different families of the village was solicited. The day before, the *naai baan* asked the village crier to announce the ceremony in the different areas of the village. Singphoon, the crier, requested the head of each village unit (*chu*) to lend a hand for repairing the *thiang seun* and clearing the shrine area. The day after, a few male adults and elders cleaned the place around 11:30 a.m.: they cut the saplings and the bush around the *lak man* and *thiang seun*, in a relaxed atmosphere. The *chao süa*, Vôngkham, was present together with close relatives; there was also Koongbun, the *chao cham*, and Thaabun. *Naai baan* Bunsoon and the deputy-chief, Khamphian, represented the political authorities. Other people, including mostly elders and children, came progressively so that there were about 20 people by 1 p.m. on the *thiang seun* terrace. Three ducks were killed and prepared on the spot: the food for the ceremony cannot be prepared elsewhere. One jar of rice beer (*lao hai*) was set in front of the entrance of each of the three *thiang seun*, together with a bucket of water (necessary to fill in the jar for drinking this kind of beer) and a pair of bamboo straws set inside the jar.

A carpet was laid on the floor of the hut on the left, the one dedicated to the spirits of the *chao süa*. An aluminum basin was set inside the hut; it contained two woven textiles (a white one and a multicolored one). The *chao süa*, helped by his brother, put food (a boiled duck, a bowl of soup, vegetables) and eating material (about five pairs of chopsticks, spoons) on a low table that he placed inside this hut. Two small cups of alcohol, two cups of *lao hai*, and two cups of herbal tea were added on the low table inside the hut; eventually, two baskets filled with sticky rice were also laid on its floor.[10] A small wooden post was erected in front of the entrance. It supported a horizontal rod with candles at both ends and an incense stick set on its middle part. Next to its base laid the jar of *lao hai* and the bucket of water. A bottle of alcohol was added next. A white cloth (originally a bag of Vietnamese cement) was laid on the ground.

Koongbun acted as the ritual leader, *chao cham*, of the ceremony. He warned us that he was not a good *moo thaam* (specialist of *thaam* prayers) but, as the last incumbent had left for Thongnamy, and because of a lack of other candidates, he had accepted taking over the position, which he had already occupied years ago. *Thaam* can be described as a 'prayer,' in the sense of an invocation addressing one or more spirits, inviting them for a meal, and asking for their help. It has a specific rhythm, being uttered with a rapid, cadenced, and monochord voice. It also has a metaphoric and poetic dimension, as appears in the translations. Performing a basic *thaam* is a capacity shared by most adults of the village, men and women. From the earliest age, children attend *thaam* addressed to the house spirits, or other spirits. They use a repertoire of expressions, often with an archaic style, which are understood by all the villagers. This verbal performance is not fixed: a good *moo thaam* is able to coin new expressions. Being the *chao cham*, that is, the *moo tham* for the village spirits, can be dangerous, due to his connection with such powerful entities. This was even more the case with the *dông khuaang* ceremony, as we shall see.

Koongbun had worn the black/dark indigo cotton suit and headdress typical of the Tai Vat. Just after the candles and incense stick were lit in front of the post at the entrance to the first hut, he began the invocation at around 1:30 p.m. He removed his headdress and put it on the white cloth, close to two pieces of bamboo cut longitudinally and resting on a third one. After prostrating himself to honor the spirits, he knelt down and began to *thaam*.

He invited the spirits of the late *chao süa* by their name (always preceded by a honorary title, *Kunkhampaan Laannyaakham*, or *Laannyaakham*, which could be translated as "Lord"): Toi, Sing, Nôô, Süaa, Phoom, names that were repeated many times throughout the prayer. The names should be given from the last incumbent (Toi) to the most ancient one (Phoom), but this order was not always respected, and the list was not always complete. Koongbun explained to the spirits the hard situation of the village, using metaphors of shortage and drought:

ອາຫັງ ໝູໝາຍັງຕາຍ ຂ່ວາຍເປັດໄກ່ຍັງຕາຍກອງ	*Ahang*! [connective ritual formula] Pigs and dogs have died by large numbers; the ducks and chicken as well.
ອາຫັງ ເຂົ້ານ້ຳມານີຍັງບໍ່ໄດ້ລີບິທາຍ ບໍ່ໄດ້ຫຼາຍປີກ່ອນ	*Ahang*! Rice and water are less than last year and the year before.
ອາຫັງ ຕາຍແລ້ງຕາຍໃຫ້ຂົບທິບ	*Ahang*! The rice stands dead with dryness.
ອາຫັງ ສາລີສາລີລອນ ຍັງບໍ່ໄດ້ຫຼາຍ	*Ahang*! There is not much corn.
ເຂົ້ານ້ຳບໍ່ມານາ ປູປານບໍ່ມາທ້ອຍກວ້າ	Rice and water are not yet in the paddy fields; crabs and fishes have not yet come to the river.
ເຮັດສັງບໍ່ຍັງມາໄດ້	Somehow, they are not able to come.
ໄຂສັງບໍ່ແຕ່ງດີເປັນ ລູກເຈັບຍັງໄດ້ໄສ້ຍັງເຖິງຢູ່	Illness has not yet come to an end. The children are still sick.
ໝູໝາຍັງຕາຍຂ່ວຍ ເປັດໄກ່ຍັງຕາຍກອງກິວ	Pigs and dogs have died in large numbers; ducks and chicken as well.
ອາຫັງ ເຍືອງມີຕໍ່ອອກ	*Ahang*! The divination can still be delivered [we can find the source of the problem by divination].

Then the *thaam* turned to invitations: the spirits of the authorities of the village and of the district were kindly invited to join; big ducks with a lot of fat had been cooked, so that the whole district could come; Koongbun requested the spirits to trust each other, to come together, in couples. He explained that the

136 *The ethnography of territorial cults*

Figure 5.14 After addressing *thaam* prayers in front of the entrance of the second house, Koongbun prepares to throw the divination sticks on the cloth. The man kneeling with a cap is Vôngkham, the *chao süa* (January 2012).

spirits should express themselves in the divination (*siang thuaai*): "when the sticks fall down, one should show its upper side, the other the opposite side."

After that last sentence (two minutes after the start of the *thaam*), Koongbun took the two small pieces of bamboo that lay on the third and threw them on the cloth (Figure 5.14). This is a divination device to know if the spirits have accepted the call: the two pieces should show different sides (one should show the green exterior side of the bamboo stalk, and the other one the white interior side).

Unfortunately, both pieces showed the white side at the first attempt, which meant that Koongbun had to go on to convince the spirits. He resumed the *thaam*, using similar sentences and, after one minute, again threw the two sticks, with no more success. He tried again and again, each attempt after a short *thaam* (half a minute to a minute). After the third unsuccessful try, he changed the place of his material on the cloth; he was reminded by the *chao süa* of the names and order of the five late *chao süa* he had to greet, because Koongbun was not always correct in his addresses. This series of failures brought funny comments and laughter from the audience, even if Koongbun seemed a bit stressed, as he acknowledged years later. Eventually, at the sixth attempt, the two sticks fell on different sides: the spirits had come at last.

Koongbun carried on his *thaam*, prolonging the description of the afflictions in the village:

ງົວຄວາຍປາຍເຂົາກໍຕ່າຍັງເຕັມບ້ານເຕັມຂ່ອງ	Cows and buffaloes with their horns are dying in large numbers in the village area.
ອາຫັງ ເສືອໃຫຍ່ຍັງເຂົ້າທາງທ່າ	*Ahang*! Big tigers roam the place where the people go to the river.
ທາດໃຫຍ່ຍັງເຂົ້າທາງບ້ານທາງເມືອງ ເຊີນີ້	Big floods affect the village and the district, it's like that.
ອາຫັງ ເຮັດຂ້ຽງຍັງບໍ່ແຕ່ງດີໄດ້	*Ahang*! Illness has not ended yet.
ອາຫັງ ເຕິ້ງຍັງບໍ່ມາເຕົ້າຕໍ່ຍັງບໍ່ມາຮັງ	*Ahang*! The small bees have not gathered together; the big bees have not returned to the nest.

He then invited the guests to take their places and to enjoy the meal:

Come and eat the rice from the paddies and from the swiddens: a soft, white rice.
Eat as you wish, follow your heart.
Make your stomach full; take as much as you can in your mouth.
Eat the big ducks that were swimming.
Please tell each other to come, trust each other.
Take the chopsticks with the left hand and the rice with the right hand.
Eat the head, the tail, the jaws, the tongue, the two sides, the gut, the neck, the backbone on all its length, the legs and the wings that used to scratch the ground and to fly.

After further invitations to the spirits, Koongbun presented requests for the well-being of the villagers:

May they have black silver and new gold, uncut cotton clothes, beautiful and tight woven textiles.
May people offer things in the right hand of the villagers, while the villagers keep them in their left hand.
Please allow them to collect in their bags.

These are common metaphors of accumulation, the idea being that the right hand receives whereas the left hand gives nothing back.

Then the *thaam* invited the spirits to drink the rice beer. At some point, Koongbun added water to the jar of *lao hai*, as one does when inviting a guest to drink. Vôngkham, the *chao süa*, put his coat (called *süa*, as any shirt) inside the house of the spirits at this moment – it seems that he had forgotten his main ritual duty, for his title means "master of the shirt." As reported page 125, the shirt in this context is used to allow one's bodily souls to travel to the invisible world – in the present case, presumably to go and convince Vôngkham's predecessors to attend the ceremony offered to them.

138 *The ethnography of territorial cults*

Koongbun resumed with his *thaam*, about the way the spirits should enjoy drinking this beer, and also the alcohol that was close to it. They should eventually enjoy chewing betel, to have smooth dispositions toward the living: they were induced to bring peace, prosperity, and good health to the villagers.

After this long *thaam*, which lasted 14 minutes altogether, the cloth on which Koongbun had been praying was removed and laid in front of the second house (dedicated to the spirits of *naai baan* and other authorities). All the contents inside the first hut were moved to the second. The cups for the different drinks were poured out and filled again. The duck was replaced by another one; the soup was also brought back to the field kitchen and changed into another bowl. The only thing that remained in front of the entrance of the first hut was the jar of *lao hai*.

The ritual process in front of the second house was similar to the one described above. However, it needed just three attempts (and four minutes) to have the two sticks of bamboo falling in the appropriate position, after which Koongbun went on with a six-minute *thaam*. The addressees of the *thaam* were Süaa and Phoom, who appeared as the two eldest *chao süa* during the prayers in front of the first house. It is not clear why these two spirits were invoked here, rather than those of former *naai baan* supposed to inhabit the house (see page 125).

The third hut turned out to be tough: the bamboo pieces had to be thrown 11 times (14 minutes of *thaam*) to appear on opposite sides; Koongbun stood up and knelt down twice to start the process again. No one seemed to consider this a sign of misfortune, however: it was, rather, fun. Five more minutes of *thaam* were needed. The addressee was Laankham, "Laankham of our great Muang Vat, the old, very old Muang Vat."

After the end of this third session, Koongbun knelt down close to the jar of *lao hai*. Following a short address to the spirits of the hut, he drank together with an elder of the *chao süa*'s lineage (Figure 5.15). This was repeated in front of the first

Figure 5.15 Koongbun drinks *lao hai* with Thaao Chüaang, in front of the second hut. Thaao Chüaang is the younger brother of the late Sing Nguan, himself the father of the current *chao süa*, Vôngkham, who can be seen at the rear (with a coat and a cap). Thaabun stands on the left of the picture (January 2012).

house, and then in front of the second one, with different guests (including our team). Around 2:30 p.m., the attendants shared a quick lunch with the food prepared at the place. The only important prohibition people had to respect for this ceremony was to eat (or drink) on the spot, and never before the spirits [4].

At 2:40 p.m., we proceeded down the path to the *lak man*. Rice, alcohol, a chicken, some other food, and utensils were laid on the plank on top of the post next to the *lak man*. Koongbun knelt down and made a five-minute *thaam*, but without any divination with bamboo sticks this time. The attendance was sparse: there remained only three elders and the *chao süa* (who laid his coat next to the *lak man*, see Figure 5.16). They joined their hands during the *thaam*, as a sign of respect.

The *thaam* was similar to the one in front of the *thiang seun*. Here, I report more precisely its ending, following the long description of the meal and the drinks offered to the spirits, which has already been reported for the ceremony on the *thiang seun*:

> Please do not eat without concern: take care of the village, of the paddy fields; bring money and valuable things.
> Please protect all the people in the village; make them rich and happy.
> Do not allow tigers to enter the village, nor epidemics.
> If enemies come, please defend the village and chase them away.
> Make streams flow to the ponds and fish come to the nets.
> Bring incomes from trading; protect our pigs, dogs, chickens.
> Do not allow buffaloes or cows to die.
> Our great *lak man*, old *lak man* of Houay Yong.
> If tigers come, chase them away; if a disease comes, protect us from it.

Figure 5.16 Koongbun leading the ceremony in front of the *lak man* of Houay Yong. Note the coat (*süa*) of the *chao süa* at the front of the picture, on the cement base of the *lak man* (January 2012).

140 *The ethnography of territorial cults*

The very last sentences of any *thaam* request the spirits to leave. If the living are very happy that the spirits have come to bring their protection, this should be limited in time, and the spiritual guests are requested to go back to their place, and not to interfere anymore:

> After I have told you to eat, I tell you now to sleep.
> Take a rest, go back to protect the farms and the gardens. After you leave, please do not come to eat again.
> Make everything well, everything good for the village, for the people.

Afterwards, the offerings were removed from the plank. Small balls of rice were stuck on it as a gift to the spirits. Koongbun had to eat some rice and some chicken before leaving the place.

Then Koongbun moved to the *phii seun* of *Naa Kuu* to proceed with the ceremony in a very similar way (Figures 5.17 and 5.18). As there is only one *thiang seun* in *Naa Kuu*, the ceremony was shorter. The divination sticks fell in the right position at the third essay, after four minutes, followed by a five-minute *thaam*.

The ceremony proceeded on in front of the *lak man*. On both spots, Koongbun was helped by Bunmaa, the *chao süa* of *Naa Kuu*. He used similar food, drinks, and material as in Houay Yong.

At the end of the day, ceremonies went on in the houses of the *chao süa* (Vôngkham for Houay Yong, Bunmaa for *Naa Kuu*) with a reception for a meal, but, as it is more directly directed to the *kinchiang* cycle, it is not discussed here.

Figure 5.17 Koongbun addressing *thaam* in front of the *thiang seun* of *Naa Kuu*. Bunmaa is sitting next to the *thiang seun* while Marie-Pierre Lissoir (left) records the prayers (January 2012).

Figure 5.18 Koongbun addressing *thaam* in front of the *lak man* of *Naa Kuu*. This panoramic view illustrates that rituals are conducted in a casual atmosphere. Kongbuun remains concentrated on his work while young adults joke, smoke cigarettes, and eat peanuts at the back (January 2012).

The *sén baan* ritual and the spirits of the village doorways

Apart from these ceremonies celebrated every year, the *thiang seun* and *lak man* are also the locus for a non-yearly ritual called *sén baan* [140, 141, 239, 244]. This can be translated as a 'curing' ceremony (*sén*) for the village (*baan*). People have to respect prohibitions (*kham, khalam*) during one or three days: no one can leave the village or come into it; no one can carry water in bamboo boxes (which no one does anymore in the present day), nor thresh the rice. A post is erected on the road, at both ends of the village, to enforce the prohibition and protect the place from bad spirits – we come to this point later. On the *thiang seun* shrine, a ritual is conducted similar to what has been described for the annual ceremonies. A big pig is killed for another ceremony carried out in front of the *chao süa*'s house.

In 2013, Marie-Pierre Lissoir attended a *sén baan* in Houay Yong (Lissoir 2016: 113–114). It was celebrated the day after the village had been awarded the title of "developed village" (see page 110), in the wake of the festivities. Anyway, it was time to hold a village ceremony, because the poultry had repeatedly been decimated by epizootics in the preceding years. Mèèthao Dèèng, an elder female medium, had been reciting prayer songs (*khap-môt*) overnight to expel the bad spirits from the village (this tempers the reported male monopoly on territorial cults, although she does not address the spirits on the village shrine). The next morning, people had an enjoyable time. After lunch, under the leadership of the *chao süa*, a procession started, including a lot of villagers and children. Two men with blackened faces led the walk, swinging the air with a wooden sword in each hand. The atmosphere was funny and noisy: a pair of gongs and a drum suspended on a bamboo pole were repeatedly beaten; some women had a pan lid in one hand and a spoon in the other, and struck them continuously; others shrieked or made noise with sticks they hit on the ground; the boys enthusiastically hit the sides of the road with bamboo sticks, as they were encouraged to do by the adults. The cortege reached one end of the village, and then turned back to the other end, with the aim to frighten and definitely expel, through this deafening performance, the bad spirits Mèèthao Dèèng had chased away during the night.

This description shows the importance of the village limits. During a visit to the northern end of the village, where the former occupants had their *vat* temple, Bunsoon conducted us to a small patch of forest that must remain unslashed. The place, he explained, is the doorway of the village (*patuu baan*) [213, 244]. Whenever there is a *sén baan, kinchiang*, or a death, a ceremony has to be carried out on the spot by the *chao cham* to "open" the village. Stalls of wood are erected, and offerings (usually a chicken) are placed on large leaves for the spirits of the place, who act as guardians of the village. Inversely, on the third day, another ceremony takes place to "close" (*at*) the village to the spirits who could enter it again. The ceremony should ideally take place at both ends of the village, but there is no more forest on the southern end, so people do not perform anything there except for the *sén baan* ceremony. According to Bunsoon, the guardian spirits of the village doorway act on behalf of the spirits of the *thiang seun*. Some people who had to spend the night in the place had dreams in which spirits appeared as soldiers in uniform and told them to leave the place.

The *dông khuaang* ritual

Although the two ceremonies described above are celebrated up to the present, the *dông khuaang* has not been performed for about two decades – I discuss the reasons why on pages 169–171. This major ceremony is also called *phii khuaang, sôn khuaang*, and *sén khuaang*. It aims to lift the *khuaang*, referring to a large-scale misfortune, or something that blocks or obstructs a flux. Our informants, in Houay Yong as elsewhere, reported on the importance of this ritual in the past [27, 61, 71, 239–244, 254, 257, 258, 262].

The ritual was performed in Houay Yong, but it necessitated the cooperation of all the villages that depended on the water of the *Huai Yoong* stream: Ban Kang, Houay Yong (and *Naa Kuu*), Nasan, Muang Van, but also Nalèng, Ban Sot, Nahit, and Muang Èt. In the past, the last four settlements got part of their irrigation water from the *Huai Yoong*, through canals. Houay Lom relied on its proper stream (the *Huai Lôm*) and consequently had its own *dông khuaang* ritual.

The ceremony had to be carried out in late May, a crucial period for the cultivation of rice in the swiddens. The *chao cham* used to officiate at a place along the *Huai Boo*, the brooklet separating Houay Yong from *Naa Kuu*, on the Houay Yong side. Long ago, it was celebrated close to the bamboo bridge that crossed the stream a few meters upstream from the present village road. There was a thick forest (*paa dông*) only a few meters from the road. When the forest was slashed down, the location of the ritual was moved about 300 meters upstream of the *Huai Boo*.

The ritual was carried out to yield various benefits, but the central point was to bring rain. Some informants hold that it was not annual, but performed every two or three years, when there was a problem such as a drought, or after somebody had a dream.

The ethnography of territorial cults 143

All the villages concerned participated in the buying of one, or two, buffalo(es): their respective *naai baan* were in charge of collecting the money from the villagers, and handing it over to the organizers of the ritual in Houay Yong. The buffalo was killed early in the morning – powerful spirits do not accept that flies touch the meat they are offered – and was chopped into pieces placed on wooden plates, with rice and other foods. Those plates were laid on stalls of wood, each of which was protected by an umbrella, as a sign of respect. Twelve stalls were built for the different addressees of the ritual, that is, the different kinds of spirits. The *chao cham* moved from one stall to another and addressed *thaam* prayers for each and every category of spirits, which together formed the generic category of *phii khuaang*. He began with the most powerful ones: the *phii faa* (spirits of the sky) and the *phii tèèn* (spirits of "heaven"). But he also had to address the *phii phuu* (spirits of the mountains), *phii paa* (of the forests), *phii din* (of the soil), *phii huai* (of the streams), *phii koong* (of the canals), *phii müang* (of the district), and *phii baan* (of the villages). As with other *thaam* prayers, the list had to be exhaustive: during her interview, Mèèthao Leua, the widow of Phongsai, the last *chao cham* in charge of this ritual, immediately listed seven brooklets that her late husband had to address.

The participants, including many villagers, stayed on the ritual area to eat the food after the spirits, because it could not be brought away. However, the *chao cham* received the back of the buffalo as a reward for his services, because it was a long ceremony beginning at 7 a.m. and ending around 11 a.m.

The *dông khuaang* retains an aura of hushed mystery. Narratives link its disappearance with the death of Phongsai, its last ritual master reputedly killed by the spirits, but also with the coming of modernity to the village. 'Disappearance' is probably not the best word to define its status: I often felt during conversations that the *dông khuaang* was, rather, indefinitely adjourned. And, in any case, if no performance had taken place for two decades, people still describe it with a strong feeling of enchantment; the powers evoked during the ceremony are still present in the valley. Chapter 6 analyzes in detail this fascinating ritual, after first starting with the ceremonies conducted up to the present day at the village shrine.

Notes

1 The conclusive chapter by O'Connor (2003) is an inspiring reflection on how founders' cults can accommodate with changing contexts, and are reframed by them.
2 Early interviews about the territorial cults in Houay Yong took place in Thongnamy [61, 64a]. Our team conducted interviews, visited the shrines, and observed the annual ritual in Houay Yong [2, 4, 10, 26, 27, 29, 91, 129, 130, 137, 138, 140, 141, 191, 239–242, 244] and in *Naa Kuu* [20, 27, 29, 30, 32, 42, 142, 245]. We interviewed elders about the 'consolidated' shrine of Houay Lom and Houay Louang, and could observe it [70–71, 195–196, 198]. We also conducted interviews and direct observations in Ban Kang [76, 208, 254]. The local shrine was briefly mentioned in Nasan [82], and we had interviews on the topic in Nangiu, Pakfèn and Ban Sot [256–258].
3 *Moo môt* are men or women who embraced that status because the guardian spirit of a late *moo môt* relative, typically their father or mother, elected them through illness or

another affliction. To be cured, they have to be initiated by a senior colleague. Thereafter, the *moo môt* is able to perform rituals and, with the help of the guardian spirit, to travel into the invisible world to deal with spirits causing misfortune to the living. In 2018, there were five *moo môt* in Houay Yong, mostly elderly women, but the villagers also relied on the *moo môt* from Ban Kang or Houay Lom, where a similar number of mediums were active.

4 The words used to describe the shrine and its inhabitants are similar to those recorded by Tanabe (2000: 303, 314) during his research in the northern districts of Houaphan in 1991.
5 Interestingly, during his second interview (see page 61), Bunmaa presented the (relatively recent) foundation of *Naa Kuu* as contemporaneous with the (ancient) foundation of Houay Yong, possibly for the sake of a smooth and consolidated narrative that connects the three Tai Vat settlements strongly together through the trope of the three founding brothers (see page 68).
6 See pages 5, 33–36, 82–83n17 about the history and the ethnic ascription of Ban Kang.
7 Different Tai–Lao groups use the same title for the ritual officer in charge of the village spirits. According to Hayashi (2003: 193–194), the *cham* is the intermediate between the community and the village spirit for the Tai–Lao living in northeastern Thailand; he reports the messages of the spirit through either possession or divinatory practices. The *cham* has to be a man, middle-aged or older; he must be unmarried.
8 Many clans or patronyms (*sing*) are distinguished in Houay Yong, and the main ones are subdivided into branches: Sing Loo (Loo Thaô, Loo Khun, Loo Noi); Sing Lüang (Lüang Ngua, Lüang Yèn, Lüang Moo); Sing Khuang (Khuang Boo, Khuang Hu Mo, Khuang Thong Tèèk); Sing Lèm; Sing Khaa; Sing Wii; Sing Lüü [63, 86, 217]. They are all based on patrilineal descent. Even if their current influence on everyday life is limited, they still play a role in ritual life, in relation to domestic shrines, exogamy, wedding, and mourning. There is, up to this day, a village leader for each clan in Houay Yong: usually a male elder, sometimes a promising young man [86]. Apart from these ritual functions, clans are not corporate units in daily life, as they have remained, for example, among the Hmong of Laos, as I could observe in Thongnamy. Clans are related to the former political order of the Tai polities in Vietnam. According to Thoongsôm, the first settler and "king" of the Tai Vat was *phanyaa* Nguu Hao, which means "the lord of the Cobra"; he belonged to the Loo clan. He had many sons who settled elsewhere to rule over other polities on his behalf; their descendants became progressively autonomous and founded new subclans. This explains why Tai Vat kings and chiefs belonged to the Loo clan, even if some *chao süa*, descendants of village founders, may belong to other clans [186, 191]. On the precedence of the Loo clan among the Tai Dam, see Lafont (1955).
9 According to Koongbun, who was the half-brother of Thaabun, their father was the younger brother of Koongbannôô [239], the grandfather of the present *chao süa*.
10 The components of the ceremony listed by elders in Houay Lom included two jars of rice beer, bottles of alcohol, two ducks, and twelve chickens [196, 198]. In Ban Kang, the ceremony takes place at the *lak man*'s place, for there is no *thiang seun*; people offer a pig for the spirits [254].

6 Territorial cults in a regional perspective

The three sets of rituals described in Chapter 5 obviously have different functions. The annual ceremony at the village shrine is devoted to honor the village spirits, in the *thiang seun* and the *lak man*, and to ask for their help and protection for the community. The *sén baan* involves, at some point, the same spirits, but it aims at expelling malevolent entities from the settlement. It is in line with the other *sén* rituals performed by *moo môt* mediums in various contexts – for example, to expel mischievous spirits from the house, or to send the spiritual 'friend' of a child back to 'heaven' due to the danger (s)he causes to a boy or a girl. Finally, the *dông khuaang* appears as a regional cult dealing with non-ancestral and apparently non-human spirits. It goes far beyond the village limits – up to the sky and the 'heaven' – and delineates a terrestrial territory that does not fit with any boundary known through either other oral sources or the archives.

Chapter 5 unpacked the ethnographic information at hand, but it also evoked larger issues in its introduction. This chapter resumes with these theoretical stakes. The following sections gradually unfold the topic from the village to the larger region and the state, and from more structural aspects to historical dynamics. The reader should, however, bear in mind that all these dimensions are integrated. The very idea of stable village structures encompassed into a changing state apparatus does not capture well the iterative process of change that I would like to develop in this chapter and in Chapter 7, in which modern monuments make their appearance as a new avatar of territorial cults.

Performing corporateness and boundaries in the village

I start with the quite obvious link between the rituals performed on the *thiang seun/lak man* shrines and the affirmation of communal identity. With no exception, the authors who discuss territorial cults highlight their importance for merging farmer households into a community. Our ethnographic data largely confirm this assumption. The shrine provides protection for the whole village; it is supposed to keep the place safe from bad spirits, wild animals, dangerous people, illness, and calamities. The annual ceremonies involve potentially the whole village community. Representatives of each and every *chu* unit are asked by the village crier to take part in the cleaning of the shrine. The *sén baan* ceremonies display this unity in an even stronger way: the prohibitions "close" the village from any outside contact during the ritual, so that it appears as a separate and integrated unit – a principle that repeatedly appears in the literature about territorial rituals in the region.[1] Furthermore, the noisy procession of the villagers to both ends of the village, and back, frames very clearly the boundaries of the community. If the annual ceremonies conducted at the *thiang seun* highlight the ritual core of the village, the prohibitions and the procession of the non-yearly rituals display clearly its human and spatial borders.

The territorial cult is instrumental in the creation of "a sovereign commonwealth of humans and spirits, a community of the living and the dead, that seeks to prosper and protect itself through rites and customs" (O'Connor 2003: 274–275). It is a clear example of how a society celebrates and re-creates itself through religious practice, to refer to the old but still relevant Durkheimian view on religion.

Making identity is a double-sided process, as evidenced by Barth in his seminal work *Ethnic Groups and Boundaries* (1998 [1969]). If the ceremonies create a social effervescence linking the villagers and marking the extension of the community, they also define what is beyond, and outside, this boundary. In 2012, the village crier made a round trip across the village of Houay Yong to announce the event, but he did not cross the *Huai Boo* brooklet that separates the old village from the hamlet of *Naa Kuu*, due to the existence of a shrine marking *Naa Kuu* as a specific ritual unit. This is a very telling example of a "cadastral religion," to refer to the concept proposed by Mus (1975: 55 [1933: 378, 396]) and reinvigorated by O'Connor in the idea of a "lingua franca of localism" that "implied the recognition of its neighbors' cults" (O'Connor 2003: 282–283). I argue there is much to gain from adopting a relational approach to territorial cults, that is, to appraise territorial cults not from a local, village-based perspective, but from a regional, intervillage-based stance. This is the kind of paradigmatic shift that Barth (1998 [1969]) and, before him, Moerman (1965), proposed to address ethnicity as a relational process, and not as an internal attribute of the group.

All villages in the valley have their own shrine, and villagers link territorial cults with the well-being of each and every place. For instance, the inhabitants of Houay Yong relate the prosperity of their own village to their commitment to honoring their *phii seun*. They contrast this welfare with the problems they endured when strict prohibitions were enforced on rituals (see pages 167–169), or with the misfortunes faced by the villagers of Ban Kang who, based on their neighbors' view, display too little regard for their own territorial spirits.

The mutual acknowledgment of social groups through territorial cults is conspicuous in the oral and ritual lore of *Naa Kuu* and Houay Louang. This illustrates how territorial cults can "balance centrifugal and centripetal pulls" at the heart of farmer societies in southeast Asia (O'Connor 2003: 279). The centripetal forces have to do with the necessity for collective work (an entrenched disposition in rice-farmer societies) and the ethos of social concord under the umbrella of kinship (for all villagers are assumed to be relatives, *phiinoong*). The centrifugal forces are related to local tensions for leadership, the growth of the population, and the need to colonize new places for cultivation. Territorial cults constitute a frame by which the balance between these opposed forces is eventually reached, presumably after a period of discussions, observations, experimentations, and negotiations. The role of religious leaders – *chao süa*, diviners and mediums – is important in this boundary-making process.

In the case of *Naa Kuu*, the centrifugal forces had the upper hand (see pages 125–129). As we have already seen, during the first half of the twentieth century, a villager from Houay Yong, Phuu Phoom, created a new settlement with the view to developing rice fields in an uncultivated area. A village shrine was erected after his death in the 1950s, elevating the pioneer to the rank of founding ancestor (*chao kôk chao lao*), and creating a lineage of *chao süa* for *Naa Kuu*.

After *Naa Kuu* was integrated into Houay Yong in the late 1950s, the incorporation of its shrine into that of the main village was considered, but, at some point, the idea was abandoned. Consequently, annual ceremonies addressed to the spirits of *lak man* and *thiang seun* are currently conducted on the same day, by the same master of ceremonies *chao cham*,[2] but separately in Houay Yong and *Naa Kuu*, and under the supervision of their respective *chao süa* who do not mix with their colleague's business.

Hence, despite the measures fixed by the administration, *Naa Kuu* hamlet has kept some corporateness and has refrained from complete inclusion into Houay Yong's main village. I have already discussed the role of oral traditions in acknowledging *Naa Kuu*'s specificity: it has been given an ancestor at the same genealogical level as the founder of the main village, despite the chronological inconsistency of such an assertion (see pages 60–61). The place has its proper toponym, *Naa Kuu*, which is still used today, even by the youth, who distinguish this part of the village from the main one that they call *baan luang*, the "principal village." The ritual is even more central in keeping this distinction. Once a year, the people of the *Naa Kuu* area, regrouped into two *chu* (the smallest administrative divisions), join together to celebrate their territorial spirit. Although *Naa Kuu* is much smaller than the central village of Houay Yong, the number of people attending was similar in the two places (see Figures 5.17 and 5.18), which demonstrates the popular adherence to this institution. The resilience of this cultual institution which persisted across the vicissitudes of history, sustaining a collective identity that is not relevant based on the current politico-administrative divisions, is striking.

The case of Houay Louang is different, but still a good example of the adaptive capacities of territorial cults in relation to the dynamics of fission and fusion. As mentioned on page 130, the fourth house on the left of the shrine in Houay Lom shelters the spirits of the former village of Houay Louang. Houay Louang used to be one kilometer southeast and upstream from the present Houay Lom village (see Map 2.1). It was reportedly created in 1938 by some Tai Vat villagers from Houay Lom and by Tai Dèng villagers who used to live close to Ban Kang [71].[3] It was a small village made up of 32 families,[4] which could be the reason why the authorities decided to merge it with Nasan: the whole population had to resettle over there [82], in all likelihood during the 1980s. However, afterwards, some Tai Vat people who had moved to Nasan eventually resettled in Houay Lom, closer to their former habitation and among people of their own ethnic group.

Despite the disappearance of the ancient village, currently returned to swidden fields, the ritual specificity of the former community did not completely disappear. There is a long story about the successive settlements of Buaphoon, the *chao süa* of Houay Louang, and the custody of the *lak man/thiang seun* of the abandoned village. Eventually, Buaphoon settled in Houay Lom. After initial refusals that led to further divination, the spirits agreed to be integrated with those of Houay Lom into a single shrine, but in a specific spirit house. They are respected because the village of Houay Louang used to be in a structural position of father-in-law to Houay Lom. However, since the consolidation of the shrine, the spirits of Houay Lom hold precedence in the ritual protocol. The ceremonies for the integrated village shrine hence involve two *chao süa* on a single spot.

Here, by contrast with what happened in *Naa Kuu*, the integration into one single village was ratified by consolidation into a single shrine. This does not amount to a disappearance of the former units, because the village spirits of Houay Louang have not been merged with those of Houay Lom; they are still hosted in a specific house and receive prayers from their direct descendant, Buaphoon, the present *chao süa*. The reason why the integration was more effective in the Houay Lom/Houay Louang case than in the Houay Yong/*Naa Kuu* case is not sufficiently documented to provide a definite explanation, but one factor is obvious: by contrast with the *Naa Kuu* community, living in a specific area, grouped into two *chu*, and possessing paddy fields, the former inhabitants of Houay Louang have lost their former area of settlement, and their (few) families are not grouped into an administrative unit of any kind. We can say that they lost their specific relationship to their original area, which makes their former territorial cult unfit to support their present identity. Significantly, their communal shrine survives only as a house for the ancestral spirits of the *chao süa*, but without a specific *lak man*, the powerful charm keeping and protecting a community in its place, as is mentioned in the next section. Deprived of their territorial cult, the community has preserved a founding ancestors' shrine, but encapsulated in the territorial cult of Houay Lom and under the protection of its *lak man*.

A commitment to stability

The name *lak man*, given to the post of the shrine, is a regional peculiarity. It contrasts with the usual denominations mentioned by the literature on Tai and Lao villages: *lak baan* (post of the village) or *lak müang* (post of the polity), the latter being reserved for political centers (Zago 1972; Hayashi 2003).[5] "*Lak man*" are reported throughout Houaphan (Tanabe 2000: 303), but also in the neighboring provinces of Luang Prabang and Xieng Khouang.[6] Archaimbault, who describes the legends and rituals related to the Luang Prabang post, translates *man* as "firm, resistant" (Archaimbault 1973: 107, 124; 2014: 191, 198). In Houay

Yong, the word also refers to a quality of stability, in the sense of 'unchanging' and 'unmoving' (Petit 2015; see also Archaimbault 1991: 36). A most revealing aspect of this immobility appeared when I asked Koongbun why he did not conduct divination for the *lak man* as he did for the spirits of the *thiang seun*, whose presence had to be verified before completing the *thaam* prayers; he answered that the *phii seun* spirits are like people: they go to paddy fields, to the forest, looking for food. But the spirit of *lak man* never moves away [239].

This quality appeared clearly in a discussion involving Thaabun, the local historian, and *Naai baan* Bunsoon, who were interviewed together in 2011 at the foot of the *lak man* [91]. Quotes from the interview are presented at length because they reveal the central values Tai Vat elders associate with the *lak man*:

ທ່າບຸນ: (...) ຫຼັກໝັ້ນນີ້ລະໃຫ້ເປັນຫຼັກແກ່ນ.
ຂໍໃຫ້ບໍ່ໄດ້ກິນຈັກເທື່ອ ບໍ່ໄດ້ຍ້າຍຈັກເທື່ອ.
ມັນເປັນຫຼັກໝັ້ນຈິດໃຈ. ເປັນຫຼັກໝັ້ນບໍ່ໃຫ້ອ່ຽງຫັກຫ້ອຍມາ.
ໃຈຄົນບໍ່ມີຕິງວອ. ເປັນຫຼັກແກ່ນ.
ຈັກກີ່ຊາດກີ່ສັດຕະວັດກໍຍັງຢູ່ນີ້ ບໍ່ໄດ້ຍ້າຍ.

ບຸນສອນ:
ເປັນຫຼັກທີ່ວ່າປະຈຳເຈືອງປະຊາຊົນທີ່ວ່າໝັ້ນເຈຢູ່ນີ້.
ຖ້າວ່າຫຼັກມີບໍ່ໝັ້ນ ລະ ຄົນກໍຢາກຫນີໄປທີ່ມາຢູ່ໆ.
ອັນນີ້ຕີວ່າເປັນໝາກທົວເຈຂອງຊາວບ້ານ ເຮັດໃຫ້ໝັ້ນເຈ.

ທ່າບຸນ: ຍ້າຍບໍ່ໄດ້ ຄັນວ່າເຮົາຍ້າຍອັນນີ້
ລະປະຊາຊົນໃນບ້ານເຮົາຈະເກີດເຊື່ອງຫັນ.

ບຸນສອນ: ມີບັນຫາ.

ບຸນສອນ: (...) ຄັນວ່າເຮົາຍ້າຍໂຕນີ້ ເໜືອດັ່ງ
ແມ່ບໍ່ໝັ້ນເຈແລ້ວຊັ້ນມາ. ຢາກຍ້າຍໄປຍ້າຍມາ.
ຢາກປ່ຽນໄປປ່ຽນມາ ບໍ່ຍ້າຍໄດ້.

ເຮົາຕ້ອງຫາບ່ອນທີ່ວ່າມັນຈະກຸ່ມດີບ ແລະ
ມີບ່ອນກໍບັງນີ້. ລະເຮົາຕ້ອງໝັ້ນເຈຢູ່ຫັນ ແສນ ໝີດ
ຮ້ອຍປີກະຢ່າ. ຕ້ອງໝັ້ນເຈ ຕ້ອງປັກຢູ່ນີ້ ລະ
ບໍ່ໄດ້ປ່ຽນແປງ.

Thaabun: (...) This *lak man*, it's the axis post. The people are requested not to dig it out, not to move it whenever. It's the *lak man* that makes the people confident. It cannot be bent down or broken, not even slightly. Our minds are the same [with *lak man*]. It's the axis post. Even after many generations and centuries, it was never moved away.

Bunsoon: the *lak man* is always in the heart of the people, making us confident to stay here.
If this *lak man* were not stable (*man*), the people would like to move away. It's the core of the heart of the villagers, to be confident.

(Later on)

Thaabun: If you move the *lak man*, bad things will happen to villagers.

Bunsoon: There will be problems.

Bunsoon: (...) If we move the *lak man*, people will not be confident anymore, they will want to scatter away. It cannot be moved.

That's why we have to find a good place where to settle the *lak man*, because it must be conserved for long. We have to be sure. After 100 years, the *lak man* is still in the same place. We have to be sure; it must remain planted here, unchanged, unrepaired.

150 *Territorial cults in a regional perspective*

Figure 6.1 Screenshots of the moment when Bunsoon explains that the *lak man* "has to remain planted here" (*toong pak yuu nii*), making a plunging gesture with the hand (June 2011).

As vividly phrased in this interview excerpt, the *lak man* is supposed to keep the people inside the village. It is the protector of the villagers, and it makes them want to stay; it anchors the people into the village in the same way as the post is planted in the ground. Bunsoon accompanied his assertion with evocative gestures (Figure 6.1). The words used during this interview excerpt are very strong and loaded with emotions: the post is an axis (*kèèn*), or the "core" (*maak*) of the heart of the villagers. The two elders really magnified the post and its effects on the village community.

In the excerpt, the commitment to stability is evidenced by all the restrictions against moving, changing, or even repairing the post. Other interviews similarly highlight the prohibitions imposed on the *chao süa*, the male patrilineal descendant of the founding ancestor of the village (see page 132). The *chao süa* embodies the *chao thin chao than*, the founders of the village. As these ancestors are supposed to remain in the place to protect their progeny, the *chao süa* cannot move away to settle elsewhere. He can just leave for a visit. This ritual obligation is pervasive in the comments villagers give about this office: they all have narratives about dreadful problems faced by *chao süa* who did not respect their prohibitions. They often refer to a former *chao süa* responsible for the *lak man* of Ban Kang, who reportedly settled in Vientiane and died afterwards; this lack of respect would also explain why a young woman of his family became mad (*phii baa*) – we could see her traveling every day on the main path until 2012, naked or half-naked and addressing her imaginary children in a language no one could understand [64a, 196]. Even the widow of the former *chao süa* of Houay Yong (the mother of the present incumbent) is under this prohibition: she wanted to move to Vientiane but fell ill after some time and had to settle back in Houay Yong [181].

The villagers of Houay Yong often referred to the story of the *chao süa* of Houay Lom, Koongthéé, as a piece of evidence of the problems faced by office holders who disobey this prohibition to move away [26]. This is a popular story Koongthéé enjoys sharing with fellow villagers. He related it to us as well [196].

He left Houay Lom a first time to settle with his son in another village in a nearby district, entrusting another of his sons with his ritual duties. After some time, he began to cough dangerously. This is exactly what happened to his late father, who died after coughing up blood. A diviner (*moo yüang*) told him that, unless he stayed in Houay Lom, he would die; Koongthéé promised to do so, addressed his father during a ceremony in Houay Lom, and recovered. Later on, he informed his father that he would leave for a while because he had to pay a visit to his son in the close district. The same complication occurred again. Koongthéé went to a hospital, but could not recover. He eventually had to go back to Houay Lom to conduct a ceremony and address his father anew. When we interviewed him in 2014, his health had improved and he did not intend to leave the village anymore.

Commitment to stability is symbolically assumed by the *chao süa*, who carries the burden of ritual prohibitions on behalf of the larger community of the village.[7] This commitment seems in line with the oft-reported concern of political authorities across southeast Asia to keep people inside their polity, in a system where farmers would be tempted to separate from the centers of power due to the multiple demands imposed by the lowland states (Scott 2009). Lehman (2003: 18–19) supports the idea that founders' cults have been instrumental in keeping the people where they were, or "fixing manpower," to the benefit of rulers or chiefs, at the higher or lower levels of polities. I do not subscribe to this idea, at least as it is phrased. Rather territorial cults provide a frame to balance centripetal and centrifugal forces, as developed on pages 145–148 (see also O'Connor 2003: 279). They do not preclude people from migrating, an age-old practice among the Tai people at large, and among the Tai Vat in particular, as appeared in Chapters 3 and 4. When people have to leave, in Houay Yong, they have no specific ritual duty to the *lak man* or the village ancestors. Domestic spirits are addressed before such a departure: during the prayers, the person in charge of the ceremony also addresses the spirits of the village. There is no further requirement [196]. There is no more problem when a whole village has to resettle: Chiao Bun explained that, when Ban Kang was moved along its three successive locations, the spirits of *lak man* were simply invited to the new settlement through due ceremonies [76]. Similarly, Koongbun, the *chao cham* of Houay Yong, explains that, when it is necessary to change the *lak man* itself, it can be done without any problem, with a ceremony where food is offered and *thaam* prayers are addressed to the spirit of *lak man* to inquire about its approval [239].[8] Such remarks demonstrate that, when people evoke the *lak man* as unchanging throughout generations and centuries, this quality refers to its quintessence, not to the materiality of the wooden post.

I argue that, among the Tai Vat, an ethos of mobility coexists with an ethos of stability. But they come to the fore in different circumstances and for different people.[9] The ethos of mobility and pioneers surfaces when people face a serious stress, or when the future of the new generations is at stake. Inversely, the ethos of stability is a kind of ideal for an abstract, unchanging society; it is more associated with the elders who secure the link between the group and a specific place,

152 *Territorial cults in a regional perspective*

and are in charge of the ritual duties in the village. But the valuation of this second ethos never amounts to 'anchoring' the community in the place, as evidenced by the continuous resettlement of villagers and villages mentioned in the preceding chapters.

An outstanding example of the link between mobility and stability mediated by a *lak müang* post comes from Mộc Châu, a Tai polity in Vietnam (see Maps 3.2 and 3.3). A prince from Laos found a gem when he bathed in the Mekong River. He undertook a series of conquests in the uplands of what is presently Vietnam, and the gem continuously grew in size during the migration, until people reached a place where it cried out "I go down!" and plunged into the earth where it became the *lak müang* of the polity (Cầm Trọng and Phan Hữu Dật n.d.: 156). In other Tai polities, embedding a *lak müang* post into the ground is the very sign of control of a territory after a conquest (ibid.: 157). Such narratives demonstrate that territorial cults are related to mobility as much as to stability, and in fact mediate them.

Verticality, hierarchy, and offerings

Territorial spirits are above the humans. The oral tradition of Houay Lom locates the widow *phii* on the cliff of *Phaa Boo*, in the mountains above the village of Nahit (see pages 66–67). The *dông khuuang* ceremony addresses first the spirits of the sky and 'heaven,' then those of the mountains and other places. Interestingly, when he described this ceremony, Koongbun said that the *chao cham* used to perform it "on a mountain," although it takes place at the foot of the mountain range to the west of the village [239].

To come back to the village shrine now, let us resume with the interview of Bunsoon and Thaabun. After they described the *lak man* (see the previous section), we went up to the *thiang seun* terrace, a bit above. At some point, Bunsoon commented on the second house, devoted to the late village chiefs and state employees. At the very moment he explained the identity of those spirits, he turned round and faced the valley. He raised his arms and then lowered them (Figure 6.2), as if embracing the landscape in the direction of

Figure 6.2 Screenshots of the interview of Bunsoon and Thaabun on the *thiang seun* of Houay Yong. The former explains how the spirits watch over the village below (June 2011).

Territorial cults in a regional perspective 153

the village below, and explained that these departed spirits still look after the village and the polity (*müang*) [91].

The same vertical ordering appeared in Houay Lom. When questioned about the reason why the village shrine was built on higher ground, Buakham, one of the elders who accompanied us (Figure 6.3), answered [198]:

ເປັນເຈົ້າກົກເຈົ້າເຫງົ້າ ເຈົ້າທື່ມເຈົ້າທານ ເຂີ ເປັນລ້ານເປັນຄຳ ຕ້ອງຢູ່ເທີງ ເຂີ ເບີງໂງມ ເອົາບ້ານ ເອົາເມືອງ ຂອງຜູ້ແມ່ປະຊາຊົນ ໄພລາດຊະກອນກະເຂົາໃຫ້ຢູ່ເທີງ [...] ຮັກສາ ບ້ານ ປະຊາຊົນ.	They are the first settlers, the founders (*chao kôk chao lao chao thin chao thaan* [see page 132]); they are *Laan*, they are *Kham* [they are Laankham]. They have to stay above, to cover and keep the village and the polity of the common people. ...They protect the common people.

Throughout the valley, the shrine should be above the village. A villager from Bang Kang told us that, a few years ago, a man from his village committed suicide after killing his wife. The reason given to explain his dreadful behavior was that the *lak man* was at the time below the village level (*yuu lum*); after the tragedy, it was moved up, above the village (*hua baan*), to protect the inhabitants from such misfortunes in the future [208].

As the last narrative illustrates, the *lak man* possesses a powerful agency and must be respected by the villagers. Apart from preserving its upper position, other forms of respect are due. In Houay Yong, a most disrespectful man who would have urinated on the *lak man* died afterwards [64a]. In *Naa Kuu*, a man died after he took some meat left to dry close to the *lak man*, without asking permission – his death, from a terrible stomachache, was reminiscent of the death of Phoom, the spirit of the shrine (see page 126). Someone else from the same village collected wood close to the *lak man* and his son became mute; the latter eventually spoke after a divination and, through his voice, Phoom asked for more respect from the living [142].[10]

The upper position of the spirits is a recurring trope in the narratives and comments that have been reported above. This is in line with a pervading principle of territorial cults of the subcontinent, according to Schlemmer (2012: 12). This

Figure 6.3 Screenshots of Buakham explaining the position of the spirits above the people (June 2014).

vertical superiority is linked to authority and respect, as the misfortunes of trespassers attest in stories that are spread by the villagers through everyday conversations. The higher position and status of territorial spirits also appear in gestural embodiments captured in the figures. Physically, the territorial spirits are above the people, as in a premodern, Tai Vat version of the panopticon (Foucault 2010 [1975]). But in the present case, visibility entails not only control, but also protection, a dimension that Foucault does not bring up in *Discipline and Punish*.

This principle is not limited to territorial spirits. Figure 5.2 shows an ancestors' shrine as it can be found in every house in Houay Yong. A comparison can be made between the place occupied by the domestic shrine in the house – always above the living, fixed on a wall or a post – and the position of the *thiang seun* and *lak man*, always above the village on a mountain slope.[11] Still referring to rituals guided by a vertical axis, there would also be much to say about the life cycle from birth to death: babies come from 'heaven' and the dead return to it through descending and ascending travel. The commonness of this principle in everyday life explains its pervasiveness in territorial cults. The house and the village share a common ritual grammar of verticality, a replication that contributes to the consistence of the religious system of the Tai Vat.

Another element shared in the ritual grammar of the house and the village is food offerings. This is an ever-present component of these rituals. The *thaam* prayers devote a lot of time to describe the deliciousness of the offerings, and to stress the completeness of the dishes: hence the exhaustive list of the body components of the duck offered on the *thiang seun* of Houay Yong (see page 137). Offerings also include alcoholic drinks and betel. The idea is to feed the spirits first. People will enjoy the food afterwards – more physically, this time, and in a joyful atmosphere. There is a logic of offering and communion, but ordered along a principle of hierarchy in which the spirits rank first. The cult for domestic spirits does not proceed in a different way, but on a reduced scale.

Such offerings trigger the process of exchange between the living and the spirits. The living show respect and care for the spirits, providing them with a house and food, with light and fire (candles are always lit during ceremonies). They make them feel comfortable with the pleasures of life. This is very close to what is expected from sons and daughters vis-à-vis their aging parents: they have to take care of them, which in Lao is the same word as "to feed" (*liang*). This moral duty goes on after their death, and is prolonged on the village scene through the cult of the local spirits.

On their side, the spirits have to protect the living. They are reminded very clearly of their duty, as appeared during the *thaam* (see pages 137–140): "Please do not eat without concern: take care of the village, of the paddy fields; bring money and valuable things." The logic of exchange is very clear. The political subjectivities mentioned on page 80, about the role and duties of the *aanyaa* chief and his subjects, follow broadly a similar pattern.

These elements are important to show that what takes place on the village shrine is intimately linked to everyday concerns for the villagers. There are continuities between the relationships children have with their parents, those that adults have with their late parents, and finally those that villagers have with their collective spirits. The village cult, in other words, is not a distant reality, but a manifestation of a larger system of asymmetric exchange that pervades the whole of Tai Vat society.

State spirits

During the early revolutionary period, the Lao State authorities opposed many rituals based on their reputedly 'archaic' character that hampered development, and because they supported social relationships of dependence that did not fit with the new regime ideology. This period is analyzed on pages 167–169, but I investigate here how the territorial cults that survived this period have been partly 'domesticated' by the current authorities – and how they have in return domesticated the latter as well. This process is much in line with Grant Evans's (1998) argument about the way kingship symbols and rituals have been taken over by the current authorities to define new legitimacies after the waning of the revolutionary project.

A clear marker of this process is the way in which the village shrine is commented on using references to the state system. The second house in the *thiang seun* of Houay Yong and Houay Lom is described as hosting the former *naai baan* who died while doing their duty or, more generally, "state agents" (*khalatsakan*), as encapsulated by Bunsoon [29]. Another example comes from Pakfèn, a village south of Muang Èt inhabited mostly by Tai Vat [257]. Here, there are three *lak man* in a line – which is different from the standards of the *Huai Yoong* valley. Our main informant told us that, when authorities of the village die, they become *phii baan* and *lak man*. His wife added that the three *lak man* were respectively *hua naa*, *hoong*, and *khana*: these are the words used today to describe the village authorities, with the *naai baan* and his two deputy chiefs. The rhetoric of the state is thus very much present when discussing the village shrine.

In Houay Yong, the materiality of the *lak man* shrine is sometimes phrased using this state rhetoric. The shrine is made of a central post surrounded by smaller ones at a lower level. Their relationship with the central post has been explained in various terms: the central one would represent the first settler of the village, who came from Vietnam, surrounded by the later generations; or their relationship would be like the relationship between an army officer and the soldiers who protect him; or between a leader and the population [4, 64a]. At some point during the interview of Thaabun and Bunsoon already presented, the link between the central post and the lesser ones was explained in reference to the relationship between the village chief and the social institutions of the population, including the mass organizations typical of Marxist–Leninist regimes [91]:

| ອຳພອນ: ເສົາອ້ອມຂອງແຕ່ລະສົນມີຄວາມໝາຍບໍ? | **Amphone Monephachan**: The surrounding posts, do they have a meaning? |
| ທ່ານບຸນ: ມີ. ຮັກສາໄຕນີ້ ຮັກສາໄຕໄຕນີ້ເອີ! | **Thaabun**: Yes. They take care of this one [showing the central post]. |

156 *Territorial cults in a regional perspective*

ອຳພອນ: ໝາຍຄວາມວ່າ ປຣຸບສະເໜືອນ ຄົນທີ່ຢູ່ອ້ອມຂ້າງ ຫຼື ວ່າຍາມເຝົ້າຮັກສາ?	**Amphone**: It means like surrounding people or guardians?
ບຸນສອນ: ເອີ ເອີ!	**Bunsoon**: Yes!
ທ່ານບຸນ: ຄືວ່າງຢ່າງແບບນີ້ ຜູ້ນີ້ເປັນຜູ້ບ້ານເບາະ ເຮົາລະເປັນຮອງບໍ ເປັນປະຊາຊົນບໍ່ຊິບໍ່ ພວກນີ້ບໍ່ ເປັນທະຫານກອງຫຼອນບໍ່ຊິບໍ່າ.	**Thaabun**: Yes. For example. This man [he shows Bunsoon] is the village chief and [making a circle gesture around himself and then around the central post] we are the deputy chief and the population, it is like this. These people are soldiers or guardians, for example.
ອຳພອນ: ຄືວ່າຍັງເປັນຕົວແທນຂອງ...	**Amphone**: It's like representatives of....
ທ່ານບຸນ: ເອີ ເອີ! ຄືວ່າເປັນໃຕແທນໃຫ້ຈຳນີ້.	**Thaabun**: Yes, yes! It's like representatives of this one.
ບຸນສອນ: ການຈັດຕັ້ງທຸກພາກສ່ວນຊັ້ນສາ ອ້ອມລ້ອມເອົາ ຮັກສາເອົາໃຕນີ້ເປັນເຈົ້າ.	**Bunsoon**: Like mass organizations of all kinds, that surround and protect the chief.

Apart from merging state rhetoric with cultual institutions, another way to reconcile the state and territorial cults (and the powers they support) lies in alliances and kinship. I have not been able to ascertain in which measure the old elites have managed to secure positions in the new political structure of the village. It seems on the whole that the ancient ruling families could not conserve their authority, contrary to the continuities that have been observed elsewhere, notably by Bouté among the Phounoy of Phongsali (Bouté 2011: 46–50), where the families who held political positions in the pre-revolutionary regime (*phanyaa* and land chiefs) retained a privileged access to positions at the village level. In Houay Yong, I could simply notice the good relationships between the two groups of authorities, as appeared notably in their joint participation in the yearly rituals on the *phii seun*. The marriage of Vôngkham, the present *chao süa*, to the daughter of Buasai, the leading political figure of the village and the head of the *kum baan* (see pages 41–42), also points to the present mutual co-optation of old and recent elites.

Dual shrines

Until now, we have discussed many aspects of the *lak man* and the *thiang seun*, but have left unaddressed the very issue of their association. In Houay Yong, *Naa Kuu*, and Houay Lom, they appear as twin shrines. It is difficult at first to assert their respective specificity: both protect the village and its population; both are concerned with the ceremonies described in Chapter 5; and both are related to the spirits of the first settlers. There is in fact no circumstance for dealing separately with just one of the two structures.

But there are also differences. *Thiang seun* are small houses related to distinct categories of spirits, the number of which may vary over time,[12] whereas *lak man* is unique and related to spirits in a less particularized way. When informants talk about the *lak man*, they describe it as a power figure, that is, as if it held a proper agency; when discussing the *thiang seun*, agency seems related to the spirits inhabiting the place. Tellingly, Koongbun has no idea about the identity of the spirit of the "old" *lak man*, contrary to the precise knowledge he must display regarding the spirits of each *thiang seun*, which are invoked nominally [239].

By comparison with the *thiang seun* that shelter spirits, the *lak man* acts both as a magnet and as a shell: a magnet to keep the people inside the village through appealing to their desire for a good life and their feeling of belonging; and a shell to protect them from outside dangers. This was very clear in the interview of Bunsoon and Thaabun quoted at length above (see page 149). The strong connection between the *lak man* and the village as a place is evidenced by the story about the resettlement of Houay Louang: after people moved to Houay Lom, they still resorted to a specific *thiang seun*, eventually re-established on the village shrine of Houay Lom, but they were deprived of their *lak man*, the function of which disappeared with the abandonment of the village (see pages 130, 147–148). *Thiang seun* appear as dealing with ancestorship and community, whereas *lak man* appertains to spatiality and settlement.

This distinction is also supported by some comments given by elders from Houay Lom [196]. When we asked them about the difference between the two ritual areas, they replied that they were similar to relatives: if the *lak man* is to be compared with the *naai baan*, the *thiang seun* would be more like *chao süa*. To unpack this comparison, we should not forget that, despite being a local authority, the *naai baan* is clearly an officer of the Lao State. This characterization of two components of the shrine seems to refer to the difference between central state authority (the *lak man*) and the local hierarchies of seniority (the *thiang seun*).

The local comments listed up to now characterize *lak man* as embodying territorial and political relations, in the sense of relationships of authority (and protection) irrespective of lineage. By comparison, the *thiang seun* fall into the domain of kinship and genealogy: they host specific ancestors – Toi, Sing, Nôô, etc. – who are known by their filiation to the living. The difference between *lak man* and *thiang seun* could thus be phrased in terms of the political relationships of authority versus the local relationships of ancestrality. This distinction is not a substantial, but a structural, one: a general principle that fits well with the local systems of representations or, more precisely, with the way male elders in charge of the rituals elaborate discursively on the village shrine. In the ritual practice, however, the two aspects are much more entangled, and many villagers would probably not phrase the distinction in such terms.

A review of the literature reveals the recurrence of similar systems of representation across the whole region. Dual structures are indeed mentioned in the texts on territorial cults throughout the subcontinent, even if this duality is not always explicitly mentioned, and takes various forms. Maspero (1950 [1929]: 24–28) explains that, among the Tai Dam of Upper Tonkin, territorial cults were organized along a hierarchy similar to the "feudal" structure of their polity. There was a spirit for the founding polity (*phii Müang Muai*) at the top of the system; under it came the spirits of the different principalities (*phii müang*), and then the village spirits (*phii baan*). The territorial cult of each *müang* was dual: on one side was the *phii müang*, the spirit of the soil celebrated for the population's well-being; on the other side was the *phii lak müang* or *phii lak süa*, the personal spirit of the current chief. The former was permanent; the latter changed at each incumbent's accession. The former took the form of a large tree in a wood at the boundary of the *müang*'s main village; the latter was a wooden post erected elsewhere, in a small wood. The duality here is between the territorial community at large and the current political incumbent, which is consonant with what is observed in Houay Yong and Houay Long, despite the 90 years that have elapsed since Maspero's early research in French Tonkin.

The introduction of Buddhism among the Tai–Lao populations certainly had many consequences for territorial cults. Hayashi (2003) addresses this issue among the Tai–Lao of northeast Thailand. The territorial spirits (*phii puta*, literally, "the spirits of both paternal and maternal grandfathers") are celebrated in a house built in a forest at the edge of the village (ibid.: 185). Yet there is another territorial cult, addressed to *phii mahesak* (a Pali word, meaning a spirit of great power/authority) at the *lak baan*, a pillar erected on a crossroad inside the village (ibid.: 196). Hayashi describes the various recompositions of territorial cults under the influence of Buddhism. In some cases, the *phii puta* are simply expelled from the religious scene, replaced in their function by Buddha images on a pillar of the *phii mahesak* type, creating a "Buddhicized guardian" also called *lak baan* (ibid.: 198); in other cases, the *phii puta* coexist with such a Buddhicized *lak baan* or with the pillar for *phii mahesak*. Whatever the transformations, Hayashi contrasts the *phii puta*, who sustains the agriculture cycle directly, is connected to the population of a specific village and none other, and is referred to as a relative (see the etymology above), with the *phii mahesak*, who is more concerned with protection and has an extra-territorial nature. "Propitiating *phi[i] mahesak* suggests an obedience to an external power that originates from the universal rulers exemplified in the literary tradition and is seen as a more sophisticated or civilized power holder than the *phi[i] puta*" (ibid.: 196–197, 200).

Archaimbault's description of the *lak man* of Luang Prabang provides another piece of evidence of a dual space for territorial cults. In the former royal capital, there used to be two shrines for the spirits of *lak man*: one outside the city, with a pillar dug into a mound, under the shadow of a tree, and another in a district of the city (Archaimbault 2014: 198). Yearly rituals related to fertility and fecundity had to be carried out successively in the two places (ibid.: 235–238). Although Archaimbault makes no comment about the reason why the *lak man* has two shrines, the duality is once more attested, and takes the form of a structure outside the built area and another one inside.[13]

Territorial cults in a regional perspective 159

As evidenced in the last paragraphs, territorial cults often display a dual structure in Buddhist contexts as well. Of course, the situation is quite different from non-Buddhist settings, notably because Buddhism introduced a new type of shrine into the earlier system: the *that*, or stupa, theoretically containing relics from the Enlightened One. But *that* should not be considered as a 'purely' Buddhist monument of devotion. Holt (2011: 250–255) argues that stupas, and other aspects of Buddhism at large, have been adopted and adapted by the Lao in a religious system that remains mostly focused on the relationship with *phii* spirits, and aims at dealing with their dangerous presence. At a general level, the religious system of the Lao could be described not so much in terms of syncretism between a cult of spirits and Buddhism, but in terms of separate and complementary ontologies (ibid.: 255). In my view, this "inspiriting" of Buddhism makes it fit to take a place in the dual structures described up to now.

Figure 6.4 The city pillar, *lak müang*, of Vientiane (June 2018).

In the 1970s, Zago remarked that, in Vientiane, the That Louang, currently the main stupa and symbol of the country, was celebrated at the same time as the city pillar, *lak müang* (located close to the temple of Vat Si Muang) (Zago 1972: 185–189, 352–353). King Setthathirat, who moved the capital of the kingdom to Vientiane in the sixteenth century, established both places as sacred centers of the city, but with different contents. According to Zago, the *lak müang* refers to an earlier layer of "beliefs." "The two centers are intertwined and intensify each other in the symbolism. The *lak müang* is the Tai popular expression of a center, while the *that* is its Buddhist and royal representation" (Zago 1972: 352; see also Evans 1998: 47). Here, again, the territory is under a dual tutelary protection, one of which is more ancient and popular, whereas the other is related to Buddhism and the king. By comparison with the situation among the Tai Vat (and Tai Dam), Buddhism has provoked a shift, because the *lak müang* no longer occupies the political pole of the duality in Vientiane. This place was taken over by the *that*, which is quite normal in a Buddhist monarchy considering that a relic of the Enlightened One embodies the highest quality of power. The *lak müang* instead incorporates the community/local pole of the dual system.

This long comparative way round aimed to show that, despite their variations, Tai–Lao territorial cults usually present a dual structure. This duality takes various forms and certainly does not refer to the same contents and meanings in all settings, especially when we compare Buddhicized and non-Buddhist contexts. But a generic pattern appears: one pole has more to do with the spiritual powers of the area, whereas the other pole is of a more supra-local nature, and projects the area onto the larger frame of a polity, a world religion, or both. In this way, the coupled shrines of territorial cults tap fertility, fecundity, and protection from both internal and external sources, which is a very effective symbolic structure for meeting the villagers' demands for well-being. The cults provide an original way to conceive and create a place, a community, and the flow of fertility powers, stressing, at the same time, the specific qualities of a locality and its inclusion into a wider entity. This duality possibly explains why the system of territorial cults has been able to accommodate various historical and social conditions, and why it allows thinking of stability and mobility, or autochthony and allochthony, as two sides of the same coin. I do not consider this duality as resulting from a succession of cultural strata, as suggested by Mus's seminal article (1933, 1975), but as an original and structural characteristic of territorial cults in the whole area.

Former presences

Throughout his life-long research, the French ethnologist Charles Archaimbault devoted much attention to the alliance between autochthonous powers and new settlers, which was, according to him, at the core of the oral lore and rituals of the Buddhist monarchies in the region. The ritual presence and symbolic potency of the 'autochthonous' forces were indeed all important in the social and religious systems of the past. For example, in Vientiane, the first inhabitants' representatives took temporally the lead over kingship in ritual competitions of cricket (*tikhi*) (Archaimbault 1973: 1–16). Autochthons also appeared at the forefront of the oral traditions of origins in Champassak's kingdom (Archaimbault 2014: 307–311), during the territorial ritual celebrated in Vat Phu (Archaimbault 1956), during the enthronement ceremonies and yearly rituals in Luang Prabang (Archaimbault 1964, 1973: 20–62; Evans 1998: 144–146; Souksavang 2014), in oral traditions of origins in Chiang Mai (Tanabe 2000), and in both oral traditions and territorial rituals of the Tai Lü (Tanabe 1988: 11; Tanabe 2000: 303).

Turning now to the close area surrounding Houay Yong, there are clear indications that 'autochthons' – which are always a constructed category (Geschiere 2009) – were much more important in ritual and oral traditions until a few decades. There used to be an annual buffalo sacrifice for the *phii müang* of Muang Èt: in two specific forests, "a cow was ritually killed using a hammer by an autochthonous Phwak (sometimes called Tai Phwak by the Tai Nüa), a Mon-Khmer group" (Tanabe 2000: 303). According to Evans (2000: 270), the ethnonym "Phwak" refers in the area to various Mon-Khmer groups, including Khmu and Singmun. In the Tai Dam village of Ban Sot, just a few kilometers from Houay Yong, one of Evans' informants told him:

> The Lao Theung [the generic ethnonym including the Mon-Khmer populations] were in charge of the land ... if we do not hold a ceremony for the *phii* of the Lao Theung before the harvest then the rice harvest will not be good
>
> (Evans 1991: 96).

At first sight, this concern does not appear either in the oral traditions of origin or in the ritual practices of the Tai Vat of Houay Yong. Their story is one of flight, occupation, and expulsion, not of transaction, accommodation, and alliance with earlier inhabitants, or spirits, of the place. They apparently have no regard for the former presence of the Tai Soi or the Khmu. And a story that will be reported later (see pages 166–167) relates that they turned to the powers of Buddhist monks to get rid of spirits that impeded their colonization of the area. Considered in their present state, the territorial cults of the Tai Vat are directed to ancestors of the present community, or protecting spirits brought by the first migrants.[14]

We should nuance this representation, because the current relationship of the Tai Vat to territorial spirits does not amount to a *tabula rasa* principle. This appears at two levels at least.

First, the Tai Vat acknowledge the existence of age-old spirits in the landscape. This appears in the story of the couple of *phii* who inhabited the cliff of *Phaa Boo*, described in the oral lore of Houay Lom; the widow spirit is still in the cave and feared by the living (see page 67). This also appears in their description of the *dông khuaang* ritual, where spirits living in different sections of the territory – mountains, forests, streamlets, canals – were addressed through prayers in front of the twelve tables representing exhaustively the landscape of the area. Despite the disappearance of this ritual, I was told in Houay Yong about a villager – a hunter – who had a personal shrine for the spirits of the water and the soil [239]; there is up to the present a tiny shrine devoted to the spirits of the forests close to the village shrine of Houay Lom (see page 130); I could also observe, in swidden fields on the mountain slopes, the presence of *taalèèo*, hexagonal pieces of wickerwork on top of a bamboo stick that represent an eye to protect the fields from the spirits of the sky (Figure 6.5) [80], and there are stories about spirits living in mountain caves, related to the former Buddhist inhabitants of the area (see page 167). These elements substantiate the occupation of the landscape by spirits who are not all ancestors and who are not all of human origin.

Second, if the earlier presence of the Tai Soi is apparently unacknowledged in the ritual system – no Tai Soi spirit seems to be addressed in *thaam* prayers – this statement must be tempered. Some minimal forms of continuity are recognized. An elder of Houay Yong acknowledged that the *dông khuaang* was originally performed by the Tai Soi [241]. Bunsoon went further: the Tai Vat learned this ritual from the Tai Soi. The latter explained to the new settlers, who were scared on their arrival in the region, that to have good rains and a good

Figure 6.5 Taalèèo. This hexagonal piece of wickerwork on top of a bamboo stick protects the swidden fields. It is erected by the household head after the forest has been slashed down and burned; he tells the spirits of the sky that the *taalèèo* represents him in the fields so that spirits would not come and leave bad seeds mixing with his crops. *Taalèèo* can also be raised in an area where someone brings his cattle to graze [80]. The village of Houay Yong appears in the background (picture taken from the ridge on the east of the village, May 2011).

harvest, they had to perform that ritual, and while doing it, they showed them how to carry it out (*phaa hét*) [257].

This demonstrates that former presences are acknowledged in the ritual system and the memory of the villagers. But they are peripheral compared with what has been reported about the area in the past – as in the mention of the Phwak sacrificer in Muang Èt, or as in addressing the 'Lao Theung' in the ceremonies of Ban Sot. There are currently only scattered signs about former 'autochthons' or the 'chthonian' presences that were so central to the writings of Mus and Archaimbault. What was a collective issue in the past seems to fall now within more individual concerns or into the realm of hearsay. This peripheralization is probably quite recent, and is possibly related to the disappearance of the *dông khuaang* ritual in the 1990s. This ritual appears more and more as a central issue to understanding a history made of continuities and ruptures. Its potential for exploring a distant past is substantive, as explored in the next section.

Müang Yoong

This title is provocative. Despite acknowledging the centrality of Houay Yong for the *dông khuaang* ceremony, no villager in Houay Yong ever described it as the former center of a *müang* polity. However, this hypothesis deserves consideration. I heard at least one very old man using the expression "*Müang Yoong*", but in another village: Chiao Bun, from Ban Kang, whose grandfather-in-law had been taken as a captive to Vietnam by the Yellow Flags, mentioned that, in the past, the whole area used to be called "*Müang Yoong*" and belonged to the Tai Soi [76].

A second toponym supports this argument. During interviews, Houay Yong was repeatedly referred to as "*baan thaao*" [30, 51, 240, 242, 244, 245, 257]. "*Baan*" means "village," and "*thaao*" is the civility used to precede a senior male name, like "Sir." This name is intimately linked to the fact that the village hosted the ritual center of the *dông khuaang* ceremony; it applies only to the 'old' village of Houay Yong, not to its hamlet *Naa Kuu*, established long after. "*Thaao*" hence seems to refer to ritual centrality and seniority, compared with the neighboring villages.

The list of villages concerned with the *dông khuaang* is a long one: beyond Houay Yong, there is Ban Kang, *Naa Kuu*, Nasan, Muang Van, Nahit, Muang Èt, Nalèng, and Ban Sot. Their common point was their dependence on the water of the *Huai Yoong* stream for irrigation of their fields. It is obvious for the villages inside the valley, but Nahit, Muang Èt, Nalèng, and Ban Sot formerly received part of their water from the stream through canals; this is not the case any longer. This 'hydraulic' dimension of the ritual also appears in the fact that the spirits of the sky (who provide rain) and of the streams (including those governing the canals) were clearly addressed, on a ritual area next to a streamlet, in the crucial season before the coming of the rain. So if the political dimension of such rituals is obvious, as is developed in the next paragraphs, one should not ignore that rain and fertility were real issues for these farmer societies. The detailed observations by Tanabe (1991: 6–7, 13, 22, 25) about the territorial cult in Chiang Mai show very clearly that the villages involved all resorted to the same stream for their irrigation, and that the prayers explicitly demanded rain. A comparison with the lowland Lao rituals asking for rain would be an interesting way to prolong this preliminary consideration.

The presence of Muang Van and Muang Èt (seats of the subdistrict and the district) in the list of involved villages is perplexing. The past ritual hierarchy does not coincide with the present political order. To disentangle this complex situation, one needs to explore in detail the role of territorial cults to support yesteryear's 'nested polities' (Scott 2009: 60) distributed throughout the region.

Archaimbault (1991) devoted a fine-grained study to the buffalo sacrifice carried out annually in Xieng Khouang, based on direct observations he made in 1955, and on interviews carried out later. In the past, Xieng Khouang used to be a polity in the orbit of Luang Prabang, similar to Houaphan, but it was more centralized until the first decades of the nineteenth century. It was much more impacted than Houaphan by the havoc prompted by the fall of Vientiane in 1828, and by the invasions of the Chinese Flags in the 1870s (ibid.: 81–82). The French eventually reinstalled the former regional dynasty, with much more limited powers. I do not unpack here the link between the local history and the development of the ritual, which is an important dimension of Archaimbault's book (ibid.: 31, 55, 82). What is more relevant to the present section is that the ritual centered on a twelve-shrine structure located in the polity center: eleven shrines for the dependencies and one for the central *müang* (ibid.: 30, 48). The different territorial components of the polity had to contribute financially to the buying of the buffalo for the sacrifice (ibid.: 1). The very long prayer addressed during the ceremony, translated on 17 pages by Archaimbault (ibid.: 12–28), is for a large part an enumeration of all the locations connected to spirits in the polity, but also to the king's ancestors and other spiritual presences. Using this exhaustive enumeration, the ritual paved a "circuit of sacredness" (*circuit du sacré*), where the central polity held the initiative for the annual renewal, whereas the 12 polities were jointly acknowledged as the favorable (*kun*) pillars of the polity (*lak müang*) (ibid.: 48, 50).

Similar ceremonies used to take place in different polities, and supported similar "circuits of sacredness" between heartlands and subordinate centers, as has been reported about the Tai Lü of Sipsong Panna, in China, by Tanabe (1988). Still dealing with the Tai Lü, Henri Deydier (1954: 108–109), another French ethnologist working for the *École Française d'Extrême-Orient*, reports his observations in Laos, in a polity where two buffaloes, a white one and a black one, were sacrificed every three years for the territorial spirit. Their meat was divided into twelve parts, each of them associated with a hamlet of the polity. The author argues that the correspondence between the local spirits, addressed in the prayers by the Tai Lü, and the territorial components of the polity is a multilayered principle that remains relevant from tiny hamlets to the kingdoms.

This principle of correspondence between the economy of the sacrifice and the territorial subdivisions of the polity applied as well in the Houaphan principalities.

Deydier observed the buffalo sacrifice carried out in Sam Neua during the Lao New Year of 1952 (Deydier 1954: 23–30). Two buffaloes, a white one and a black one, were successively sacrificed close to two territorial spirit shrines. They were butchered into nine parts, each of which corresponded to the territorial spirit of a subdivision of the *müang*.

Tanabe also collected information about the *phii müang* rituals in Houaphan. His observations deserve a long quote, due to their importance to the present research:

> Among the Tai Nüa of Hua Phan province, northern Laos, where I stayed in 1991, the propitiation of *phi müang* had been held in many localities under colonial administration until the 1950s. Ten buffaloes and two cows were sacrificed in the fourth month (around March) at seven different locations including *lak man* (*lak müang*). In the *phi müang* cult rites at Müang Et, at the two most important groves (Dong Süa and Dong Kham) a cow was ritually killed using a hammer by an autochthonous Phwak (sometimes called Tai Phwak by the Tai Nüa), a Mon-Khmer group. In the case of the *phi müang* cult at Xiang Kho, the last of which was held in 1952, twelve buffaloes were killed at different places, including *lak man*, and a cow sacrifice was assigned to a Tai Daeng (Red Tai) village within the domain. In this case the Tai Daeng are regarded as autochthonous (and non-Buddhist) vis-à-vis the Lao, having been resident before Xiang Kho was established.
>
> (Tanabe 2000: 303)

Unfortunately, the first series of sacrifices referred to (ten buffaloes and two cows at seven locations) is not well contextualized: it seems to refer to the whole province, or a whole district. But Tanabe is more precise about the sacrifices taking place in twelve places resorting to the *müang* of Xiang Kho having a *lak man*. At the time, the *Huai Yoong* valley resorted to the *müang* of Xiang Kho, and I argue that the *dông khuaang* celebrated in Houay Yong was one of the twelve rituals. The reference, in the descriptions I collected, to the twelve shrines, the participation of the incumbents of other villages, their financial contribution to the buying of the buffalo to sacrifice,[15] and the minute reference to the territorial components of the area in the *thaam* prayer all allow the casting of the *dông khuaang* of Houay Yong as another politico-ritual enactment of the multilayered *müang* rituals described by the two French ethnologists mentioned earlier. Tellingly, Buasai described the *dông khuaang* ceremony of Houay Yong as addressed to *phii müang* or *phii taasèèng*, the spirit(s) of the district or subdistrict, a clear affirmation of the political dimension of the ritual [27].

All the rituals described share a similar principle. The flow of life and prosperity is secured when the territorial components of the polity, embodied through their territorial spirits, acknowledge the centrality of the *müang*, and when the *müang* center reciprocally acknowledges the necessity of its components to be involved as a whole. The centripetal and centrifugal movements of the dignitaries, the payments, the prayers, and partaking of the meat make up a large ritual operation re-enacting the organic and hierarchical nature of the *müang*.

One can only be struck by the recurrence of number 12 in these rituals: 12 animals to sacrifice, 12 areas involved, 12 tables. A comparative analysis could easily show that this is reported in many other occurrences of territorial cults, as among the Tai Lü (Tanabe 1988: 9) or in Chiang Mai (Tanabe 1991: 10–12), for example. In Tai societies 12 is a number related to completeness (Condominas 2006: 270). As I have shown, the territorial rituals are greatly concerned with exhaustivity – of locations, of spirits – which I interpret as a sign of their involvement with the territory as a whole. They are – they were, in fact – a way of revitalizing annually and extensively the social, political, and religious relationships between higher and lower polities, villages, and natural areas in the whole province of Houaphan.

But why was this ritual celebrated in Houay Yong rather than in the political seats of authority, Muang Van and Muang Èt? The simplest answer is that it reflects a centrality of a distant past, certainly before the Siamese came into the region (1886) and reshaped the ancient *müang* hierarchies (see page 86). The former presence of a *vat* temple in Houay Yong, attributed to the Tai Soi but possibly more ancient, the celebration of the *dông khuaang*, acknowledged by all neighboring villages as taking place in Houay Yong, and the very name of *Baan Thaao* all hint at the possibility that Houay Yong had been the seat of a minor *müang* long ago. I argue that at some point during the nineteenth century, it lost its political status; it kept some kind of ritual preeminence until the end of the twentieth century and it holds up to the present day a symbolic notability in the nearby area.

Buddhist exorcisms

In the 1960s, Buddhist monks were invited to Houay Yong to expel the spirits inhabiting the forest at the bottom of which the *dông khuaang* ceremony took place. They wrote letters telling the spirits to go elsewhere to find their food, because the ceremonies would not take place anymore. After this, the ritual did not disappear: it was displaced about 300 or 400 meters upstream of the *Nam Boo* brooklet. The spirits were told, once more by written notes – made this time by the villagers, one may presume – that the celebration would take place on this new spot. The ritual was performed in this second spot for the last time in the 1990s by Phongsai, the late husband of Mèèthao Leua, who acted as *chao cham*, and died soon after [242, 244].

The coming of the monks mentioned above is also related to a second exorcism ritual they carried out in the present location of Ban Kang. This is well remembered and narrated by the inhabitants of Houay Yong [87, 90, 244, 245, 248]. At the time, the place was a huge forest called *Dông Yoong*, that is, the forest of the *Huai Yoong* River. The place had been chosen to resettle Ban Kang for the third time (see page 5). The monks were reputedly of high religious rank (*maahaa khaao*), and had *mon*, magical powers. According to Thaabun, they were sent by the central administration. They wrote sentences on white sheets of paper that they stuck on the trees of the *Dông Yoong* forest. After this, they announced that the trees could be cut safely because the spirits would go away. The villagers of Ban Kang slashed these huge trees down with the help of fellow villagers from Houay Yong.

The motivations underlying these Buddhist exorcisms are not easy to define. Bunsoon, as *naai baan*, suggests a voluntary and pragmatic initiative. The villages needed to be extended and the people were greatly limited by the presence of the forests. So they asked the subdistrict authorities of the *taasèèng* to help them, and the latter recruited monks from Muang Èt to get rid of the spirits protecting the forests [244, 248]. But a less voluntary process appears in some comments: according to Bunmaa, the objective was rather to "reduce the beliefs" (*lut kwaamsüa*) [245], a point that is discussed in the next section.

The two motivations are not contradictory. It is very possible that some villagers desired to get rid of dangerous spirits and that their demand was received positively by state agents concerned with the policy of "reducing the beliefs," who delegated monks to exorcize the dangerous spirits of the place. In any case, the episode reveals the connections the local non-Buddhist Tai have with Buddhism. Buddhism sometimes appears as a religious competitor linked to the Lao majority and the state system at large: we see in the next section that many villagers consider that Buddhism had been given an advantage by the state during the policy to "reduce beliefs." But sometimes, also, Buddhism appears as an external power to tap when facing a danger such as dangerous spirits,[16] or as a resource more than a competing religious system putting at stake the local representations. This second process is in line with the argument proposed by Holt (2011) that Buddhism can be "animated," rather than animism Buddhicized as often asserted in the literature.

The place of Buddhism in a non-Buddhist, 'animist' context certainly deserves more research, in the region of Muang Èt as elsewhere. There are many stories related to the discovery of Buddha statues hidden in mountain caves, possibly during the period of the wars of Chüang or of the Chinese Flags, in the 1870s and 1880s. Some of them have been found over the last decades in the area of Houay Yong and Ban Sot [66, 239, 242, 246–247, 258]. The caves turned out to be inhabited by spirits of monks, who spoke with a typical Lao accent when they manifested themselves orally. The Buddha statues discovered were mostly sold, or melted down to extract the gold, but misfortunes befell many of those who took part in this business – they became crazy or died. Such stories are statements on morality and power, on Buddhist and non-Buddhist agency, and deserve more attention in the future.

The revolutionary struggle against 'beliefs'

If the village shrine is currently referred to with pride by all villagers, it has not always been the case. For five or six years after the 1975 revolution, many religious practices were forbidden by the new regime. They were despised as "beliefs" (*kwaamsüa*), in the negative sense of 'superstitions,' especially if they involved the sacrifice of animals, which was denounced as detrimental to the village economy (Évrard 2006: 314; Petit 2008b). Territorial rituals were particularly targeted by this struggle, due to their intimate link with the hierarchies of the past. They have been vividly denounced by Vietnamese ethnographers such as Cầm Trọng, who presented them in Marxist terms as the support of the exploitation of the population by the nobility (Cầm Trọng 2004: 235).[17] In Laos, the *lak man* shrine in Luang Prabang was destroyed soon after the 1975 revolution (Tanabe 2000: 302).

Villagers from Houay Yong contend that, during the early revolutionary period after 1975, the prohibition touched nearly all ritual practices [61, 64a, 181]. Some of them stressed that the prohibition lay mostly on ethnic minorities, because their ceremonies were reportedly extravagant and an obstacle to economic development. The authorities urged the population to stop making rituals; a strict prohibition was enforced for three years. During this time, it was forbidden to go and see diviners (*moo yüang*). As a consequence, many people reportedly died because of the uncontrolled agency of the *phii*. No respect was paid to the *phii* of the village; a drought ensued and many people left the place during that period of five or six years. But, after some time, things changed: the preservation of traditions was at stake, and new government policies encouraged "reconstructing the traditions of the different groups" (*hai saang hai saa kheuun mai hiit khoong phai hiit khoong man*). The key date for the introduction of the 'New Economic Mechanism' in Laos, 1986, is sometimes presented as the turning point.

Elders of Houay Lom remember vividly the period of prohibition as well [196]. According to them, the government had a policy of restriction on rituals, and only Buddhists could perform theirs. The villagers of Houay Lom had to remove the domestic shrines from their houses – as well as those outside the houses for the ancestors of the householder's wife – which they did after explaining to their ancestors why they had to do so. Fortunately, the ancestors understood they had no choice, and no misfortune ensued from such inauspicious behaviors. *Moo phii*, diviners and mediums, were forbidden to exert their ritual duties: if one of them had come at someone's request for a cure, she or he could be apprehended by the authorities and punished with one week of forced labor for the subdistrict. No ceremony could be organized at the *thiang seun* terrace: the huts were decaying but could not be restored. People could just whisper a few words out of respect for the spirits when passing close to the shrine. Fortunately, after a rather short period, the authorities became less strict and people could resume their traditions, on the principle that Laos is made up of different groups that have each their own way.

It is interesting to note that, in the two villages, people report that Lao or Buddhists were not affected by those measures. The situation was not so clear, in fact (Hours and Selim 1997; Evans 1998: 57–68, 71–75), but this reflects the perception non-Buddhists had on this policy. Commenting on the coming of Buddhist monks to exorcize the forests (see pages 166–167), Bunmaa described it as part of the policy to "reduce beliefs" [245], another sign of the feeling that Buddhist and state authorities worked hand in hand in the struggle against 'beliefs' and 'animism.'

The village shrine, as has been repeatedly argued in this chapter, encapsulates much more than a bunch of old and distant traditions. It materializes the origins of Houay Yong, the attraction of the place, the link between families, their identity as a corporate group, the protection of the inhabitants, and the power of ancestors and spirits on the local world. The revolutionary prohibitions endangered all that at once, which explains why they have been remembered as a deep alienation.

The memories related to the vagaries of village and domestic shrines are in my view a central trope of a larger narrative on the acting powers of this world. It appeared clearly in an interview of Mèè Ua, the late sister of *Naai baan* Bunsoon. She was a reputed medium, *moo môt*, traveling back and forth between Houay Yong and Thongnamy, where some of her children had settled. In 2008, we had a stimulating discussion in Thongnamy with her and with two other Tai Vat I consider friends, which explains the trusting tone of the interview on a sensitive topic [61]. They explained how the prohibitions on rituals had been enforced until the mid-1980s. Mèè Ua reported that such prohibitions ran against the fact that the spirits are leading the people's lives "for doing, for speaking, and for going" (*phaa hét, phaa waô, phaa pai*). She related the eventual lift of the interdiction against rituals to a specific event. Nouhak Phoumsavanh, the former president of the Lao PDR (1992–1998), fell ill. He went to different hospitals but could not be cured. A woman performed a divination with his shirt and revealed that the *phii* wanted to eat buffalo. Nouhak reportedly complied with the demand, and recovered. After that, people from all the country could resume with ceremonies, and feed the *phii* when the latter asked.[18]

Similar stories about the deadly consequences of disrespect for the *phii* and about the fact that the leaders of the country resorted secretly to their power have been reported elsewhere (Hours and Selim 1997: 312–314; High and Petit 2013: 12–13). They all point to the fact that the humans rely on the spirits for living. *Phii* cannot be discarded, and any attempt by the state to do so inevitably leads to a disaster, because it creates a rupture in the encompassing order of the world. This is why the revolutionary authorities had to back off, and eventually resume respecting and relying on these acting powers of the world, as captured by Mèè Ua's story on the former president – an interesting example of the way history is phrased by a female medium's voice in Houay Yong.

The disappearance of *dông khuaang*

However, despite the resurgence of the domestic and village shrines in Houay Yong, the *dông khuaang* ceremony eventually disappeared after a final celebration in the 1990s. Three comments by villagers divulge the range of local explanations. The first is from Mèèthao Leua, the widow of Phongsai, the last *chao cham* who carried out this ceremony [242]. She explained that, if the ritual were to be performed every year, it would have been a very good thing. But it was not the case anymore when her husband took up the position. The spirits were unhappy with this; they made Phongsai ill, and eventually "took" him. Mèèthao

170 *Territorial cults in a regional perspective*

Leua insisted that, despite her own wish, her husband could not see the development (electricity, pipes) that reached the village soon after his death. The second comment is from Koongbun, the present *chao cham* of Houay Yong, who argues that the tough point for Phongsai was that the ritual was not celebrated annually anymore, due to the difficulty in raising from the different villages the funds for buying the buffalo; this is why the spirits killed Phongsai [239]. Koongbun added he would never himself accept performing the ceremony, for fear of sharing the fate of his fellow. The third statement is from Bunsoon, who alleges that the *dông khuaang* made sense only when people relied on swidden cultivation (*hai*), which was directly dependent on rain; today, people cultivate their rice in paddy fields, for which the coming of the rain is less consequential [244].

These three accounts are not as casual as they might seem. Mèèthao Leua relates the end of the ritual and the death of her husband to the period preceding the implementation of infrastructure in the village, as if there was a contrast between this ceremony encapsulating the values of the past and the development of the modern nation. The remark made by Koongbun about the difficulty to raise funds to organize the ceremony annually suggests that the current values are far from the solidarity on which the *dông khuaang* used to rest in the past. As for the explanation given by Bunsoon, it reflects the trope of modernity accessed through stopping swidden cultivation, a grand narrative on development widely circulated by the Lao regime in the highlands. The three accounts articulate the past, the present, and the future. They link the disappearance of the *dông khuaang* to the current transformations of the local community and its inclusion into the modern development state.

There is, however, another layer of analysis. A ritual makes sense only if it is related to a community, in the sense of a group of people who share some ideas on their identity, or carry something out together. The former system of nested polities certainly produced a strong sense of community at different levels. Similarly, dependence on the same water in a hydrographic basin must have triggered a sense of unity among farmers when this dependence was high. But currently, the old system of *müang* has been dismantled, and the new irrigation systems made outlying villages less and less dependent on the *Huai Yoong* River. Evans remarked long ago that in Laos:

> the overthrow of the old Tai aristocracy by the communists saw the disappearance of religious rituals associated with the *lak müang* which defined intermediate political spaces [that is, between the village and the nation-state], and these rituals devolved to the village (*ban*) level where only *phi ban* and *phi heun* [*phii heuan*, spirits of the house] are now observed.
>
> (Evans 2000: 284)[19]

This is exactly what happened in Houay Yong, where the spirits of the house and the village are still honored, because they refer to corporate units that are still active today. If the rituals addressing the spirits of the house, the village, and the *müang* have been similarly affected by the policy against "beliefs," only the first two were plainly revived after this period, because their resilience rested on social institutions that had not disappeared. The former territorial unit appearing in the *dông khuaang* does not constitute a corporate unit anymore, in any sense of the term.

However, the presentation of the *dông khuaang* as a disappeared tradition does not capture, in my view, the intimate feeling of the Tai Vat for this ritual. Many people simply say that it has not been carried out for many years, as if some opportunity could prompt the performance again. And when he guided us to the place upstream the *Nam Boo* brooklet where the ceremony was held by Phongsai for the last time, Bunsoon showed us a small patch of forest that had been voluntarily conserved there till the present, despite most of the forest having been slashed down: "one never knows for the future, we could carry on with the ceremony."

Notes

1 Maspero (1950: 28) mentions that Black Tai close the whole territory of their *müang* to any stranger during the yearly worship to the territorial spirits, allowing no one to trespass the borders. During rituals for territorial spirits among the Tai–Lao of northeast Thailand, posts of wickerwork (*taalèèo*) are erected to prevent outsiders from trespassing the village boundaries, while the villagers are not allowed to leave the village and refrain from working (Hayashi 2003: 193). The same remark applied to territorial cults among the Lü of China: during the rituals for the village spirits, "the village territory was sealed off with magical hexagons, the two gates at either end of the village were closed, and all villagers were confined within" (Tanabe 1988: 10). As for the ritual for the *müang* district:

> all the villages closed their gates and the entire *moeng* was sealed off with magical hexagons and written notices prohibiting people from moving in and out of the territory. It is said that those who violated this prohibition were fined.
> (Ibid.: 11–12)

2 In the past, *Naa Kuu* used to have a specific *chao cham* [242].
3 The Tai Dèng were no more than four families living in the place called *Taat Ling* (the waterfall of monkeys) just before they settled in Houay Louang.
4 The population amounted to 25 families in 1983 (see Map 2.1).
5 Maspero uses both names, as well as a third one: *lak süa*, by reference to the shirt used to invite the spirits to come during ceremonies (Maspero 1950: 27).
6 Archaimbault (1991: 26, 64) argues that the *lak man* mentioned in the recitation during the annual sacrifice of a buffalo in Xieng Khouang referred to the post of Luang Prabang. As nothing in his text substantiates his opinion, I rather hold that it is another local occurrence of that word used throughout northern Laos.
7 The literature reports many cases where incumbents of territorial shrines have to respect ritual prohibitions for the sake of the community's welfare. This has been reported in detail by Coville (2003: 94, 97), for example, about the (male) "mothers of the land" among the Toraja: by respecting prescriptions, the mothers of the land allow the uninterrupted flow of fertility and fecundity to the benefit of the whole territory. Going one step further, this extensive set of prohibitions on behalf of the community's well-being seems very close to the one surrounding the "sacred kings" evoked by de Heusch (1987) in his neo-Frazerian analyses.
8 Archaimbault edited a document authored by Maspero about the ceremony for changing the *lak süa*, or *lak müang*, among the Black Tai; this does not contradict the

172 *Territorial cults in a regional perspective*

rhetoric on stability embodied by the post, as appears in a casual remark about the necessity that the post should never lean, which would cause trouble (Archaimbault 1991: 49, 165–166).

9   I adhere here to Dumont's (1966) theory about moral hierarchies and the way they can be reversed in specific contexts.
10 Lévy reports that the invasion of Luang Prabang by the Tai of Đèo Văn Tri in 1887 was attributed to the discontinuation of the territorial cult that included a buffalo sacrifice (Lévy 1956: 855). The lack of respect or piety for the city pillar of Chiang Mai similarly triggered tragic consequences (Tanabe 2000: 300).
11 The homology between the ritual post of the village or polity, and the posts of the house, should be investigated thoroughly. According to Cầm Trọng (2004: 233–234), among the Tai of Vietnam, the *müang* polity is conceived as a house: this is why it needs posts, *lak müang*, as a house needs foundation posts.
12 Koongvaa declared that there used to be five *thiang seun* in Houay Lom in 2011 [71]. And according to Koongbun, long ago, there used to be up to five such houses in the shrine of Houay Yong [239].
13 Deydier (1954: 186–197) provides an interesting and lively description of the ritual taking place in the two shrines devoted to the *lak man* of Luang Prabang.
14 See Tannenbaum and Kammerer (2003: 4) and Hayashi (2003: 190) on this distinction.
15 Archives dated 1906 report similarly that, in the principality of Houa Muang (see Map 3.1), each village contributed to the buying of the buffalo to be sacrificed during the annual ceremony in the center of this *huaphan* (RSL E4, 22/11/1906).
16 Similarly, the Khmu of Nangiu faced a tough situation after they were forcibly resettled from Nong Thop in the early 2010s: many deaths occurred in the new settlement [256]. They discussed the problem and decided to resort to monks, who performed a ceremony in 2018 in their new village to lift misfortunes, in replacement of their annual ceremony devoted to the village post (*klak*, in the local Khmu idiom). In fact, they have five village posts: one in the middle of the village, and four disposed in a square at the corners of the village. The annual celebration is normally organized in April/May.
17 See also Tanabe (1988: 19) who analyzes territorial cults among the Lü in terms of "an ideological apparatus employed by a ruling class as an alternative to the use of violence," and the criticisms against this Marxist approach by Evans (1991: 94–95), who stresses the need to consider the issues of identity as well.
18 The chronological discrepancy between the relaxing of the prohibitions (in the mid-1980s) and the presidency of Nouhak (in the 1990s) is not uncommon when dealing with oral history; this leaves open the question of why Nouhak had been chosen in this narrative, rather than another political figure.
19 Similarly, Tanabe (1988: 14–18) notes that house and village spirits among the Lü are still honored today in Communist China, whereas those of the former *müang* disappeared with the policy of the Great Leap Forward (1958). He explains this by referring to the persistence of the two lower units in the new administrative frame (the former villages became "production teams" during collectivization), whereas the new "communes" did completely supplant the former *müang*, making rituals at this level obsolete.

7 Conclusion

In a nutshell

Despite its peripheral status in a 'remote' area of Laos, Houay Yong turned out to be a stimulating place to investigate ethnohistory, that is, history as it is locally remembered, narrated, and set in motion, notably through oral traditions and rituals. This has never precluded a deep interest in a more classical, chronological, event-based history, for which the engagement with written sources was imperative. In my view, these two orientations of research should be linked. To phrase it differently, the quest for the objective aspects of history has never been exclusive to research on the ideological and performative aspects of historical narration, in line with Vansina's (1985) recommendations. I have analyzed the way in which people imbue the past with political assertions and moral values, and use it as a resource for the present. I also introduced materiality and embodiment in the discussion on memory and history, and I adopted a comparative stance on territorial cults in the whole region, changing the scale of the research to insert this ethnography into larger debates. I hope this book can serve as a heuristic model for other scholars pursuing similar aims in other contexts.

Let us summarize important achievements of this research and conclude this work on the past and present with some considerations of the way the Tai Vat appraise their future.

After introductory remarks on the relational nature of Tai Vat ethnicity and the ongoing process of Laoization, and after a glimpse of the intricacies of the village political scene and the everyday presence of the Lao State, I launched the core argument of this book with a discussion on orality and written culture to give an idea of the different regimes of history in the valley. Former administrative centers, such as Muang Van, have a more text-based form of history, whereas the nearby villages rely more exclusively on orality. Orality is not to be opposed to materiality: I have highlighted throughout the text how landscapes, shrines, and rituals also elicit memory, or are evoked during narration. History turned out to be an unequally shared competence: it is a prerogative of male elders from the leading families, that is, patrilineal descendants of the first settlers, or local state agents. This uneven distribution of historical authority across the population, especially across genders, definitely deserves further research. If event-based history (*pavat*) is the domain of men, then how do women appropriate the past? Biographies or family-oriented stories are an option, but there should be much more to say.

Oral history brought to the fore the massive impact of the invasion by the Chinese Flags armies, in the 1870s. These invasions caused the departure of Tai Vat families from Yên Châu, or Muang Vat as it was called at the time. This period of havoc is vividly remembered today through the founding myth of the brothers coming from Yên Châu, which serves as a political charter about the links between the different segments of the Tai Vat population in the valley, erasing chronological differences to present an integrated image of the different settlements through a sibship story.

Oral accounts were most useful to disentangle the progressive settlement of the valley, with the Tai Soi 'first' inhabitants, the coming of the Tai Vat from Yên Châu, and the fluxes of the population in the neighboring villages. Further research should be conducted about the Tai Soi and their perplexing settlement in different areas of Muang Èt district, and about their presumptive expulsion from Muang Soi in the early nineteenth century. It would be most useful to connect with the descendants of those who left Houay Yong in the 1940s, after the Japanese occupation – I devoted time to do so, in vain. The Buddhist presence in the valley, which possibly predates the settlement of the Tai Soi, is another issue left largely unpacked for lack of information: archaeology could be helpful to sort out this vexed question. As for the presence of the Khmu, who reportedly moved out due to the coming of the different Tai Dam/Tai Vat groups, further research should be carried out with those living west of the valley, in Nangiu.

I tried to avoid too parochial a focus on Houay Yong through an insistence on the regional context, based on archives and other colonial documents. Such sources were instrumental to understanding the colonial regime, which turned out to be grounded on indirect rule due to the shallow presence of the French in the region, and their limited access to the hinterland. The archives were also a captivating source to investigate the economic history of the region, replacing the area in the precolonial long-distance trade networks and in the international capitalism of the colonial era (notably through the local production of raw shellac).

The First Indochina War had a massive demographic, social, political, and cultural impact in the valley. The climate of tension and the fighting in northwest Vietnam before the battle of Điện Biên Phủ led to a large-scale migration of Tai Vat and Tai Dam into Laos. Due to the origins of its population, Houay Yong became a hotspot of concentration for the refugees. Soon after General Giap's campaign (April 1953), the political order of *phanyaa* lordship was definitely overthrown, provoking a major break with the lineage hierarchies of the past. Here, also, pending issues remain. Why did so many refugees settle permanently in Houay Yong rather than coming back to Yên Châu after the end of the First Indochina War? How did they concretely access land and positions in their new settlement? What were their links with the administration of the time? The present-day contacts between Houay Yong and Yên Châu also deserve more attention. As for the overthrown elites, we have seen that the leading lineages of the past have not lost all prerogatives: their members still play a central role in the communal rituals of the village and are acknowledged as authorities on history and traditions. Their links with the current official elites are part and parcel of their resilience. The mutual co-optation of new and old elites is one of the possible reasons explaining the primacy of Houay Yong in the political arena of the valley.

The history of the region during the Second Indochina War has just been glossed over. I felt less comfortable with that period which raised sensitive issues. War did not appear very often in conversations, but I did not inquire explicitly about it, because it involved living people and traumatic memories. I am convinced that research conducted with care on that period would be a great contribution on the role of highlanders during the conflict, but also on the early transformations of peasant societies during the initial phase of the communist regime.

The next steps of history – the period following the communist victory of 1975, the "New Economic Mechanism" of 1986, the post-revolutionary present – were marked as the former periods by mobility, in two senses at least. First, there has been a constant process of village divisions and fusions, geared by the successive administrations, but also by the war, and the fear of bombing. Second, the flux of migration, launched on a limited scale and under state control during the last years of the twentieth century, has enormously expanded since the year 2000, leading to the creation of a large Tai Vat neighborhood in Thongnamy, and eventually to a massive youth migration to Vientiane that has deeply changed the social and economic life of Houay Yong, mostly populated nowadays by elders and children.

The second focus of this book – territorial cults – inspired a material and performative turn to the approach of the past, usually carried out through archives and oral accounts. The *lak man* and *thiang seun* turned out to be central institutions for the village as a corporate unit: their transformations through time are telling and have been analyzed in a comparative perspective. They help to address the relationship of the villagers to the past, the representations of authority and power, and the resilience and creativity of local society through the vicissitudes of the last decades.

Mus (1933) and others after him developed the hypothesis that territorial cults form a "cadastral religion." I have been able to scrutinize and extend this hypothesis through the ethnography of neighboring village shrines in the valley, exploring their role in the creation of corporate groups and boundaries, and showing how 'cultual units' are interrelated with the history of fusions, fissions, and resettlement. The present research gives credence to Mus's seminal idea, but based on empirical evidence that was lacking in his text.

I have explored the category of *lak man* both in its distribution, unmapped before, and in its semantics of "stability," which does not preclude the acknowledgment of mobility in societies that cultivate an ethos of pioneers. The link of such cults with the old lineage precedences, the generational and familial hierarchies, and the current political order is manifest. The respect due to the shrine, as well as its position above the village, puts it at the top of the local society, similar to the position family ancestors occupy in the domestic sphere. The homology between domestic ancestor cults and territorial cults deserves further analysis, through minute attention to ritual practices and the content of prayers.

The aptitude of the village's shrine to adapt to the current political order is striking, and attests that resilience relies on transformative capacities. People use references to the *naai baan* institution, mass organizations, or state agents when explaining the functions and the structure of the shrine. Despite this, the shrine is still under the ritual authority of the founding lineage, in potential friction with the current state order. Such continuities are ethnographic nuggets for rethinking social change under revolutionary transitions.

The dual character of territorial cults is attested to throughout the whole area. A review of the literature on Tai–Lao territorial cults, from the text of Maspero (1950 [1929]) to the volumes edited by Tannenbaum and Kammerer (2003) and Schlemmer (2012), reveals that duality is a recurring attribute more than an exception. This duality takes varying forms, depending on the context and on the possible Buddhicization of the society, but it usually contrasts a local, community-oriented pole, with an extraterritorial, polity-oriented pole. This duality makes the territorial cult fit to adapt to changing contexts, because the poles may be loaded with different contents.

'Autochthony' hardly appears as a category in the present ritual practices linked to territorial cults, in sharp contrast with what is asserted in many earlier studies devoted to this question. However, until the early 1990s, the category was still relevant in the territorial cults of the close region, as attested to by the research of Evans and Tanabe. This observation could probably be confirmed in other provinces of Laos, which raises the issue of the status of autochthony in the country at large. The Lao State has rejected any distinction based on precedency among the different peoples of the nation; it does not acknowledge the notion of "indigenous people" (Goudineau 2000; Pholsena 2006: 77–118). This paradigm disavowing the autochthon/allochthon divide extensively used in the past triggered many consequences – still to explore – on rituals or ceremonies, and sparks frictions with those who consider themselves as first comers – remember the Khmu leader of Nangiu asserting that their ancestors were "born here" and did not come from anywhere else (see page 79; see also Petit [2013a: 14] on the Khmu's self-proclaimed anteriority). Another research avenue would be to work more closely with villagers familiar with the village territory, such as hunters or upland farmers, to investigate their own representations and practices in relation to the landscape: personalized accounts about those who were there 'before' and left traces in the landscape could be rewarding.

In past periods, the hierarchical principle mentioned above went well beyond the village limits. The *dông khuaang* ritual inserted Houay Yong into a larger network of territorial cults celebrated across yesteryears' *müang* polities through-

Conclusion 177

out Houaphan. It connected political structure to the flow of life and prosperity. The analyses developed by Maspero (1950) about the Black Tai of northern Vietnam and by Archaimbault (1991) about the former kingdom of Xieng Khouang are relevant to Houaphan as well. Strangely enough, the celebration of the *dông khuaang* until the 1990s in Houay Yong proves that everything did not disappear after the 1953 revolution, contrary to an opinion shared by many scholars.

The link between Buddhism and territorial cults among non-Buddhist people of the highlands is another fascinating topic for further research. The connection between the two religious systems cannot be appraised through the paradigm of resistance and conversion. I feel much more in line with Holt's (2011) seminal idea on the "inspiriting" of Buddhism. This does not preclude the possibility of antagonistic relations, especially as Buddhism is related to the state elites in Laos, but there is mutual embedment as well, and mutual instrumentalization of the two systems that have cohabited for centuries.

Eventually, I questioned the place of territorial rituals in the recent history. The revolutionary struggle against the so-called "beliefs" had a profound impact at the turn of the 1970s and 1980s, creating a shared traumatic memory for the evaluation of moral politics and for thinking the acting powers of the world. The resilience of the local religious institutions has been strong, and could have been deciphered using Scott's (2009) theories of resistance against the state. However, I did not follow that perspective because it does not consider properly the role played by the local state employees, or the selective evolutions of territorial cults at large. The persistence of cults turned to domestic and village spirits contrasts with the disappearance of the rituals linked to *müang* polities: this in my view cannot be understood based on concepts of domination and resistance.

With all these elements in mind, it seems obvious that territorial cults are a central institution – in their material, social, and symbolic dimensions – to think the past and the present, and to lift the veil on some layers of history that do not surface easily in the narratives of the past.

Epilogue: of spirits, cement, and the future

The village shrine, I should add, is also a good place to think about the future. To end this volume about the relationship that Tai Vat have with their past, let us take a last breath of ethnography to show how the village shrine is not just a memory device: it also helps villagers to articulate their expectations for the times to come. I engage more directly with the circumstances that led to using cement to strengthen the village shrines, an episode I have already outlined before (pages 8–9, 122–125).

In 2009, during our very first visit to the village shrines in Houay Yong, *Naai baan* Bunsoon ended the visit asking if we could provide funds for renovating the *lak man* and the *thiang seun* [4]. At the time, they were built in wood, and hence vulnerable to termites. Bunsoon thought it would be much better to have constructions in cement that should not be built again and again, every year; he

178 *Conclusion*

listed the materials and the budget to do so, around $US80 at the time. I was surprised by this request presented ten minutes after his strong assertion about "no change, no repair" (*boo pian boo pèèng*). I felt a bit desperate (as an old-fashioned, nostalgic art historian) but I promised to help the village community during our next stay (as a dedicated anthropologist of contemporary worlds).

The following month, we met Mèè Ua, the sister of Bunsoon living in Thongnamy. I have already presented this reputed medium (*moo môt*) on page 169. We were discussing with her and her son-in-law and had disclosed the intent of her brother to strengthen the village shrines with cement. Both of them felt that it was an odd idea: the spirits are not accustomed to such houses; how could they remain in them? The shrines (*hoo*) of *phii* cannot be changed (*pian*). Eventually, the son-in-law said that one could try, and that the spirits would elicit dreams to express their reaction; according to him, the domestic shrines and the *lak man* are very similar to the shrines Buddhists build on their side, but only Buddhists have "solid" *vat* (temples), compared with the wooden ones of the Tai [64a].

We did not come back in January 2010 as expected, but in June. Soon after our arrival, Thaabun, the respected elder, told us incidentally that "the state" had committed to funding the renovation of the village shrines, but eventually didn't, so that villagers had to contribute to it [10]. It took our team a few minutes to understand that we were "the state" – presumably due to our position as researchers mandated by the National University.

Two days later, we visited the village shrines with *Naai baan* Bunsoon. The *lak man* had been embedded in cement and a pedestal lay at its base, surrounded by the bottoms of bottles (see Figures 1.3 and 5.4). A date had been molded on the cement when it was fresh: 2 February 2010. The roof of thatch and the wooden posts of the *thiang seun* had been similarly replaced by new ones in cement. Bunsoon explained to us what had happened: as *kinchiang* was approaching and we had not come yet, the villagers contributed to the capital for the renovation, and the missing amount of money was borrowed from an enterprise; however, they hoped we could return the capital for funding (which I did, of course). The villagers thought it was a good idea to protect the *lak man* and *thiang seun* in this way, because cement makes the shelters of the spirits, as they phrased it, "like our houses," that is, "complete, perfect" (*sômbuun*). Bunsoon further explained that they had proceeded like the Buddhists who share the costs for building their village temple [29]. So they renovated the shrine as planned, taking the precaution to make a ceremony (with offerings of alcohol and *thaam* prayers) to announce the forthcoming change to the spirit of *lak man* [91].

Changing the "unmovable," "never-to-be-mended" *lak man* in this way is not a village fancy. It takes place in a broader, national context, as the reference to Lao religious culture reflects in the preceding accounts. Interestingly, the reference to the Lao Buddhist temples was raised twice, but with different meanings. Against the use of cement, Mèè Ua and her son-in-law objected that Tai spirits are not used to living in permanent temples as the Lao Buddhist spirits do. Inversely, her brother Bunsoon explained that the change was made possible by the solidarity the villagers displayed, similar to the solidarity of the Lao when

Figures 7.1 and 7.2 An old house and a new house in Houay Yong. The new house (Figure 7.2) belongs to Buasai, the head of the *kum baan* (see pages 41–42); it was the most imposing house in the village at the time (June 2010).

180 Conclusion

they build a temple. Hence the material innovation attunes the local cult to national standards, that is, to the Lao "solid" temples. In a similar way, the reference to "perfected" (*sômbuun*) buildings is in line with the current discourse on development and progress (*chaleuun*), which unequivocally values hard structures in concrete and cement rather than wood and thatch. Such values have gone well beyond the state's modernist agenda: they are currently shared by the vast majority of the population, as mentioned by Bunsoon when he compared the renovated shrine with the houses of the villagers ("like our houses"). In Houay Yong, having a "solid" house is an explicit sign of prosperity (Figures 7.1 and 7.2). It is the most usual form of investment, especially as remittances have allowed forms of capitalization.

What happens in Houay Yong is not an isolated fact. On Road 6A, alongside the River Ma, new village posts and monuments have been built in cement, as we observed in the villages Nahit and Sop Hao (Figures 7.3 and 7.4) [232, 233].

These buildings are recent (2013 for Nahit; "a few years ago" for Sop Hao). The one in Nahit, advertising a commercial company at its base, has no proper ritual function. The one in Sop Hao has been built on the initiative of the deputy chief of the village; some people died after its building, until a small house was erected (see to the right of Figure 7.4), presumably to offer a shelter to the spirits. But it seems that this modern building has no cultual function, which is devoted to another shrine in the village.

Figure 7.3 The *lak baan* of Nahit, next to the village board (June 2017). The jar of rice beer (*lao hai*) represented on the top has recently become an icon of the ethnic or village solidarity for highland societies in Laos (Oliver Tappe, personal communication).

Figure 7.4 The *lak baan* of Sop Hao (June 2017).

Figure 7.5 The *lak müang* monument in Sam Neua (June 2010).

182 *Conclusion*

All these new village monuments take their inspiration from a larger building: the *lak müang* of the provincial capital, Sam Neua (Figure 7.5). A link between that monument and the village shrine of Houay Yong was explicitly made by Thaabun, the historian of the village, who argued that the two buildings held similar functions for their respective places [10].

According to an article published in a Lao magazine (*Vatthanatham* 2008), the construction of the *lak müang* monument in Sam Neua started in 2007 for a total cost of above 4 billion kip (about $US500,000). The building was inaugurated by provincial authorities on 17 May 2008. After Buddhist ceremonies (*tak baat, yaat nam*), there were official parades and entertainment. On the top of the four posts is a kind of jewel that is 'sacred' (*saksit*); the *lak müang* is a symbol (*sannyalak*) of origins (*muunsüüa*), of bravery, of the people of Houaphan; it unifies the people through solidarity; it is the center that unifies the hearts and commits people (*chitchai*). An officer interviewed by Tappe (2017: 72) explained that the stylized gemstone on top of the monument represents the indestructibility of Sam Neua and its people, which survived despite the massive bombing by American planes during the war.

The designs in red and white on the lower half of the *lak müang* are inspired by the well-known traditional fabrics of the province. Slogans are written on the four posts, each with a message of the kind often seen on propaganda boards: "Let us all work for development and progress"; "Leading the people to ensure peace and good fortune"; "Keeping together provides peace and happiness"; "Governing the homeland with justice."[1]

The monument has been built in front of the main offices of the province (which were moved to a building nearby afterwards). The wall facing the monument represents allegories of the "liberation war," showing fighters and people with the communist and the national flags on their back (Figure 7.6). Such scenes are in line with the representations of the national liberation struggle

Figure 7.6 Revolutionary scenes on the side of the *lak müang* park in Sam Neua (June 2009).

Conclusion 183

displayed everywhere across the country as a token of the legitimacy of the present political order (Tappe 2013a, 2013b, 2017).

The monument is famous across the whole nation, due to the publicity given to its inauguration and its quick adoption as an icon for the province, as one can see in Figures 7.7 and 7.8.

The gap with the territorial spirit shrines discussed up to now is manifest. Questioned about the relationship between these recent monuments and the *lak man* of Houay Yong, Bunsoon drew a sharp distinction [259]. The new monuments are all *lak baan*: they are symbols (*sannyalak*), intended to show the specific identity (*éékalak*), to host public celebrations of the traditions (*sadèèng paphéénii*), as a reminder of the history of the place, but they host no spirit (*phii*). By contrast, the shrines in the villages are *lak man*; they date back to a remote past and are places of religious respect (*napthüü*) for all villagers. Bunsoon considers building a *lak baan* monument in the central area of the village in the years to come, to ornament public celebrations.

Other differences can easily be enumerated, such as the use of writing on the Sam Neua monument – an important device to grant authority to the past, as argued by Scott (2009: 226–228). The materiality of cement must also be considered. It is endowed with connotations of modernity and development, the ubiquitous tropes of the present regime. Besides, the 'monumental turn' solidifies cultural practices that used to previously be carried out more flexibly. The area for the *lak man* in Luang Prabang did not support permanent structures in the past. The yearly ritual began with the sacralization of the ritual space (as was apparently the case with the *dông khuaang* ceremony in Houay Yoong, for which no permanent structure has been reported): pieces of wood and bamboo

Figure 7.7 Painting of the Sam Neua *lak müang* on the side of a long-distance bus linking the provincial capital to Vientiane. The gem-like ball on top of the monument is pictured as shinning, which reinforces its reputation to be sacred/animated (*saksit*) (June 2010).

184 *Conclusion*

Figure 7.8 The *lak müang* of Sam Neua pictured on a scenery décor in the city's cultural hall. Concerts and other performances were held to celebrate a meeting with (mostly Vietnamese) investors. The *lak müang* appears (on the left) with a woman spinning cotton, a man playing a mouth organ, another one crafting a basket, vestiges of the local megalithic cultures, a limestone karst mountain with an entrance to a cave, and traditional houses on stilts close to a river with fishers and boats (June 2011).

were cut and fixed together; candles were lit; invocations were voiced; and the spirits came. "Why make a solid shrine?" asked Deydier (1954: 190), apparently reporting the comments of the attendance in 1952.

Despite all these differences, parallels have to be investigated as well. As reported above, Thaabun insisted on the similar functions the *lak man* of Houay Yong and the monument of Sam Neua held in their respective places [10]. The various comments on the two structures underscore their resilience, the presence of something 'sacred' (*saksit*) inside, the unity of the people around them, and the deep commitment (*chitchai*) they elicit. Oliver Tappe more recently developed a larger argument about the continuity between the old and the new city monuments in Laos (Tappe 2013a, 2013b, 2017; see also Evans 1998: 114–128). He shows, for example, that the recent statues of the former kings in Vientiane have been animated through ceremonies (Tappe 2017: 69), a process described in detail by Ladwig (2015), who stresses the continuity of those ceremonies with the old rituals to empower Buddha statues and endow them with agency. It is likely that the ceremonies carried out for the inauguration of the monument in Sam Neua, including *tak baat* and *yaat nam*, aimed at inviting some kind of generic spirit into the monument as well: the reference to the sacredness (*saksit*) of the gem-like sphere on top of the post makes it like a power figure more than a purely commemorative space.

Another similarity between the two sets of buildings is their embodiment of the system of nested polities. Maspero (1950), Deydier (1954), and Archaimbault

Conclusion 185

(1991) discussed, in different ways, how the territorial cults enacted the political hierarchies among the Tai polities of the past. In the present day, diffusing a common pattern of posts across Houaphan Province practically re-establishes a pyramid of rank topped by the *lak müang* monument of Sam Neua, in line with the current political order.

The Sam Neua monument must certainly be put in perspective with other attempts of the modern states – revolutionary or not – to forge legitimacy through the appropriation of components of the old territorial cults.[2] This is another instance of "the invention of traditions" (Hobsbawm and Ranger 1983), by which local and national identities are crafted using bits and pieces of the past. For example, during the colonial era, when Paksane (central Laos) was raised to the level of a province, a shrine was built to honor the *phii müang* of the new entity (Zago 1972: 188). And the very first revolutionary journal of the Vietminh-inspired Tai Association for Saving the Homeland, in Sơn La Province (see page 101), was titled *Lắc Mường*, the Vietnamese transliteration of *lak müang*, with the view to promote the revolution (Cầm Trọng 2004: 303; Le Failler 2014: 418; Lentz 2019: 25, 256).

However, the villagers of Houay Yong and their neighbors do not seem to feel overwhelmingly constrained or disturbed by these recent transformations. Bunsoon explained that it would be good to build a monumental post in the central place of the village, even if this would never replace the *lak man* as a place of religious power. His approach on the issue was rather unflustered, and I would like to stress in my last two vignettes the casualness people can adopt when dealing with those issues. This is a friendly corrective to the sense of awe, hierarchy, and political concern that appeared in many ways in the preceding chapters.

Figure 7.9 Laughter in Houay Lom: "Spirits are like people, and people are like spirits." From left to right: Buaphoon, *chao süa* of Houay Louang; Koongthéé, *chao süa* of Houay Lom; Amphone M.; and Buakham, an elder of Houay Lom (June 2014).

186 *Conclusion*

In 2014, we visited the village of Houay Lom, together with Bunsoon [195–196, 198]. We had a walk with the two *chao süa* of the place (see page 148) and some elders, to visit the village shrine. The elders eventually asked me if I could help them strengthening the shrine with cement as I did in Houay Yong. Here again, I asked about the suitability of such houses for the spirits: could the latter easily accept such a major change? I was answered jokingly by Buakham: "spirits are like people, and people are like spirits" (*phii khüü khôn, khôn khüü phii*), which provoked laughter from all (Figure 7.9).[3]

Of course spirits want good houses like people do. They went on to explain that, sometimes, the *phii* make people dream that they want their shelters to be repaired; sometimes, also, this lack of repair explains why a sick person has not been able to recover. Inversely, if the spirits are provided with good houses, they bring good things to the villagers. Bunsoon, who attended this conversation, approved the arguments of his neighbors, and confirmed: no specific problem had occurred in his own village since the *thiang seun* had been cemented. With such convincing arguments, our research team was eager to offer as a gift this small amount of money to our hosts.

Four years later, in 2018, our team visited the village shrine of Houay Yong with Bunsoon for the first time since the ceremony of 2012 [260]. We were most surprised to discover a new post, without any cement (Figure 7.10).

Figure 7.10 The *lak man* of Houay Yong as it appeared in 2018 (December 2018).

Conclusion 187

Figure 7.11 The *lak man* of Houay Yong in 2018. The removed blocks of cement appear in the front; the old post lies horizontally on the ground, just a bit above the main block in the lower center (December 2018).

Bunsoon explained that the cement used in 2010 progressively crumbled and cracked. As for the wood structure inside, it was worn out. A ceremony with *thaam* was hence organized to know if the spirit agreed to have a new post. The *chao süa* sculpted it, in a strong wood, *mai khuun*, the name of which evokes richness (*kham khuun*). They made a new ceremony and planted the new post, while the old post and the blocks of cement were thrown a few meters away (Figure 7.11).

A sign of the spirits? Certainly not. The preparation of cement had been poor, and the termites had completed their patient destruction of the wood. Bunsoon had not given up his idea to strengthen the shrine, and in our presence elaborated new plans with cement, a platform, and a little wall. Indeed, the Tai Vat – or their authorities? – face the future with confidence.

Notes

1 Respectively: *Buk büün saangsaa kuaamchaleuun, Nam phaa pasaasôn yuu yén pén suk, Yuu huamkanyaang, santisuk, Pôk khoong baan müang dôôi nyut dii tham.*
2 See Tannenbaum (2003) for Thailand or Diem Hang Ngo Thi (2018) for Vietnam.
3 Laughter often reveals ambiguous feelings. This is a reminder that the very casual nature of the spirits in Tai Vat society contradicts the polished presentation of spirits as entities beyond contingencies, especially in a Buddhist environment.

References

Archaimbault, Charles, 1956. "Le sacrifice du buffle à Vat Ph'u," *France-Asie* **118–119** (special issue: *Présence du Royaume Lao*): 841–845.
Archaimbault, Charles, 1964. "Religious structures in Laos," *Journal of the Siam Society* **52**(1): 57–74.
Archaimbault, Charles, 1973. *Structures religieuses lao (mythes et rites)*. Vientiane: Vithagna.
Archaimbault, Charles, 1991. *Le sacrifice du buffle à S'ieng Khwang (Laos)*. Paris: École française d'Extrême-Orient.
Archaimbault, Charles, 2014. "Chefferie lao. Cosmogonies, structures religieuses et rituel," in Jacques Lemoine and Bernard Formoso (eds), *Boudhas, Nagas et lieux de mémoire en R.D.P. Lao. Essais à la mémoire de Charles Archaimbault*, pp. 183–351. Bangkok: OI Publishing.
Baird, Ian G., Keith Barney, Peter Vandergeest, and Bruce Shoemaker, 2009. "Reading too much into aspirations: More explorations of the space between coerced and voluntary resettlement in Laos," *Critical Asian Studies* **41**(4): 605–614.
Barth, Fredrik, 1998 [1969]. "Introduction," in Fredrik Barth (ed.), *Ethnic Groups and Boundaries. The Social Organization of Culture Difference*, pp. 9–38. Long Grove, IL: Waveland Press.
Becker, Benjawan Poomsan and Khamphan Mingbuapha, 2003. *Lao–English, English–Lao Dictionary*. Bangkok: Paiboon Publishing.
Berliner, David, 2005. "The abuses of memory: Reflections on the memory boom in anthropology," *Anthropological Quarterly* **78**(1): 197–211.
Berliner, David, 2018. *Perdre sa culture*. Brussels: Zones sensibles.
Billig, Michael, 1995. *Banal Nationalism*. London: Sage.
Bobo (Capitaine), 1898. "Les habitants du Laos," *Revue française de l'étranger et des colonies et Exploration, Gazette géographique* **23**: 505–516, 571–582, 725–733.
Bouté, Vanina, 2011. *En miroir du pouvoir. Les Phounoy du Nord-Laos. Ethnogenèse et dynamiques d'intégration*. Paris: École française d'Extrême-Orient.
Bouté, Vanina, 2018. *Mirroring Power. Ethnogenesis on the Margins of the Lao State*. Chiang Mai: Silkworm Books.
Boutin, André, 1937. "Monographie de la province des Houa-Phan," *Bulletin des amis du Laos* **1**: 69–119.
Brubaker, Rogers, 2004. *Ethnicity without Groups*. Cambridge, MA and London: Harvard University Press.
Cầm Trọng, 2003. "Préserver et promouvoir la langue et l'écriture: l'exemple du thaï," in Yves Goudineau (ed.), *Laos and Ethnic Minority Cultures: Promoting Heritage*, pp. 75–79. Paris: UNESCO.
Cầm Trọng, 2004. *Les Thai du nord-ouest du Viêt-Nam*. Paris: Cahiers de Péninsule.

References

Cầm Trọng and Phan Hữu Dật, n.d. *La culture thai au Viet-Nam*. Paris: Cahiers de Péninsule.
Carmack, Robert M., 1972. "Ethnohistory: a review of its development, definitions, methods, and aims," *Annual Review of Anthropology* **1**: 227–246.
Condominas, Georges, 2006 [1980]. *L'espace social. À propos de l'Asie du Sud-Est*. Paris: Les Indes Savantes.
Coville, Elizabeth, 2003. "Mothers of the land. Vitality and order among the Toraja highlanders," in Nicola Tannenbaum and Cornelia Ann Kammerer (eds), *Founders' Cults in Southeast Asia. Ancestors, Polity, and Identity*, pp. 87–112. New Haven, CT: Yale University Southeast Asia Studies.
Davis, Bradley C., 2017. *Imperial Bandits. Outlaws and Rebels in the China–Vietnam Borderlands*. Seattle, WA: Washington University Press.
de Heusch, Luc, 1987. *Écrits sur la royauté sacrée*. Brussels: Éditions de l'Université.
Deydier, Henri, 1954. *Lokapâla. Génies, totems et sorciers du nord Laos*. Paris: Plon.
Diem Hang Ngo Thi, 2018. "Venerating the swearing stone at the Hung temple," communication presented during the workshop "Stone Masters: The Territory Cults of Moonsoon Asia," 22nd biennial conference of the Asian Studies Association of Australia (Sydney, 3–5 July 2018).
Dumont, Louis, 1966. *Homo Hierarchicus. Essai sur le système des castes*. Paris: Gallimard.
Evans, Grant, 1990. *Lao Peasants under Socialism*. New Haven, CT and London: Yale University Press.
Evans, Grant, 1991. "Reform or revolution in heaven? Funerals among the Upland Tai," *Australian Journal of Anthropology* **2**(1): 81–97.
Evans, Grant, 1998. *The Politics of Ritual and Remembrance. Laos since 1975*. Chiang Mai: Silkworm Books.
Evans, Grant, 2000. "Tai-ization: Ethnic change in Northern Indo-China," in Andrew Turton (ed.), *Civility and Savagery. Social Identity in Tai States*, pp. 263–289. Richmond, Surrey: Curzon Press.
Évrard, Olivier, 2004. La mise en œuvre de la réforme foncière au Laos. Impacts sociaux et effets sur les conditions de vie en milieu rural. Working paper for the Livelihood Support Programme (LSP). Rome: Organisation des Nations-Unies pour l'Agriculture et l'Alimentation (FAO).
Évrard, Olivier, 2006. *Chroniques des cendres. Anthropologie des sociétés khmou et dynamiques interethniques du Nord-Laos*. Paris: IRD Éditions.
Fabian, Johannes, 2007. *Memory against Culture. Arguments and Reminders*. Durham, NC and London: Duke University Press.
Le Failler, Philippe, 2014. *La rivière Noire. L'intégration d'une marche frontière au Vietnam*. Paris: CNRS.
Finot, Louis, 1956. "Les écritures lao," *France-Asie* **118–119** (special issue: *Présence du Royaume Lao*): 981–998.
Fiskesjö, Magnus, 2010. "Participant intoxication and self-other dynamics in the Wa context," *Asia Pacific Journal of Anthropology* **11**(2): 111–127.
Foropon, J., 1927. *La province des Hua-Phan (Laos)*. Hanoi: Éditions de la Hanoi.
Foucault, Michel, 2010 [1975]. *Surveiller et punir. Naissance de la prison*. Paris: Gallimard.
Geschiere, Peter, 2009. *The Perils of Belonging. Autochthony, Citizenship and Exclusion in Africa and Europe*. Chicago, IL: University of Chicago Press.
Gibson, William M., 2018. "Mission Raquez: A forgotten ethnographic expedition through Laos in 1905," *History and Anthropology* **29**(4): 446–468.

190 References

Goudineau, Yves, 2000. "Ethnicité et déterritorialisation dans la péninsule indochinoise. Considérations à partir du Laos," *Autrepart* **14**: 17–31.

Ha Thi Hong Lan, Nguyen Manh Cuong, Luong Thi Tuoi, and LyHour Hin, 2011. Process of mobility and migration in Chiềng Pằn Commune. Field report in the frame of the MA seminar "Rural sociology" under the direction of Pierre Petit, Hà Nội University of Agriculture.

Hardy, Andrew D., 2003. *Red Hills: Migrants and the State in the Highlands of Vietnam*. Copenhagen: NIAS Press.

Hayashi, Yukio, 2003. "Reconfiguration of village guardian spirits among the Thai-Lao in Northeast Thailand," in Nicola Tannenbaum and Cornelia Ann Kammerer (eds), *Founders' Cults in Southeast Asia. Ancestors, Polity, and Identity*, pp. 184–209. New Haven, CT: Yale University Southeast Asia Studies.

High, Holly, 2008. "The implications of aspirations. Reconsidering resettlement in Laos," *Critical Asian Studies* **40**(4): 531–550.

High, Holly and Pierre Petit, 2013. "Introduction: The study of the state in Laos," *Asian Studies Review* **37**(4): 417–432.

Hobsbawm, Eric and Terence Ranger (eds), 1983. *The Invention of Tradition*. Cambridge: Cambridge University Press.

Holt, John, 2011 [2009]. *Spirits of the Place. Buddhism and Lao Religious Culture*. Chiang Mai: Silkworm Books.

Hours, Bernard and Monique Selim, 1997. *Essai d'anthropologie politique sur le Laos contemporain. Marché, socialisme et génies*. Paris: L'Harmattan.

Ivarsson, Søren, 2008. *Creating Laos. The Making of a Lao Space between Indochina and Siam, 1860–1945*. Copenhagen: NIAS.

Jenkins, Richard, 1997. *Rethinking Ethnicity. Arguments and Explorations*. London, Thousand Oaks, CA and New Delhi: SAGE Publications.

Jonsson, Hjorleifur, 2014. *Slow Anthropology. Negotiating Difference with the Iu Mien*. Ithaca, NY: Cornell University Press.

Kilani, Mondher, 1994. *L'invention de l'autre. Essais sur le discours anthropologique*. Paris-Lausanne: Payot.

Ladwig, Patrice, 2015. "Worshipping relics and animating statues. Transformations of Buddhist statecraft in contemporary Laos," *Modern Asian Studies* **49**(6): 1875–1902.

Lafont, Pierre-Bernard, 1955. "Notes sur les familles patronymiques Thai Noires de Sơn-la et de Nghĩa-lộ," *Anthropos* **50**: 797–807.

Lao National Front for Construction, 2005. *The Ethnics Groups in Lao P.D.R.* Vientiane: Department of Ethnics.

Le Boulanger, Paul, 1930. *Histoire du Laos français*. Paris: Plon.

Le Failler, Philippe, 2014. *La rivière Noire. L'intégration d'une marche frontière au Vietnam*. Paris: CNRS.

Lefèvre, Eugène, 1898. *Un voyage au Laos*. Paris: E. Plon, Nourrit et Cie.

Léger, Alain, 2018. "La Gomme-Laque J.-B. (Besnard & Cie), La-Pho," online. Available at: www.entreprises-coloniales.fr (accessed 16 December 2018).

Lehman, F. K., 2003. "The relevance of the founder's cult for understanding the political systems of the peoples of Northern Southeast Asia and its Chinese Borderlands," in Nicola Tannenbaum and Cornelia Ann Kammerer (eds), *Founders' Cults in Southeast Asia. Ancestors, Polity, and Identity*, pp. 15–39. New Haven, CT: Yale University Southeast Asia Studies.

Lemoine, Jacques, 2014. "Charles Archaimbault et son œuvre," in Jacques Lemoine and Bernard Formoso (eds), *Boudhas, Nagas et lieux de mémoire en R.D.P. Lao. Essais à la mémoire de Charles Archaimbault*, pp. 151–182. Bangkok: OI Publishing.

Lentz, Christian C., 2019. *Contested Territory. Điện Biên Phủ and the Making of Northwest Vietnam*. New Haven, CT and London: Yale University Press.
Lévy, Paul, 1956. "Le sacrifice du buffle et la prédiction du temps à Vientiane," *France-Asie* **118–119** (special issue: *Présence du Royaume Lao*): 846–858.
Lissoir, Marie-Pierre, 2016. Le *Khap tai dam*, catégorisation et modèles musicaux. Étude ethnomusicologique chez les Tai des hauts plateaux du Laos. PhD dissertation, Université libre de Bruxelles.
Lissoir, Marie-Pierre, 2017. "Boire, chanter, et créer des liens. Ethnomusicologie et alcool chez les Tai Dam du Nord Laos," *Civilisations* **66**: 159–175.
Lorrillard, Michel, 1999. "Quelques données relatives à l'historiographie lao," *Bulletin de l'École française d'Extrême-Orient* **86**: 219–232.
Lorrillard, Michel, 2006. "Lao history revisited: paradoxes and problems in current research," *South East Asia Research* **14**(3): 387–401.
Lorrillard, Michel, 2015. "Sceaux et autres symboles de l'autorité dans l'espace lao ancient," *Péninsule* **71**(2): 7–34.
Martin, Jean-Marie, 1899. "Voyage au Laos," *Les missions catholiques*, 13 October: 488–491.
Maspero, Henri, 1950 [1929]. "La société et la religion des Chinois et celles des Tai modernes," in *Les religions chinoises*, pp. 139–194. Paris: Bibliothèque de diffusion du Musée Guimet. Available at: www.chineancienne.fr.
Michaud, Jean, 2007. *'Incidental' Ethnographers. French Catholic Missions on the Frontier of Tonkin and Yunnan, 1880–1930*. Leiden: Brill Academic.
Michaud, Jean, 2010. "Editorial. Zomia and beyond," *Journal of Global History* **5**: 187–214.
Michaud, Jean, 2015. "Livelihoods in the Vietnamese Northern Borderlands recorded in French colonial military ethnographies 1897–1904," *Asia Pacific Journal of Anthropology* **16**(4): 343–367.
Michaud, Jean, Meenaxi Barkataki-Ruscheweyh, and Margaret Byrne Swain, 2016. *Historical Dictionary of the Peoples of the Southeast Asian Massif*. Lanham, MD: Rowman & Littlefield.
Mignot, Fabrice, 2009. *La France et les princes thaïs des confins du Viêt-Nam et du Laos: des Pavillons noirs à Điên Biên Phu (1873–1954)*. Paris: L'Harmattan.
Mironneau, J. 1935–1936. "Le district de Muong-Xôi. Province des Hua phan. Laos," *Bulletin de la Société des missions étrangères de Paris* **14**: 710–718, 767–776; **15**: 4–17, 88–98.
Moerman, Michael, 1965. "Ethnic identification in a complex civilization: Who are the Lue?" *American Anthropologist* **67**(5): 1215–1230.
Moniot, Henri, 1999. "Faire du Nora sous les tropiques?" in Jean-Pierre Chrétien and Jean-Louis Triaud (eds), *Histoire d'Afrique. Les enjeux de mémoire*, pp. 13–26. Paris: Karthala.
Monpeyrat, J., 1904. "Monographie de la province de Muong-Son (territoire des Huas-Phans-Thang-Hoc)," *Revue coloniale* **4**: 125–140, 283–302.
Mus, Paul, 1933. "Cultes indiens et indigènes au Champa," *Bulletin de l'École française d'Extrême-Orient* **33**: 367–410.
Mus, Paul, 1975 [1933]. *India seen from the East. Indian and Indigenous Cults in Champa*. Translated by I.W. Mabbett, edited by I.W. Mabbett and D.P. Chandler. Caulfield, Victoria: Monash University Press.
Nguyen Van Huy, Le Duy Dai, Nguyen Quy Thao, and Vu Xuan Thao, 2009. *The Great Family of Ethnic Groups in Viet Nam*. Hà Nội: Nha Xuat Ban Giao Duc Viet Nam.

References

Nora, Pierre, 1997 [1984, 1986, 1992]. *Les lieux de mémoire* (3 vols). Paris: Gallimard.

O'Connor, Richard A., 2003. "Founders' cults in regional and historical perspective," in Nicola Tannenbaum and Cornelia Ann Kammerer (eds), *Founders' Cults in Southeast Asia. Ancestors, Polity, and Identity*, pp. 269–311. New Haven, CT: Yale University Southeast Asia Studies.

Pavie, Auguste, 1919. *Mission Pavie Indo-Chine. 1879–1895. Géographie et voyages. VII. Journal de marche (1888–1889). Événements du Siam (1888–1889)*. Paris: Leroux.

Petit, Pierre, 2006. "Migrations, ethnicité et nouveaux villages au Laos. L'implantation des Hmong, Tai Dam et Khmou à Thongnamy (province de Bolikhamsay)," *Aséanie* **18**: 15–45.

Petit, Pierre, 2008a. "Rethinking internal migrations in Lao PDR. The resettlement process under micro-analysis," *Anthropological Forum* **18**(2): 117–138.

Petit, Pierre, 2008b. "Les politiques culturelles et la question des minorités en RDP Laos," *Bulletin des séances de l'Académie royale des sciences d'outre-mer* **54**(4): 477–499.

Petit, Pierre, 2012. "Émergence d'un pluralisme religieux en contexte multiethnique: l'exemple du village recomposé de Thongnamy (Bolikhamxay)," in Vatthana Pholsena and Vanina Bouté (eds), *Sociétés et pouvoirs au Laos contemporain*, pp. 139–161. Paris: Les Indes savantes.

Petit, Pierre, 2013a. "Ethnic performance and the state in Laos. The *bun greh* annual festival of the Khmu," *Asian Studies Review* **37**(4): 470–490.

Petit, Pierre, 2013b. "The backstage of ethnography as ethnography of the state. Coping with officials in the Lao People's Democratic republic," in Sarah Turner (ed.), *Red Stamps and Gold Stars. Fieldwork in Upland Socialist Asia*, pp. 143–164. Vancouver–Toronto: UBC Press.

Petit, Pierre 2015. "Mobility and stability in a Tai Vat village (Laos)," *Asia Pacific Journal of Anthropology* **16**(4): 410–423.

Petit, Pierre, 2017. "Land, state, and society in Laos: Ethnographies of land policies," *World Food Policy Journal* **3**(2) and **4**(1): 83–104.

Petit, Pierre, 2020. "L'exode rural au Laos. Mobilité, jeunesse et parenté à Houay Yong (province de Houaphan)," *Bulletin des séances de l'Académie royale des sciences d'outre-mer* **63**(1).

Phimphan Phaibunwangcharoen, 2000. *Baichum: Saranithet bon singtho*. Bangkok: National Library (in Thai).

Pholsena, Vatthana, 2006. *Post-War Laos. The Politics of Culture, History and Identity*. Singapore: Institute of Southeast Asian Studies.

Pholsena, Vatthana and Ruth Banomyong, 2006. *Laos. From Buffer State to Crossroads?* Chiang Mai: Mekong Press.

Pholsena, Vatthana and Oliver Tappe (eds), 2013. *Interaction with a Violent Past. Reading Post-Conflict Landscapes in Cambodia, Laos, and Vietnam*. Singapore: National University of Singapore.

Proschan, Frank, 1998. "Chüang in Khmhu folklore, history and memory," in Sumitr Pithipat (ed.), *Proceedings of the First International Conference on the Literary, Historical and Cultural Aspects of Thao Hung Thao Chüang*, pp. 174–209. Bangkok: Thammasat University.

Raquez, Alfred, 1905. "Au Laos," *Revue indochinoise* **17**: 1225–1233; **18**: 1320–1332; **19**: 1394–1406; **20**: 1481–1485; **21**:1528–1538.

Reinhorn, Marc, 2001. *Dictionnaire laotien-français*. Paris: Editions You-Feng.

Revel, Jacques, 1996. "Présentation," in Jacques Revel (dir.), *Jeux d'échelles. La microanalyse à l'expérience*, pp. 7–14. Paris: Le Seuil-Gallimard.
Rigg, Jonathan, 2007. "Moving lives: Migration and livelihoods in the Lao PDR," *Population, Space and Place* **13**(3): 163–178.
Salemink, Oscar, 2011. "A view from the mountains. A critical history of Lowlander-Highlander relations in Vietnam," in Thomas Sikor, Nghiem Phuong Tuyen, Jennifer Sowerwine, and Jeff Romm (eds), *Upland Transformations: Opening Boundaries in Vietnam*, pp. 27–50. Singapore: NUS Press.
Salemink, Oscar, 2017 [2003]. *The Ethnography of Vietnam's Central Highlanders: A Historical Contextualization, 1850–1990*. London: Routledge.
Schlemmer, Grégoire, 2012. "Rituels, territoires et pouvoirs dans les marges sino-indiennes," *Moussons* **19**: 5–18.
Scott, James, 2009. *The Art of Not Being Governed: An Anarchist History of Upland Southeast Asia*. New Haven, CT and London: Yale University Press.
Souksavang Simana, 2014. "Légende et tradition des Cao Ai-Cao Nong," in Jacques Lemoine and Bernard Formoso (eds), *Boudhas, Nagas et lieux de mémoire en R.D.P. Lao. Essais à la mémoire de Charles Archaimbault*, pp. 137–149. Bangkok: OI Publishing.
Sprenger, Guido, 2016. "Dimensions of animism in Southeast Asia," in Guido Sprenger and Kaj Århem (eds), *Animism in Southeast Asia*, pp. 31–51. London: Routledge.
Street, Brian V. (ed.), 2001. *Literacy and Development. Ethnographic Perspectives*. London and New York: Routledge.
Stuart-Fox, Martin, 1997. *A History of Laos*. Cambridge: Cambridge University Press.
Stuart-Fox, Martin, 1998. *The Lao Kingdom of Lan Xang: Rise and Decline*. Bangkok: White Lotus.
Tanabe, Shegeharu, 1988. "Spirits and ideological discourse: The Tai Lü guardian cults in Yunnan," *Sojourn* **3**(1): 1–25.
Tanabe, Shegeharu, 1991. "Sacrifice and the transformation of ritual: The Pu Sae Ña Sae spirit cult of Northern Thailand," paper presented at the symposium "Spirit Cults and Popular Knowledge in Southeast Asia" at the National Museum of Ethnology, Osaka (Japan), November 1991.
Tanabe, Shegeharu, 2000. "Autochthony and the Inthakin cult of Chiang Mai", in Andrew Turton (ed.), *Civility and Savagery. Social Identity in Tai states*, pp. 294–318. Richmond, Surrey: Curzon Press.
Tannenbaum, Nicola, 2003. "Phaya Sihanatraja and the founding myth of Maehongson," in Nicola Tannenbaum and Cornelia Ann Kammerer (eds), *Founders' Cults in Southeast Asia. Ancestors, Polity, and Identity*, pp. 210–226. New Haven, CT: Yale University Southeast Asia Studies.
Tannenbaum, Nicola and Cornelia Ann Kammerer (eds), 2003. *Founders' Cults in Southeast Asia. Ancestors, Polity, and Identity*. New Haven, CT: Yale University Southeast Asia Studies.
Tappe, Oliver, 2013a. "Faces and facets of the *kantosou kou xat* – the Lao 'national liberation struggle' in state commemoration and historiography," *Asian Studies Review* **37**(4): 433–450.
Tappe, Oliver, 2013b. "National *lieu de mémoire* vs. multivocal memories: The case of Viengxay, Lao PDR," in Vatthana Pholsena and Oliver Tappe (eds), *Interactions with a Violent Past. Reading Post-Conflict Landscapes in Cambodia, Laos, and Vietnam*, pp. 46–77. Singapore: National University of Singapore.
Tappe, Oliver, 2015. "A frontier in the frontier: Sociopolitical dynamics and colonial administration in the Lao-Vietnamese borderlands," *Asia Pacific Journal of Anthropology* **16**(4): 368–387.

Tappe, Oliver, 2017. "Shaping the national topography. The party-state, national imageries, and questions of political authority in Lao PDR," in Vanina Bouté and Vatthana Pholsena (eds), *Changing Lives in Laos: Society, Politics and Culture in a Post-Socialist State*, pp. 56–80. Singapore: Singapore University Press.

Tappe, Oliver, 2018. "Variants of frontier mimesis. Colonial encounter and intercultural interaction in the Lao-Vietnamese uplands," *Social Analysis* **62**(2): 51–75.

Turner, Sarah (ed.), 2013. *Red Stamps and Gold Stars. Fieldwork in Upland Socialist Asia*. Vancouver–Toronto: UBC Press.

Vansina, Jan, 1985. *Oral Tradition as History*. London: James Currey.

Vatthanatham/Culture, 2008. "Peeut lèèo! Suan lakmüang sannyalak khoong khuèèng Huaphan" [Already open! The park of the district post, symbol of the province of Houaphan], issue 22, page 7 (in Lao).

Zago, Marcel, 1972. *Rites et cérémonies en milieu bouddhiste lao*. Rome: Universita Gregoriana.

Zasloff, Joseph J., 1973. *The Pathet Lao. Leadership and Organization*. Lexington, Toronto and London: Lexington Books.

Archives

See page xv for an explanation on the reference system used. All the archives come from the *Archives Nationales d'Outre-Mer* (Aix-en-Provence, France), more especially from two funds: GGI and RSL.

GGI – Gouvernement général de l'Indochine

GGI 9211, 10/12/1893. *Rapport du commandant Bertin sur la région de Muong Het (1893–1894)*.
GGI 9211, 6/1/1894. *Arrêt du Gouverneur général de l'Indochine*, annexed to *Rapport du commandant Bertin sur la région de Muong Het (1893–1894)*.
GGI 20666, 11/10/1899. *Rapport économique des mois de mars et de septembre 1899 du Haut-Laos* (by the Résident Supérieur du Laos).
GGI 20671, June 1896. *Rapport politique* (by Vacle).
GGI 20671, 24/9/1896. *Rapport politique* (by Vacle).
GGI 20672, 7/1/1899. *Rapport politique du mois de décembre 1898* (by Vacle).
GGI 20691, 21/1/1897. (Telegram by the *Commandant supérieur p.i. du Haut Laos*), folder *Création du Commissariat de Hua Panh (1897)*.
GGI 20724, 18/10/1894. *Rapport général* (by Hardy), folder *Rapport de M. Hardy, chef du poste administratif de Muong Het sur la situation des Hua Panh tang Hoc (1894–1895)*.
GGI 20724, 3/4/1895. *Situation politique des Hoa panh ha tang hoc*, folder *Rapport de M. Hardy, chef du poste administratif de Muong Het sur la situation des Hua Panh tang Hoc (1894–1895)*.
GGI 20770, 1895–1899. *Rapport du garde principal Marol sur la route en construction de Louang Prabang à Muong Het*.
GGI 26509, 8/6/1896. *Monographie du territoire Ua phan thang hoc* (by Monpeyrat), folder *Rattachement à la province de Thanh Hoa (Annam) des trois huyêns de Man Duy, Sam Na et Xam Tu faisant partie des Hua panh ha tang hoc (Laos), 1894–1898*.

RSL – Résidence Supérieure au Laos

RSL E2, 4/12/1894. (Report by Hardy to *Commissaire du Gouvernement à Luang Prabang*), folder *Commissariat de gouvernement des (Muong-Son) Hua-Phans. Correspondance avec le commandant supérieur du Haut-Laos à Luang-Prabang*.

RSL E2, 15/12/1894. *Trams, routes, déplacement du poste et divers* (by Hardy), folder *Commissariat de gouvernement des (Muong-Son) Hua-Phans. Correspondance avec le commandant supérieur du Haut-Laos à Luang-Prabang.*

RSL E2, 25/4/1896. (Letter by M. Roux), folder *Muong Son 1896–1901. Tournées administratives.*

RSL E2, 14/8/1896. *Rapport* (by Monpeyrat), subfolder *1896*, folder *Muong Son 1896–1901. Tournées administratives.*

RSL E2, 1/12/1896a. *Situation politique* (by Monpeyrat), folder *Muong Son 1896–1901. Tournées administratives.*

RSL E2, 1/12/1896b. (Report on the navigability of the River Ma, by Monpeyrat), folder *Muong Son 1896–1901. Tournées administratives.*

RSL E2, 1/9/1897. *Rapport commercial* (by Monpeyrat), folder *Commissariat de gouvernement des (Muong-Son) Hua-Phans. Correspondance avec le commandant supérieur du Haut-Laos à Luang-Prabang.*

RSL E2, 21/6/1899. *Saisie d'opium* (by Besson), folder *Muong Son 1896–1901. Tournées administratives.*

RSL E2, 28/7/1899. *Barêmes comparatifs pour la vente de l'opium*, folder *Muong Son 1896–1901. Tournées administratives.*

RSL E2, 22/1/1900. *Tableau de recensement de la population des Hua Phans Ha Tang Hoc au 31 décembre 1899* (by Macey), folder *Muong Son 1896–1901. Tournées administratives.*

RSL E2, 31/12/1900. *Rapport* (by Macey), folder *Muong Son 1896–1901. Tournées administratives.*

RSL E2, 2/11/1901. *Transmission d'une supplique des mandarins des Huas Phans* (by Macey), folder *Muong Son 1896–1901. Tournées administratives.*

RSL E3, 1898. (Letters from Monpeyrat addressed to the *Commandant supérieur*), folder *Commissariat de gouvernement des (Muong-Son) Hua-Phans. Correspondance avec le Commandant supérieur du Haut-Laos à Luang-Prabang.*

RSL E3, 13/4/1898. *Culture du pavot* (by Wartelle), folder *Commissariat de gouvernement des (Muong-Son) Hua-Phans. Correspondance avec le commandant supérieur du Haut-Laos à Luang-Prabang.*

RSL E3, 26/7/1898. *A.s. du morcellement du territoire des Huaphans* (by Monpeyrat), folder *Commissariat de gouvernement des (Muong-Son) Hua-Phans. Correspondance avec le Commandant supérieur du Haut-Laos à Luang-Prabang.*

RSL E3, 2/8/1898. *A.s. des travaux à exécuter pendant l'année 1898 et du rachat des corvées* (by Monpeyrat), folder *Commissariat de gouvernement des (Muong-Son) Hua-Phans. Correspondance avec le commandant supérieur du Haut-Laos à Luang-Prabang.*

RSL E3, 5/10/1898. (Letter from Monpeyrat addressed to the *Commandant supérieur*), folder *Commissariat de gouvernement des (Muong-Son) Hua-Phans. Correspondance avec le Commandant supérieur du Haut-Laos à Luang-Prabang.*

RSL E3, 14/11/1898. *A.s. des impôts de l'année 1898* (by Monpeyrat), folder *Commissariat de gouvernement des (Muong-Son) Hua-Phans. Correspondance avec le commandant supérieur du Haut-Laos à Luang-Prabang.*

RSL E3, 5/4/1902. *Tournée administrative* (by Wartelle), folder *Muong Son 1902–1906, tournées administratives.*

RSL E3, 4/5/1902. *Rôle primitif des permis d'armes* (by Wartelle), folder *Muong Son 1902–1906, tournées administratives.*

RSL E3, 1/6/1904. *Au sujet des linhs, et des habitants de Mg Soi, etc.* (by Wartelle), subfolder *1904*, folder *Muong Son 1902–1906, tournées administratives (suite).*

RSL E4, undated. *Réseau routier de Son La*, folder *Débloquement de la province de Houa-Phan*.
RSL E4, 1904–1906. (Report on claims from local officers in Houa Mong, by Wartelle), sub-subfolder *1905–1907*, subfolder *1905–1935 Province de Sam Neua*, folder *Rapports de tournée 1925–1931*.
RSL E4, 27/6/1904. (Report by Wartelle), folder *Février 1904*.
RSL E4, 20/7/1904. *Au sujet de la division des Hua phans* (by Wartelle), folder *Février 1904*.
RSL E4, 22/11/1906. (Complaint of the dignitaries of Muang Houa Muang) (by Wartelle), subfolder *1905–1907*, folder *1905–1935*.
RSL E4, 10/3/1907. (Report on a fire in Muong Poune, by Wartelle), sub-subfolder *1907*, subfolder *1905–1935 Province de Sam Neua*, folder *Rapports de tournée 1925–1931*.
RSL E4, 2/8/1909. *Au sujet de la demande de M. le Résident supérieur de l'Annam pour laisser partir les habitants à Than Hoa* (by Wartelle), sub-subfolder *Émigration et immigration. Province de Sam-Neua*, subfolder *1905–1935 Province de Sam Neua*, folder *Rapports de tournée 1925–1931*.
RSL E4, 21/8/1911. *Au sujet des Houa phans de Houa Muong et Mg Vèn* (by Wartelle), subfolder *1908–1912*, folder *1905–1935*.
RSL E4, 11/9/1911. *Au sujet des territoires de Muong Ven et Houa-Muong* (by Nivau), subfolder *1908–1912*, folder *1905–1935*.
RSL E4, 1/11/1911. *Rapport de tournée, Muong Soi* (by Nivau), subfolder *1910–1914*, folder *1905–1935*.
RSL E4, 3/12/1911. (Letter to the Résident supérieur, by Wartelle), subfolder *1911–1914*, folder *1905–1935*.
RSL E4, 1/3/1925. *Province de Sam Neua, rapport de tournée 1925* (by Lagreze), folder *Rapports de tournée 1925–1931*.
RSL E4, 3/4/1926. *Notice à l'attention de voyageurs se rendant à Sam Neua* (by Lagrèze), folder *Rapports de tournée 1925–1931*.
RSL E4, November 1926. *Tournée administrative du 18 au 28 novembre 1928* (by Foropon), folder *Débloquement de la province de Houa-Phan*.
RSL E4, 1927–1928. (Document on the damages caused by buffaloes in the Gomme-Laque plantation), sub-subfolder *Divers*, subfolder *1905–1935 Province de Sam Neua*, folder *Rapports de tournée 1925–1931*.
RSL E4, April 1928. *Rapport de tournée du Commissaire du Gouvernement à Sam Neua et de son adjoint en avril 1928*, folder *Rapports de tournée 1925–1931*.
RSL E4, 22/3/1930. *Rapport de tournée dans la province des Houa-phans* (by Le Boulanger), folder *Débloquement de la province de Houa-Phan*.
RSL E4, 8–15/3/1931. *Compte-rendu de tournée du commissaire du Gouvernement à Samneua* (by Thierry), folder *Rapports de tournée 1925–1931*.
RSL E4, 15/11/1931. (Report), subfolder *Rapport de tournée du Commissaire du gouvernement à Sam Neua, mai 1931*, folder *Rapports de tournée 1925–1931*.
RSL E4, November 1933. Folder *Incidents survenus dans la concession appartenant à la société "Gomme Laque J.B." à Muong Het (Houaphans) Novembre 1933*.
RSL E4, 12/1/1935. Folder *A.s. Inauguration de la route Sonla-Samneua par Sopsane, janvier 1935* (by Bouton).
RSL F6, 1941–1942. *Houaphan*, folder *Rapports généraux politiques 1941–42*.

Fieldnotes

See pages xiv–xv for explanations of the references to field data throughout this book. The place of interview or observation is Houay Yong, unless stated otherwise after the date.

[2]: 28/6/2009, fieldnotes and discussion with Bunsoon. Visit to the *lak man* and *thiang seun*.
[4]: 28/6/2009, interview of Bunsoon. The *lak man* and *thiang seun* of Houay Yong; the first settlers; the annual ceremonies; the *lak man* in *Naa Kuu*.
[6]: 2/6/2010, discussion with Bunsoon. Migrations to Thongnamy and Nam Mo; the water and electricity supply.
[8]: 3/6/2010, interview of Thaabun. The foundation of Houay Yong; the departure of the Tai Soi; the French administration.
[10]: 3/6/2010, interview of Thaabun. The cementing of the *lak man*; ceremonies linked to the shrine; comparison with the monument in Sam Neua.
[13]: 3/6/2010, interview of Bunsoon. List of the former *naai baan*; his own biography; the collectivization period.
[19]: 4/6/2010, discussion with elder men during a meal. The coming of migrants from Yên Châu in 1953; traveling to and trading with Yên Châu.
[20]: 5/6/2010, interview by Sommay in *Naa Kuu*. The shrine in *Naa Kuu*.
[24]: 4/6/2010, discussion with the attendees of a *sén* ceremony. The differences between Tai Vat and Tai Dam.
[26]: 4/6/2010, interview of Buasai. How authorities become Langkham after their death and go to *phii seun*; the succession and prohibitions of *chao süa*.
[27]: 4/6/2010, interview of Buasai. Annual and non-annual ceremonies on the *phii seun* of Houay Yong and *Naa Kuu*; the division and reunification of the two villages; biography of Buasai.
[29]: 5/6/2010, visit to the *lak man* of Houay Yong with Bunsoon and Phèèngsoon. The cementing of *lak man*; the annual ceremonies; function of the three *thiang seun*.
[30]: 5/6/2010, visit to the *lak man* of *Naa Kuu* with Bunsoon and Phèèngsoon. The division and reunification of Houay Yong and *Naa Kuu*; ceremonies for the *lak man* in *Naa Kuu*.
[32]: 5/6/2010, visit of the village. The *lak man*; the school and the health center; the boundary between Houay Yong and *Naa Kuu*.
[34]: 6/6/2010, interview of Bunheuan. His genealogy and biography.
[36]: 6/6/2010, interview of Thoongsôm. His genealogy and biography.
[40]: 7/6/2010, interview of Bunhoom. His genealogy and biography.
[41]: 7/6/2010, visit of the fields with Bunsoon. The implementation of development projects; the issue of electricity.

Fieldnotes 199

[42]: 7/6/2010, interview of Bunmaa and Bunsoon. History of *Naa Kuu* and its *phii seun* shrine; the coming of refugees from Vietnam; the departure of the Tai Soi.

[43]: 8/6/2010, discussion with Bunsoon. History of his father Koongvaakhuu.

[44]: 7/6/2010, interview of Khamphét. His genealogy and biography; the electrification project proposed to the Vietnamese authorities in Yên Châu.

[50]: 9/6/2010, fieldnotes. The maintenance work for the canals; the history of the different canals.

[51]: 9/6/2010, interview of Bunsoon. The Tai Soi and their departure; history of the peopling of the villages nearby.

[55]: 11/1/2005, Thongnamy, fieldnotes. The *kinchiang* New Year; discussions with the attendance; program of the ceremony; the Tai Dam guests; the Vietnamese origins of the Tai Vat; their reasons for leaving Vietnam in the 1950s.

[56a]: 11/1/2005, Thongnamy, interview of Vannaa. The subgroups of Tai Dam.

[60]: 7/1/2008, Thongnamy, interview of Bunphèng. The *kinchiang*; the subgroups of Tai Vat.

[61]: 27/1/2008, Thongnamy, interview of Mèè Ua, Banliu, and Mèè Chét. The *kinchiang* New Year; the *sôn khuaang* ceremony; the past prohibitions on ceremonies and their relaxing.

[62]: 8/1/2009, Thongnamy, discussion with Banliu. The wartime in Houay Yong; the prisoners from the Royal Army.

[63]: 10/1/2009, Thongnamy, discussion with Phoonsikéo. The clans and subgroups of Tai Dam and Tai Vat.

[64a]: 12/7/2009, Thongnamy, interview of Mèè Ua and Nooi. The annual ceremony for the *lak man*; Vôngkham's ancestors; the prohibitions about and the protection from *lak man*; the revival of the ceremonies.

[65]: 24/5/2011, fieldnotes. The new road and the new school; the contact with Hmong and Khmu villages; the close mountains.

[66]: 25/5/2011, fieldnotes. Climbing up *Phuu Kup* Mountain; the mountains nearby; the Buddha statues discovered in caves in the close mountains.

[70]: 26/5/2011, fieldnotes, discussion with Bunsoon. The trip to Houay Lom; the prohibition to move for *chao kôk chao lao*.

[71]: 26/5/2011, Houay Lom, interview of Koongvaa Phèèng. The history of Houay Lom and Houay Louang; the *dông khuaang* ceremony; the *kinchiang*.

[73]: 27/5/2011, interview of Phèèngsoon. His genealogy and biography.

[75]: 28/5/2011, Ban Kang, fieldnotes. The successive settlements of Ban Kang; the different villages in the valley.

[76]: 28/5/2011, Ban Kang, interview of Chiao Bun. The history of the village; Tai Dèng and Tai Soi in the valley; the *lak man*.

[80]: 29/5/2011, a visit to the upland fields. Name of the mountains; *taalèèo* wickerworks in the fields.

[81]: 30/5/2011, Muang Van, interview of Buasoon. History of the village.

[82]: 30/5/2011, Nasan, interview of an elder. History of the village; the Tai Soi; the settlers from Houay Louang; the family of *chao kôk chao lao*.

[86]: 31/5/2011, interview of Bunheuang and Bunsoon. The naming system; the clans (*sing*) among the Tai Vat.

[87]: 31/5/2011, fieldnotes and video. *Eeun khuan* ceremony for someone whose father died a month earlier; discussions among elders on the foundation story of Houay Lom; the successive resettlements of Ban Kang; the Tai Vat as a moving people.

[90]: 1/6/2011, interview of Thaabun. The first settlers and the Tai Soi; the colonial period; the refugees during the First Indochina War; the successive *naai baan*; the resettlements of Ban Kang; the Tai Vat as a moving people; the recent migrations.

[91]: 1/6/2011, interview and video of Thaabun and Bunsoon. The meaning and functions of *lak man*; its recent cementing; the spirits in the three *thiang seun*.

[103]: 3/6/2011, discussion with Khamphian and Thoongsôm. The recent political incumbents in the village and the region.

[106]: 4/6/2011, interview of Thoongsôm. The resettlement of his family from Yên Châu to Houay Yong; the Tai writing; the refugees during the First Indochina War; Tai Soi and Tai Dèng; the period of collectivization; his self-presentation as keeper of traditions; his opinion on migrations.

[107]: 4/6/2011, discussion with Thoongsôm. Tai Vat as a moving people; the differences between Tai Vat and Tai Dam; his life.

[110]: 4/6/2011, discussion with Bunsoon. The location of the former Buddhist temple.

[111]: 4/6/2011, interview of Bunsoon. The cemetery of the Tai Soi.

[113]: 5/6/2011, Muang Van, interview of Oon Sii, Lii Vông, Viang Sii, and Vông. History of the village; the political organization during the colonial period; the Tai Soi in the area.

[129]: 23/1/2011, fieldnotes and videos. Lunch with and interview of Thaabun. The opening day of the *kinchiang* New Year.

[130]: 23/1/2012, interview and video of Thaabun. Interview on the relationship of *chao süa*, *chao kôk chao lao*, and *chao cham*.

[137]: 26/1/2012, fieldnotes and videos. The rituals for the *lak man* and *tiang seun* of Houay Yong and *Naa Kuu*. The closing ceremony of *kinchiang* in *Naa Kuu*.

[138]: 26/1/2012, video of the crier Singphoon. Public announcement about the *lak man* ceremony to come.

[140]: 26/1/2012, interview of Thaabun, Vôngkham, Koongbun, and Bunsoon. The program for the *phii seun* ceremony; history of the local *thiang seun*; the *sén baan* ceremony.

[141]: 26/1/2012, interview of Thaabun, Vôngkham, Koongbun, and Bunsoon. The origins and functions of *chao süa* and *chao kôk chao lao*; description of the *sén baan* ceremony.

[142]: 26/1/2012, interviews and video of Koongbun and Bunmaa. The *phii seun* of *Naa Kuu*; the related prohibitions and their infringement; Koongbun's taking over as a *chao cham*; historical relations of *Naa Kuu*, Houay Yong, and Houay Lom.

[153]: 12/2/2012, Thongnamy, interview of Mèè Ua. Genealogy of Mèè Ua.

[154]: 12/2/2012, Thongnamy, interview of Mèè Ua. The migration of her family from Vietnam to Laos; the current mobilities of the youth.

[155]: 12/2/2012, Thongnamy, interview and video of Mèè Chét. The migration from Vietnam; the migration to Thongnamy; the current mobilities of the youth.

[179]: 31/5/2014, fieldnotes. The ceremony of graduation at the secondary school; the population of Ban Kang.

[181]: 1/6/2014, interview of Nang Hian. Her biography; the prohibition to move away in relation to the *lak man* of *Naa Kuu* and Houay Lom; the prohibitions on rituals during the revolutionary era.

[186]: 2/6/2014, interview of Thoongsôm. The story of Chiềng Đông (Vietnam) as the ritual center of the Tai Vat; the Sing Loo clan.

[191]: 4/6/2014, interview of Thoongsôm. The story of Chiềng Đông (Vietnam) as the ritual center of the Tai Vat; the diverging evolution of Tai Vat in Vietnam and in Laos; the *lak man* as a token of protection and stability.

[195]: 6/6/2014, Houay Lom, fieldnotes. Visiting the *thiang seun* shrine of Houay Lom. Discussion on upgrading the *thiang seun* because the spirits want to feel comfortable like the men.

[196]: 6/6/2014, Houay Lom, interview of Buaphoon, *chao süa* of Houay Louang; Koongthéé, *chao süa* of Houay Lom; Chanphiu, former *naai baan*; in the presence of *Naai baan* Bunsoon. The old dome-shaped houses; the integration of the two villages; the foundation story of Houay Lom; the Tai Soi; the resettlement of Houay Louang; the *thiang seun*; the prohibitions after the revolution; the problems faced by Koongthéé when he left Houay Lom; the death of the *chao süa* of Ban Kang after he removed the *lak man*; the relationship between *lak man* and *thiang seun*; the ceremonies; the intended cementing of the shrine.
[198]: 6/6/2014, Houay Lom, fieldnotes and video, in the presence of Buaphoon, Koongthéé, Buakham, and *Naai baan* Bunsoon. The four *thiang seun* and the *lak man* of the village.
[208]: 9/6/2017, discussion with Phoonsuk Phèng Sidaa, *moo môt* from Ban Kang. The *lak man* of Ban Kang.
[211]: 9/6/2017, fieldnotes. *Sén* ceremony conducted by Phoonsuk Phèng for a young woman enduring blood loses after delivery; the use of the shirts during the ceremony.
[213]: 10/6/2017, fieldnotes. The guardian spirit groves at both ends of the village; the new *khana baan*.
[215]: 11/6/2017, interview of Bunsoon. Biography of his father, Koongvaakhuu; the present population; village infrastructure; migration; the new *khana baan*; the *chu* (units) in the village; links with Yên Châu; the boards in the central place of the village.
[217]: 12/6/2017, interview of Koongbun and Bunsoon. The annual harvest ceremonies; the *kinchiang*; the different clans of the Tai Vat; the Tai Soi; the village chiefs before the revolution.
[218]: 13/6/2017, fieldnotes. A *sén* ceremony; the eastern fields reserved to the village chiefs under the former regime.
[219]: 14/6/2017, interview of a youth (anonymous). Biography.
[222]: 15/6/2017, discussion with Thoongsôm. The different villages of the *kum baan*; the ethnic composition of the villages nearby.
[230]: 17/6/2017, Muang Èt, interview of the staff of the lower secondary school of Houay Yong. History and organization of the school.
[232]: 17/6/2017, Nahit, fieldnotes. The *lak baan* in Nahit.
[233]: 18/6/2017, Sop Hao, fieldnotes. The *lak baan* in Sop Hao.
[235]: 24/6/2017, Vientiane, interview with two elders from Ban Hap (anonymous). The Tai Soi; the Tai Vat and Tai Dam war refugees; the different Tai subgroups.
[237]: 28/11/2018, fieldnotes, Houay Yong and Muang Èt. Territorial divisions and ethnicity in Muang Èt.
[239]: 29/11/2018, interview of Koongbun. The *chao süa* position; the *lak man* and *thiang seun*; the Tai Soi; the ceremonies of *dông khuaang* and *sén baan*.
[240]: 30/11/2018, fieldnotes. The *dông khuaang* ceremony according to Bunsoon; Houay Yong as *baan thaao*.
[241]: 30/11/2018, interview of Bunheuang. The *sén khuaang* ceremony; the Tai Soi and their ceremonies; the village protected by spirits during the war.
[242]: 30/11/2018, interview of Mèèthao Leua. The flight of her family from Yên Châu; the *phii khuaang* ceremony as performed by her late husband; the coming of the monks to chase away the spirits; the spirits living in mountain caves.
[243]: 30/11/2018, fieldnotes. Visit with Bunsoon to the two locations where the *dông khuaang* ceremony used to be held; the San Kadi area and the ritual entrance to the village.

Fieldnotes

[244]: 30/11/2018, interview of Bunsoon. As [243]; the coming of the monks to chase away the spirits.

[245]: 30/11/2018, interview of Bunmaa. The coming of the monks to chase away the spirits; Tai Soi and Lao as the former occupants of the village; the departure of the Tai Soi.

[246]: 1/12/2018, fieldnotes. Visit of the *Tham Chao* cave; memories about the war; the successive settlements of Ban Kang.

[247]: 1/12/2018, interview of Bunsoon. The discovery of *Tham Chao* cave; the discovery of the Buddha statues in Ban Sot; memories about the war.

[248]: 1/12/2018, interview of Bunsoon. The successive settlements of Ban Kang; the coming of the monks; the Khmu in the valley.

[250]: 3/12/2018, discussion with Bunsoon. The transmission of oral history.

[251]: 4/12/2018, fieldnotes. Discussion on the translation of the *thaam* prayers for the *lak man* ceremony held on 26/1/2012.

[252]: 4/12/2018, interview of Phèèngsoon, Buasai, Bunsoon. The story of the *phii* in Nahit; the Tai Soi in Houay Yong; how Phèèngsoon learned history; the Tai Soi as Buddhists and 'animists'; the successive *naai baan*.

[253]: 4/12/2018, Ban Kang, fieldnotes. The *lak man* in Ban Kang.

[254]: 4/12/2018, Ban Kang, interview of a male elder. The *lak man* and the *chao süa*; the participation of Ban Kang to the *dông khuaang* ritual in Houay Yong.

[255]: 5/12/2018, Nangiu, Pakfèn, Ban Sot, fieldnotes. Travel observations.

[256]: 5/12/2018, Nangiu, interview of Leuangphon. History of the village; the *lak baan* (*klak*, in Khmu).

[257]: 5/12/2018, Pakfèn, interview of Khamyoong, his wife Nang Toi, and Bunsoon. History of the village; the *lak man* and the *thiang seun* of Pakfén; the *sông khuaang* ceremony carried out in Houay Yong.

[258]: 5/12/2018, Ban Sot, interview of Phoonsai. History of the village; the *lak man*; the *dông khuaang* in Houay Yong; the caves in the mountain cliffs and their Buddha statues; the trade on the River Ma, and to Muang Ngoi; the stick-lack.

[259]: 6/12/2018, fieldnotes. Visit to the *lak man*; the stick-lack.

[260]: 6/12/2018, interview of Bunsoon. The recent transformations of the *lak man* in the village; the new administrative acknowledgments of the village; the history of Houay Yong, including economic history; comparison of the *lak man* of the village and the *lak müang* of Sam Neua; the conservation of cultural traditions; the *aanyaa* positions in the past; names of the successive *chao süa* in Houay Yong; translation of *thaam* prayers.

[261]: 11/12/2018, Vientiane, interview of Thoongsôm. The Tai Soi and the *vat* temple of Houay Yong; the caves with Buddha statues.

[262]: 22/12/2018, Vientiane, interview of Thoongsôm. Biography; the successive *naai baan* and *chao süa* of Houay Yong

Index

aanyaa *see phanyaa*
access to the field 13–14, 19–21
agriculture *see* opium, paddy fields, swidden fields
animism 39, 46n11, 67, 78–9, 98, 167–8
Archaimbault, Ch. 17, 117–19, 122, 129, 133, 148–9, 158, 160–1, 163–4, 171n6, 171n8, 177, 184
archives xv, 12, 28–29, 29n10, 46n13, 48–56, 85, 87–99, 102, 110–12, 118, 174, 195–7
autochthony 79, 118–18, 160–3, 165, 176; *see also chao kôk chao lao, chao thin chao thaan*

Ban Kang xvii, 27, 33, 40, 143n3; ethnicity and history 4–7, 33, 36, 57, 72, 76, 79, 82n17, 83n30, 86–7, 103, 147, 163; territorial cults 131, 142, 143n2, 144n10, 146, 150–1, 163, 166–7
Ban Sot xvii, 32, 44n1, 46n12; ethnicity and history 33, 46n4, 46n7, 72, 83n20, 86–8, 91, 95, 167; territorial cults 142, 143n2, 161, 163
Barth, F. 34, 38, 146
beliefs (struggle against) 9, 109, 167–71
Berliner, D. 9, 11
Black Flags *see* Chinese Flags
Black River 12, 34, 69–70, 74, 82n15, 97
Black Tai *see* Tai Dam
Bobo (Capitaine) 54, 83n26
Bouté, V. 12, 20–21, 82n6, 84n31, 156
Boutin, A. 76, 78–9, 82n5, 86, 112, 113n3–113n5, 115n10
brotherhood trope 56, 60–1, 65–8, 83n20, 126, 132, 144n5
Buddhism 46n6, 46n11, 51, 52, 66, 83n28, 93, 98, 187n3; Buddhicization 37, 118, 120; exorcism 161, 166–7; in Houay Yong 4, 61–2, 67, 76–9; and the Lao nation state 10, 30, 35, 39, 168; and territorial cults 122, 158–60, 162, 165, 177–80, 182, 184
buffalo sacrifice *see* sacrifice
Burma 95–7, 115n15

cadastral religion 17, 120, 122, 146, 175
Cầm Trọng 34, 46n6, 49, 82n15, 102, 133, 152, 168, 172n11
canton 50, 56, 86–7, 89, 91–3, 112
caves 62, 67, 76, 81, 161–2, 167, 184
cement 8–10, 18, 122–5, 139, 177–87
chao cham 132, 134–5, 142–3, 147, 151–2, 166, 169, 170, 171n2
chao kôk chao lao 60, 62, 82n17, 126, 129, 132, 147, 153
chao süa 42, 61, 66, 125–6, 130–41, 144n8, 147–8, 150–1, 157, 185–7
chao thin chao thaan 62, 132, 150, 153
Chiang Mai 118, 133, 161, 166, 172n10
Chiềng Đông 14, 72
Chiềng Pắn 14, 41, 104
Chiềng Sàng 14, 60, 66, 69, 71–2, 74
China 20, 83n18, 117, 164, 171n1, 172n19; Guangxi 70; Yunnan 12, 71, 97, 118
Chinese Flags 12, 16, 60, 63, 69–75, 77, 82n16, 83n27, 163–4, 167
Christianity *see* missionaries
chu 1, 41, 134, 145, 147–8
Chüang wars 72, 75, 83n18, 83n27, 167
clan (*sing*) 36, 132, 144n8
clothes 29n5, 34–5, 37–40, 96, 105, 135, 137
collectivization 42, 109, 172n19
colonial administration 29n10, 50, 83n28, 86, 112, 114n5; and censuses 91–3; conflicts inside the 54–6, 82n9, 94; inspection tours 88–91; *see also* taxes

Index

dance 23, 29n5, 39, 113–14
Davis, B.C. 12, 70, 82n16
demography 11, 13, 20, 32–3, 36–7, 41, 46n3, 46n5, 72, 76, 82n17, 87, 91–3, 103, 106, 110, 112, 115n10, 148, 171n4
Điện Biên Phủ 12, 102–3
district: component polities of Houaphan 29n10, 53–6; functions of 19–20, 89, 94, 110, 112; of Muang Èt 40, 86, 91; and spirits 135, 143, 164, 171n1; of Xiang Kho 82n10, 99–100, 115n10; of Yên Châu 14, 34, 69, 113
Đèo Văn Long *see* Tai Federation
Deydier, H. 119, 164–5, 172n13, 184
divination 135, 136, 139–40, 144, 148–9, 153, 169
dông khuaang 49, 58, 116–17, 133, 135, 142–3, 145, 152, 161–6, 169–71, 176–7, 183
drinking 22–24, 120, 154; *see also lao hai*
duality 119, 156–60

electricity 33, 113, 170
ethnicity 5–6, 33–8, 61, 76, 99, 107; and colonial administration 91–2; and state policy 13, 19–20, 30, 34, 38–40, 79, 110, 168, 180; Tai Dam subgroups 46n7; *see also* Lao (Laoization), Tai Vat ethnicity
Evans, G. 7, 10, 37, 46n4, 46n7, 83n20, 109, 116, 155, 160–1, 168, 170, 172n17, 176, 184

First Indochina War 99–107, 111–13, 174, 185
first settlers *see* autochthony, *chao kôk chao lao, chao thin chao thaan*
food 21–24, 29n9, 80, 103–5, 108, 149, 166; ritual offering of 120–1, 132, 134–5, 137–40, 142–3, 144n10, 151, 154, 164–5
forest 31, 63; as refuge 49, 66, 74, 102, 108–9; slashing of 5, 29n2, 60, 64, 132, 166–7; and spirits 120, 122, 130, 133, 142–3, 149, 158, 161–2, 166–8, 171
Foropon, J. 29n9, 89–90, 114n5
Franco-Siamese Treaty 52, 54, 70, 86
gender 24–5, 35, 38, 41, 54, 56–9, 92–4, 108, 133, 141, 143n3, 168

Giáp (General) 103, 107, 115n17

Hayashi, Y. 144n7, 148, 158, 171n1, 172n14

health 33, 43, 88, 91, 98, 110, 113; and spirits 125, 135–9, 143n3, 151, 168–9
heritage and traditions 11, 25, 34–6, 38–9, 46n10, 64, 110, 115n25, 118–19, 168, 183, 185
High, H. 29n6, 44, 110, 115n25, 119
history: ethnohistory 7, 12, 29n3, 173; and gender 57–9, 113, 169; and literacy 48–52; local definition of 56; oral performance of 5–6, 57–8; oral traditions 6, 12, 48, 60–81, 116, 133, 147, 161; *see also* archives
Hô *see* Chinese flags
Holt, J. 118, 159, 167, 177
Houa Muang 54, 172n15
Houaphan: history of the province 16, 29n10, 37, 52–6, 70, 72, 76, 78, 82n4, 82n9, 83n28, 86, 91–8, 112, 114n4–114n5; revolution 39–40, 102, 107, 109, 115n23; territorial cults and *lak müang* 164–6, 181–5
Houay Lom xvii, 27, 33, 40, 143n3; history 46n3, 57, 62–72, 75–6, 80–1, 85–6, 99, 103, 107, 152, 161; territorial cults 113, 120, 129–30, 142, 143n2, 144n10, 147–8, 150–3, 155–7, 162, 168, 172n12, 185–6
Houay Louang xvii, 33, 46n3, 66, 76, 99, 130, 143n2, 147–8, 157, 171n3, 185
house 11, 21–2, 24, 37, 43, 76, 93, 110, 116, 120–1, 145, 154, 168, 170, 172n11, 172n19, 178–80, 184, 186
Huế 52, 54, 82n9
Hưng Yên 106

irrigation 1–4, 32, 99, 109, 126, 142–3, 163–4, 170

Japanese occupation 61, 98–9, 101, 104

Kammerer, C.A *see* Tannenbaum
Kengtung 115n15
Kha 72, 75, 83n27, 92–3
khana baan 41, 46n13, 155
khap songs 34, 58–9, 82n10, 141
Khmu 4–6, 13, 35–6, 72, 75, 79, 83n18, 161, 172n16, 174
khuan 125
kinchiang New Year 11, 28, 29n5, 29n7–29n8, 36, 113–14, 121, 133–4, 140, 142, 178
Kinh 12, 100, 102, 106–7
kuum baan 40–4, 86, 110

Index

Laankham 64, 125, 129, 138, 153
Ladwig, P. 184
Lai Châu 76, 101–2
lak baan 148, 158, 180–1, 183
lak man 17, 148, 154–7, 165, 175; of Ban Kang 131, 144, 151; of Houay Lom and Houay Louang 129–30, 148, 153, 157; of Houay Yong and *Naa Kuu* 8, 122–3, 125–7, 134, 139–41, 145, 147, 149–53, 155–7, 177–8, 183–7; of Luang Prabang 133, 158, 168, 171n6, 172n13
lak müang 148, 152, 158, 164–5, 170, 171n8, 172n11, 185; of Sam Neua 181–5; of Vientiane 159–60
landscape xiv, 7, 10, 15, 31, 85, 119, 152, 161–2, 176
Lao: ethnicity and Laoization 13, 15, 30, 33–40, 66, 82n13, 91–3, 106–7, 178, 180; language and script xv–xvii, 25–6, 29n1, 49, 53–6; people 46, 61–2, 64, 66, 70, 75–80, 83n27–8, 83n30; territorial cults 144n7, 158–60, 165, 168, 171n1
lao hai 21–3, 29n9, 125, 134, 137–40, 180
Lao Front for National Construction 34, 37, 39
Lao Issara 102–3, 126
Lao Theung 5, 38, 161, 163
Le Boulanger, P. 36–7
Le Failler, Ph. 12, 82n15–82n16, 106
Lehman, F.K. 151
Lentz, Chr. 12, 101–5
Lévy, P. 133, 172n10
Lissoir, M.-P. xvii, 29n7, 29n9, 46n7, 58–9, 82n10, 140–1
Lorrillard, M. 29n4, 51–2
Lü *see* Tai Lü
Luang Prabang: history 38, 52, 54–6, 77–8, 82n8–82n9, 86–7, 114n5, 164; territorial cults 117, 133, 148, 158, 161, 168, 171n6, 172n10, 172n13, 183; trade 95–6, 115n14

Macey, R. 91, 94, 97
mandatory labor 93
Maspero, H. 17, 86, 117–19, 158, 171n1, 171n5, 171n8, 176–7, 184
mass organizations 1, 11, 39, 41–3, 113, 155–6
mediums (*moo môt*) 18, 57, 120–1, 125, 133, 141, 143n3, 145, 147, 168–9, 178
memory xii, xiv, 6–7, 9–11, 56–9, 108, 116, 169
Michaud, J. xiv, 12, 49, 98
migrations 118, 152; from Houay Yong to the lowlands 13–15, 18–19, 25, 29n5, 29n7–29n8, 39, 41, 46n13, 110, 113, 120, 151, 175; of the Kinh to Yên Châu 106–7; from and to Muang Soi 3–4, 61, 65, 67, 75–9, 83n28; self-perception as migrants 34, 113; from Vietnam to Laos 60–75, 82n18, 103–7, 113, 125; *see also* resettlement of villages
Mironneau, J. 37–8, 83n27, 96–7, 115n18
missionaries 12, 37, 82n9, 83n28, 98
mobility *see* stability and mobility
Mộc Châu 104–5, 152
modernity 9, 18, 118, 143, 169–70, 183
Monpeyrat, J. 52, 54–6, 78, 83n26, 83n29, 84n31, 91, 93–4, 96, 115n13–115n14
monuments 7–9, 159, 180–5
moo môt see mediums
mountains xvii, 4, 11, 30–2, 44n1, 53–4, 74, 108–9, 184; and spirits xviii, 17, 62, 67, 76, 81, 122, 133, 143, 152, 154, 161–2, 167
müang see district
Muang Èt xvii, 19, 24, 26, 32–3; ethnicity 36–40, 46n9; history 28, 40–2, 50, 52–6, 67, 70, 72–4, 77–8, 80, 82n9, 83n26, 84n31, 85–6, 88–92, 95–8, 102, 108, 114n5, 115n10–115n11, 174; territorial cults 117, 161, 163–7
Muang Kham 71
Muang Ngoi 95
Muang Pun 67
Muang Soi xvii, 3, 37, 61, 65, 67, 76–9, 83n27, 96, 98–9, 174
Muang Son 55, 82n9, 86, 91, 94, 96
Muang Sum 56, 92, 114n3
Muang Van xvii, 32–3, 40, 122; history 50–1, 53, 56, 63–4, 66, 72, 74, 77–8, 80, 83n30–1, 85–93, 97, 99–100, 103, 108–12, 114n1, 114n6, 115n12, 166
Muang Vat *see* Yên Châu
Muang Ven 86
Muồi Nọi 83n20
Mường Muồi 46n9
Mus, P. 7, 17, 117–20, 146, 160, 163, 175
Myanmar *see* Burma

Naa Kuu 163; history 61, 68, 144n5; territorial cults 125–9, 132, 134, 140–2, 143n2, 146–8, 153, 156, 171n2
Naa Soo 61, 63, 66–7, 75
naai baan 1, 58, 66, 68, 82n17, 107, 127, 130, 169; functions of 11, 24, 41–2, 110; relation with spirits 125, 130, 134, 138, 143, 155, 157, 167, 177–8; succession of 46n13

Nahit 32–3, 46n12, 61, 63–4, 66–7, 75, 86, 142, 152, 163, 180
Nam Định 95
Nam Èt *see* River Èt
Nam Ma *see* River Ma
Nam Mo 46n5, 46n13, 110
Nangiu 79, 83n18, 143n2, 172n16, 174, 176
Nasan xvii, 33, 40, 46n3, 46n5, 57, 65, 76, 86–7, 89, 103, 109, 115n24, 130, 142, 143n2, 148, 163
nested polities 85–7, 163–6, 170, 184–5
Nong Thop xvii, 4–5, 79, 83n18, 172n16
Nora, P. 9–11

O'Connor, R.A. 120, 143n1, 146, 151
opium 95–7
Oudomxay 95

paddy fields 3–5, 29n2, 31, 61, 63, 65–6, 72, 75, 83n30, 109–10, 135, 139, 148–9, 154, 170
Pakfèn 46n5, 87, 143n2, 155
Pathet Lao 21, 40, 102, 107–9, 115n21, 115n23
Pavie, A. 70–4, 82n14, 95, 114n9
phanyaa (or *aanyaa*) 53, 63–4, 66, 77, 80, 84n31, 86, 103, 107, 114n7, 144n8, 154, 156
phia 64, 66–7, 80, 85–6, 93, 99–100, 103, 114n6
phii see rituals
Pholsena, V. 7, 10–11, 109, 116, 176
phông 50, 86, 93, 103, 114n6, 115n12
Phothisarat 52–3, 82n7–82n8
phuu nyai 1, 59, 100
Phwak *see* Singmun
prohibitions 98, 139, 141, 146, 150–1, 171n1, 171n7
Proschan, F. 83n18, 83n27

Raquez, A. 29n9, 37–8, 46n9, 72, 79, 96
raw shellac 95–7, 115n16–115n17
Red Tai *see* Tai Dèng
refugees *see* migrations
resettlement of villages 4–7, 13, 29n6, 33, 46n5, 79, 110, 130, 148, 157, 166, 172n16
rituals 10, 15, 18, 25, 29n5, 35, 64, 84n31, 104, 119–22, 132–3, 144n7–144n8; and history 7, 109, 116–18; *see also* beliefs (struggle against), Buddhism, divination, *dông khuaang*, food (offerings), *lak man, lak müang,*

mediums (*moo môt*), prohibitions, sacrifice, *sén, thaam, thiang seun*
River Èt 32–3, 52–3, 74, 79, 83n25, 86, 96–7
River Ma 32–3, 40, 52–3, 69–70, 73–5, 79, 86, 88, 95, 106, 115n14
River Vat 34, 71–2, 82n13
roads 32–3, 44n2, 76, 79, 88–91, 95, 109, 141, 180

sacrifice 98, 118, 161, 163–8, 171n6, 172n10, 172n15
Salemink, O. xv, 11–12
Sam Neua 19, 44n2, 98, 103, 112, 114n4, 165, 181–5
Schlemmer, G. 7, 117, 119, 153, 176
school 7, 28, 33, 39, 43–5, 49, 81n2, 98, 108
Scott, J. xii, 12, 49, 51, 81, 151, 164, 177, 183
Second Indochina War 107–9
sén 11, 22, 145; *sén baan* 133, 141–2, 145–6; *sén khuaang* 142
Setthathirat 52, 82n7, 160
shellac *see* raw shellac
Siam 38, 52, 54, 70, 72–5, 77–9, 86, 97, 166
sing see clan
Singmun (Phwak) 33, 46n4, 92, 161, 163, 165
Sip song chu thai 70, 82n15
Sop Èt 52–3
Sop Hao 180–1
Sop San 74, 88, 95
Spirits *see khuan*, Laankham, rituals
Sprenger, G. 46n11
stability and mobility xiv, 15, 17, 34, 113, 122, 148–52, 160, 171n8; *see also* migrations, resettlement of villages
state 6, 10, 12, 20–1, 34, 39–44, 49, 79, 81, 110; colonial 82n9, 89–91, 112; and rituals 118, 125, 152, 155–7, 170, 176, 178–85; *see also* beliefs (struggle against), canton, colonial administration, district, *kuum baan*, mass organizations, *naai baan, phông,* subdistrict, *taasèèng*
stick-lac *see* raw shellac
Stuart-Fox, M. 102, 107, 115n23
subdistrict 46n13, 49–50, 58–9, 66, 164, 168; *see also* canton, *kuum baan, phông, taasèèng*
swidden fields 2, 28, 31, 66, 79, 105, 107, 109–10, 137, 142, 162, 170

taalèèo 162, 171n1
taasèèng 41–2, 50, 80, 89, 103, 165, 167
Tai Dam (Black Tai): of Ban Kang 5–6, 79, 82n17; of Ban Sot 44n1, 46n4, 46n7, 72; clans 85, 144n8; ethnicity 15, 19, 33–40, 91–2, 99; history 60–1, 46n9, 85, 103, 106, 118; language and script 26, 49, 167; territorial cults 131, 133, 158, 160–1
Tai Dèng (Red Tai) xvii, 33, 38, 46n3, 66–7, 76–9, 83n21, 83n27–8, 92, 147, 165, 171n3
Tai Federation 101, 103, 106
Tai Khao (White Tai) 61, 76, 101, 106
Tai Lü 96, 118, 161, 164, 166
Tai Nüa 37–8, 91, 161, 165
Tai Soi xvii, 2–4, 6–7, 33, 35, 46n3, 61–2, 65–8, 75–9, 83n25, 83n30, 87, 98–100, 161–3, 166
Tai Vat ethnicity xvii 5, 11, 14, 25, 33–6, 39, 46n3, 46n5–46n7, 69, 78, 82n14, 99–100, 103, 106, 113, 125, 147–8, 155
Tạ Khoa 97
Tanabe, Sh. 37, 118, 122, 133, 144n4, 148, 161, 163–6, 168, 171n1, 172n10, 172n17, 172n19, 176
Tannenbaum, N. (& C.A. Kammerer) 7, 118, 172n14, 176, 187n2
Tappe, O. 7, 10–11, 29n10, 46n10, 82n4, 82n9, 83n26, 84n31, 94, 112, 114n5, 116, 180, 182–4
taxes 28, 48, 53, 80, 86, 88–9, 93–4, 97, 106, 111–12
territorial charters 52–3, 82n6
thaam ('prayers') 120–1, 133–41, 143, 149, 151, 154, 162, 165, 178, 187
Thailand *see* Siam and Chiang Mai
Thanh Hóa 76–7, 82n9, 115n14

thiang seun 131, 144n10, 145–6, 154–7; of Houay Lom and Houay Louang 130, 148, 168, 172n12, 186; of Houay Yong and *Naa Kuu* 122–8, 132–4, 136, 138–42, 147, 149, 152, 177–8, 186
Thongnamy xix, 13–14, 19, 29n8, 36, 46n5, 106, 110, 113–14, 121, 134, 143n2, 169, 178
trade 33, 70, 77, 94–7, 104, 115n13–115n15; *see also* opium, raw shellac, and taxes
traditions *see* heritage

Van Bu 70
Vansina, J. 6, 48, 59, 68, 80, 173
verticality 152–4
Vientiane 14, 18, 25, 29n5, 29n8, 39, 42, 52, 55, 78, 82n8, 83n28, 109–10, 117, 133, 150, 159–60, 164, 184
Vietminh *see* First Indochina War

Wartelle, L.-A. 53, 86, 88–9, 93–4, 97–8
White Tai *see* Tai Khao

Xiang Kho xvii, 28, 33, 40, 50, 53, 55–6, 70, 73–5, 77–8, 82n10, 86, 89–92, 95–6, 98–100, 108, 113, 114n5, 115n10, 165
Xieng Khouang 71, 96, 106, 109, 114n2, 117, 129, 148, 164, 171n6, 177

Yanling kingdom 70
Yao 33, 40
Yellow Flags *see* Chinese Flags
Yên Châu xix, 20, 34, 46n6, 49, 63, 81n2, 82n14, 94–5, 101–7, 112–14, 174–5; *see also* Chiềng Đông, Chiềng Pặn, Chiềng Sàng

Zago, M. 119, 148, 160, 185

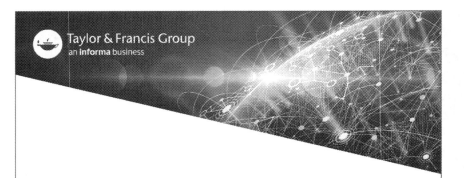

Taylor & Francis eBooks

www.taylorfrancis.com

A single destination for eBooks from Taylor & Francis with increased functionality and an improved user experience to meet the needs of our customers.

90,000+ eBooks of award-winning academic content in Humanities, Social Science, Science, Technology, Engineering, and Medical written by a global network of editors and authors.

TAYLOR & FRANCIS EBOOKS OFFERS:

- A streamlined experience for our library customers
- A single point of discovery for all of our eBook content
- Improved search and discovery of content at both book and chapter level

REQUEST A FREE TRIAL
support@taylorfrancis.com